Linden Walcott-Burton

Linden Walcott-Burton is an actor, director, producer and workshop facilitator.

His acting credits include work for HBO/Punchdrunk, the Royal Court Theatre, the Sherman Cymru, Shakespeare's Globe and the BBC.

He is a regular facilitator for the National Theatre and was involved in the development of their facilitator-training programme. His facilitating credits also include The Old Vic, the Barbican, Battersea Arts Centre and Punchdrunk Enrichment, as well as corporate facilitation work for Oxford University's Said Business School. He is also an Associate Artist for the National Youth Theatre.

He was formerly the producer of the free actor's showcase MonologueSlamUK at Theatre Royal Stratford East, and was a councillor for Equity. He has also worked as a Culture Policy Officer for the London Mayor, as the lead officer for theatre in London and artificial intelligence in the creative industries.

THE DRAMA WORKSHOP LEADER

A Practical Guide to Delivering Great Sessions

Linden Walcott-Burton

NICK HERN BOOKS
London
www.nickhernbooks.co.uk

A Nick Hern Book

The Drama Workshop Leader
first published in Great Britain in 2023
by Nick Hern Books Limited,
The Glasshouse, 49a Goldhawk Road,
London W12 8QP

Designed and typeset by Nick Hern Books
Printed and bound in Great Britain by Severn, Gloucester

A CIP catalogue record for this book is available
from the British Library

ISBN 978 1 83904 079 5

Contents

Foreword

Jackie Tait
Primary Programme Manager, National Theatre Learning

I first met Linden Walcott-Burton in 2018 when he achieved a place on the National Theatre Facilitator Training Course – an intense ten-day programme specifically designed for actors, directors and other theatre professionals who already have some experience of facilitation. Alongside a successful acting career, Linden had spent ten years working as a facilitator with a variety of different participant groups. His talent was, and is, obvious – he has the ability to make the most of every experience and opportunity that comes his way; to wring out every possible bit of learning – an essential quality when learning the art of facilitation. Since completing the course, Linden has been employed as a freelance facilitator by National Theatre Learning and has become a true expert in his field.

To many of us working in participatory drama, Linden's journey will be a familiar one. He was motivated to become a drama facilitator because of the impact that being a participant had had on him as a young person. If you ask any of the staff in the learning team at the National Theatre you will find, more often than not, that this was the reason why they wanted to work in the arts in the first place. The power of participatory drama is something that, once experienced, you want to share.

It is a common misconception, however, that participation in drama exists solely to encourage people to become an actor or to work in theatre. Drama is an extremely powerful, multi-faceted tool for learning and self-development. Participation in a creative, well-facilitated drama-based process can really transform lives. In terms of practical application, it can help to develop problem-solving and decision-making skills, improve cognitive function, and increase concentration and memory retention, as well as developing the imagination. Social-skills development is another key area of impact. Time and again,

I have witnessed this kind of learning process helping people to develop their speaking, listening and communication skills, their ability to cooperate and work as a team, and their empathy skills. It frequently helps to improve their social lives, due to the special connection that a drama-based process can create between people.

Furthermore, the broader impact on wellbeing is palpable. The opportunity that creative learning and drama provides for self-expression not only improves self-awareness, but can significantly boost self-esteem and confidence. It can reduce stress and anxiety, improving participants' emotional wellbeing. I have even seen instances of it improving physical health. Particularly when the outcome is performance-focused, a drama process can create a real feeling of pride and achievement and foster a desire for lifelong learning.

Twenty years ago, I walked into the very first session of my post-graduate course in Community Theatre. We were asked to make a list of all the different roles of a drama facilitator. It took us about an hour and, as I recall, we ended up with thirty-two on the list.

All of which is to say, facilitation comprises an extremely complicated set of skills to learn and takes many years to truly master. In my role heading up the primary-school programme for National Theatre Learning, I have had the privilege of working with many of the most experienced facilitators in the UK; not one of them would say that their learning journey is complete.

Facilitation is emphatically not the same as teaching (although both are similarly challenging, multi-role pursuits). *Teaching* is predominantly about imparting knowledge in such a way that students are able to remember it, with that journey led largely by the teacher. *Facilitation* is far more about devising a creative journey for participants in order for them to discover new insight, new solutions and perhaps also new knowledge. The direction of travel on that journey is led largely by the participants and only *managed* or *facilitated* by the leader. Participants thus have ownership of what they discover and therefore it automatically becomes more memorable. The best educators are, of course, able to master both of these approaches to learning.

Learning to be a drama facilitator can be a solitary journey, offering little opportunity to observe and learn from others. You have no choice but to learn on the job. You make your mistakes, learning by trial and error over many years. This practical experience is vital to finding your own style, strengths and weaknesses as a facilitator.

But how brilliant to finally have a bit of extra help in your hands. This important book provides an extensive account of Linden's journey into facilitation and what he has learnt along the way. Rooted in practical experience, it also offers valuable contributions and examples from some of the most experienced facilitators in the field (including the leaders of the NT's Facilitators' Training Programme). There are many books out there offering games and exercises to draw on when planning workshops but, to my knowledge, this is the first to showcase the art of facilitation to this level of detail and success.

Every practitioner, no matter their level of experience, will gain so much from this book. It will take you from the basics of planning a workshop and setting up the room, right through to advanced skills, such as using your voice effectively and how to frame the right questions. For some just starting out it will be entirely new and vital information, for some a useful refresher of what all-round good practice looks like, and for some simply a reassurance and reaffirmation that what they have been doing in practice for years has been on the right track!

To anyone wanting to excel as a facilitator, my advice would be to read this book. Dip into it or read it cover to cover. I so wish it had existed when I started out.

Introduction

You might be wondering why I'm qualified to teach you how to run a workshop. Or maybe you're curious to know how this book came about. If so, then sit down, grab a cushion and get comfy, because a brief (!) story of my life will tell you all you need to know about why I've written this book for you.

Part one – the opening chapter (of my life)

The first part of my life was rocky, to say the least. By age thirteen, as a family we'd moved house eleven times. I'd been to three different primary schools, back to my first school again, and then three secondary schools – half of which were in London, half in the West Midlands. Six schools, with a grand total of one drama class (as part of an English lesson), which nobody took seriously. So the odds of me going into the arts weren't great.

I'd need a separate book to explain why we moved house so much, but I was pretty unfazed by it all. It was my life; I didn't know any different. I just took it on the chin and got on with it. I didn't have any other upbringing to compare it to, and why stress about something you can't control?

We ping-ponged between London and the West Midlands throughout this time, until we finally settled in a cosy little house in my mum's hometown of Dudley, a former industrial heartland. The contrast to London couldn't have been greater. It was a peaceful community; with an auntie five doors down the road, my nan and grandad at the top of the hill, and enough friends within a five-minute radius for a small army of us to walk to school every day. It was during this period of stability that for the first time ever, I landed in a school that did drama.

To my shock, I was good at it. Seeing as I'd spent my previous school years as the biggest geek of all time – with big glasses, braces, and a bag so big it could (and did) carry every book for the week, being good at drama didn't make sense. How could I go from being top of the class academically but bottom of the social ladder in London, to suddenly being the cool drama kid in the Midlands? What if they found out who I really was...?

I didn't complain. After a few years at Hillcrest School and Community College in 2004, our school was approached by a company called Leaps and Bounds, who came to pitch to us a once-in-a-lifetime opportunity. Two hundred disadvantaged young people were to take part in an eighteen-month project to see if the arts could change their lives, with the not-so-minor task of staging Birmingham Royal Ballet's *Romeo and Juliet* at the Birmingham Hippodrome alongside their professional company, as part of a Channel 4 documentary.

I can remember clear as day that I barely even listened to the sales pitch. I heard the words 'this'll be on TV', and I signed right up.

Fast forward, and two years later I was on the Birmingham Hippodrome stage before a live audience of two thousand people and a TV audience of four million, playing the role of Tybalt – with all the major sword-fighting scenes alongside the Birmingham Royal Ballet dancers. And I'd only just turned seventeen. It was quite the journey, having only encountered drama quite recently, my only experience being my school plays, and my only experience of dance being the odd moves I'd bust out to some nineties Usher in my bedroom.

The whole idea of the project was insane – but it never felt that way. We had a goal and we set out to achieve it. I remember sitting in the rehearsal room two weeks before the performance, looking down at a newspaper with the headline 'it's impossible, it can't be done', in reference to the fact that there was no logical way that a bunch of street youths could stage one of Kenneth Macmillan's most prominent ballets having just walked in off the street – only to look up at the rehearsal to see that, in fact, it was possible, because we'd just finished our first run-through. Clearly we got the memo too late.

But looking back, it was such a different experience to the culture that I'd later experience in the theatre world. This was ballet. Ballet is about perfection. The perfect dance sequence, the perfect poise, everything. In rehearsals, my head would be repositioned and lengthened if it were even a centimetre dipped out of alignment.

The project was tough love. We had to be there on time, and we had to commit. There were no excuses. It didn't matter what was going on in our lives (and for most people, there was a lot) – we had a job to do and we had to rise to it. I think the world has a very different idea about tough love now, but certainly, nobody can deny that the project took us from being rowdy teenagers to achieving the 'impossible'. And I don't think any other approach would've worked.

Having then spent two years getting my A Levels at King Edward VI College in Stourbridge, I spent a gap year with the National Youth Theatre. As chance would have it, they'd set up a second headquarters in Brierly Hill – which happened to be a thirty-minute walk from my mum's house. With my mum in the Midlands and my dad in London, I spent three days as an actor on their first Playing Up acting course in London during the week, and spent Saturdays as an assistant director to Paul Edwards on their Saturday community workshops in Brierly Hill. The ping-ponging between the two areas that I'd done throughout my life was now being mirrored on a weekly basis through theatre. The world works in mysterious ways.

It was there that I learnt the foundations of being a workshop facilitator. The Saturday workshops were free for the local young people, and our register soon ballooned from seven in the first week to forty-two at its peak, with three full performances across the local area – from a church, to a shopping centre, to the local high street. It was during this year that the first spark of this book happened; from one of the most throwaway comments you could imagine.

At the end a rehearsal for our show one day, our director, Daisy Douglas, recalled her time at drama school and said something along the lines of:

'When I was at drama school, I wrote down everything I did.'

And that's what changed everything. From that point on, every new drama exercise I saw, I typed up into a scraggly table in a

Windows 98 document. That same file has made it through time, space, computer backups, hard-drive failures and a computer explosion; and ballooned from a single page with nine games on it in the mid-2000s, to a thirty-five-page document by 2021.

Part 2 – The middle chapter (of my life)

Fast forward some years and I'd graduated from drama school and was working as an actor. Like most creatives, I juggled a thousand things at once. From acting for the Royal Court, the National Theatre of Scotland, the Sherman Cymru, Soho Theatre and Punchdrunk, to producing the high-profile free actors' showcase MonologueSlamUK in London, to being an elected Councillor for Equity – all alongside workshop-leading and the general hustle that comes with being a creative. I'd started in the arts from zero – I had to work for everything.

It was also during this time that I worked as a special needs teaching assistant in a special educational needs and disability (SEND) school. I'd had a lot of experience with young people from having a big family and from my facilitating work, and I was also a backup carer for my dad, who was a foster-carer to incredibly challenging young people. But I'd never worked with disabled young people before. It was helpful because being agency staff meant I could take time off and be relatively flexible for acting work when it came along, but it actually proved more valuable than I expected.

I had the fullest experience you could imagine. Over the seven years, I worked in seven schools plus a special needs playscheme. I worked with every year group (from nursery to post-sixteen), with the full range of special needs (from autism to Down syndrome), across the whole spectrum (from children with mild learning disabilities, to those who were four-to-one, needing four members of staff with them at all times). There was even a school where I worked with every class and almost every student, to the point that most teachers were requesting for me to be in their class. I also became the person who'd be parachuted in to work with the most challenging students.

There were challenges as well as triumphs. Over the time, I'd been punched, kicked, scratched, headbutted, spat at,

I'd sprinted down hallways to stop students hitting people, sprinted down hallways to stop students hitting me, saw people go to A&E, stopped hair-pulls, dealt with epileptic fits, and barricaded doors from students on a rampage. But I also saw students who were never expected to walk, learn to. I saw selective mutes find their voice to speak. I built bonds with non-verbal students who'd run the whole school ragged, but were always responsive with me. I made connections with kids who'd break down in tears when they got to the school gates and refuse to enter, but would perk up straight away and come in with a hop and a skip as soon as I came over.

It was only by having the full range of those experiences that I learnt to handle pretty much anything that came my way. I wouldn't be able to say the same if I'd been on the outside intellectualising about it. I started in that sphere like many things I'm faced with – having absolutely no idea what I was doing or how I got there, and feeling well out of my depth; but I rose to the challenge and I learnt so much. About people, and about myself. And so much of what I learnt didn't just apply to young people with special needs, but to adults and facilitating as well. But it was during this period that the second stage of the making of this book began.

It was around this time that I ran my first summer course for the National Youth Theatre (NYT): a two-week junior course for fourteen- to seventeen-year-olds, with thirty talented young people from across the UK, an assistant, and the complete freedom to plan and deliver the course in whatever way I saw fit – so long as it was ensemble-based and we devised a final performance. Great if you know what you're doing, daunting if you're relatively new.

Having delivered my course, I'd been reflecting a lot on how it went, and brought up some of my experiences with another NYT associate, Lukas Angelini, when we were co-facilitating some NYT auditions. NYT courses for many are seen as a completely life-changing experience, with the group starting as strangers, then usually in tears at the end of their two or three weeks because they don't want to part ways. I had a group of teenage boys who were so sad it was over that they spent the entire goodbye session with sunglasses on, trying (and failing) to cover the tears streaming down their faces.

So I had two questions. The first was: Why was this the case? What was it about the courses that made them so fulfilling and life-changing? Yes, people loved it for the theatre aspects, but they loved it just as much, if not more, for the personal and social side.

But there was a second question too. That same year, there were other courses that had really struggled with a host of mental health challenges from participants, and internal rifts within the groups. It was often said that more young people were struggling with their mental health over recent years than ever before (which mirrors the national data on the issue), and that the courses were almost expected to have pastoral challenges along those lines. But I didn't have any of that on my courses. Why not? What was different? Was my experience a fluke? Or were there things happening that I just wasn't aware of?

There was something else that confused me too. Towards the end of my first NYT course, one of my participants had written to me saying they'd been in a bad place before it started – to the point that they weren't even going to attend – but for the first time in a long time they'd felt happy and part of a family. Again, I was confused. I hadn't done anything special. I just did the theatre. I didn't understand. Was Zip Zap Boing and some script work really all that? Surely not. Why did it have so much of an impact?

But it kept on happening. Similar things happened in every course I ran. From a disabled participant saying it was the first time they'd ever felt 'normal', to another who had never committed to anything in their life but turned up to every single session of mine on time (their mum was in tears with pride), to another having had nightmares every night for months but none whatsoever throughout the course, to more and more people saying in our final checkouts that they'd been in bad places before the course, but hadn't felt any of that during it. You can see what I mean from the 'Thank-yous from the Past' section on page 271.

This was all great. Fantastic feedback. Absolutely brilliant to have made such an impact. But the question I kept coming back to was:

Why?

Why??

It made no sense to me. There were other directors whose whole ethos was around compassion, happiness and changing lives, yet for some of them their courses were riddled with far more conflict and unhappiness than mine, and after a few years of doing it, I realised that it couldn't just be down to the random selection of young people we were getting.

To be clear, this wasn't about me or about patting myself on the back. I don't care about that. The reality was that if I couldn't pinpoint what was effective and what wasn't, I wouldn't be able to replicate the success, and I'd have no way of addressing any problems if I did eventually run into them. You can't replicate luck, but you can replicate skill.

Having aired some of these thoughts with Lukas, the second spark to this book happened, when he said:

'The facilitator has more of an impact on the room than you think.'

It wasn't until I did a facilitation course with the National Theatre a few years later that this really hit home, and I realised just how much of my experience I'd taken for granted. For the first time ever, I was consciously taught the skills to run a room, rather than learning them on the job. I already knew a chunk of what the course covered, but it was good to reaffirm what I knew, and it was interesting to see others' reactions to the fundamentals that I'd assumed were just common knowledge. But I realised that of all the companies I'd worked for, only two of them had ever actively trained their facilitators in how to run a room. It was always just assumed that you could. Training would happen, but it'd usually cover topics such as safeguarding or diversity and inclusion. And those won't be of much use when you're in a room with thirty feral young people hanging off the walls, with Jeremy and Philip more interested in making fart noises than listening.

Especially for successful actors. The assumption was always: 'Oh great! You're fresh from the Royal Shakespeare Company? You'd be great to run these workshops.' Well, no. Delivering your finest Romeo or Juliet to a paying audience and delivering a theatre workshop may have some crossover, but they're different disciplines. And in some respects, captivating thirty half-sleeping teenagers who don't want to be there can be way harder than engaging an audience who have willingly paid to see you.

Plus, I realised there were no resources on how to facilitate, and given that most of us work alone, how could you learn from other people? There were a few accredited courses in drama schools, but those were for newcomers to the industry, not those already in it. There were certainly no books. The only things that existed were books on drama games, but knowing an exercise and knowing how to deliver it (and a workshop) are two different things. Never mind a course.

So I decided to write one. If nobody else had done it, I would. Go me.

Part 3 – The writing of this book chapter (of my life)

This book had always been on my 'one day, I'd really like to...' list, until the day came when I unlocked my phone and started making notes. From that point on, my life went from 'If I had more time, I'd write a book' to 'I'm writing a book, I have no time.'

I already had a fair amount to say on the subject. During my NYT courses, I'd always sit down with my assistants and talk them through my workshop plans and the craftmanship of my delivery, which served as a starting point. I originally planned for the book to be about how to run a workshop and to include all of the exercises that I'd built up over the years in my Word document. But it quickly became clear that there was far more to this book than I expected, and that it should be a standalone book in itself.

And then the pandemic hit. Before Covid-19, I was fiercely political and spent far too much time on social media trying to change the world. But in the wake of the pandemic and the death of George Floyd in America, it was almost as if a circuit breaker kicked in for me. All of a sudden, the internet had become so angry, frustrated and toxic that I pulled myself off social media entirely. The fuse had blown. There was too much coming down the power lines.

It was one of the best things I could've done. I got my life in order, spent more time in the real world rather than the digital, and I channelled the newfound time into the things I chose rather than on endless scrolling. It also meant I had a whole year to dedicate to writing during the Covid-19 lockdowns. Perfect timing. So like most of us would do under the circumstances, I began to write this book...

...once lockdown had lifted, and I was busy with a thousand other things.

But two years later, it was complete. So what you have here is everything I've learnt over fifteen years of both the successes and mistakes from running hundreds of workshops, as well as the insight from having worked with many who I'd consider to be some of the finest practitioners of our time; some of whom have made contributions to this book to offer their perspective. This book isn't a complete replacement for going out there and gaining experience, but it should serve as a guide through your journey and career.

It's important to note that I've written this book while actively working in the field – scribbling down notes or key points of learning while I was delivering workshops, to share with the world in these pages. So it's not a theoretical book that's been written from a distance, it's been written from me being on the ground and getting my hands dirty. I also didn't want it to be an intellectual pursuit or self-indulgent – so I hope that it's accessible enough that you can dive into it mid-workshop and get the guidance you need within minutes, while still being given the level of depth that you need.

All the many life experiences I've had have fed into who I am and the way that I work. From the tough love of Birmingham Royal Ballet and Leaps and Bounds, to my extensive experience with the National Youth Theatre, to my challenges and successes in SEND schools; as well as the wide range of acting and theatre jobs I've done, alongside my facilitation work in general. I don't have a dedication to any particular worldview or perspective – I simply do whatever works to bring out the best in the people that I work with. I ditch anything that doesn't.

I'd wager that good facilitation can prevent most of the problems you may encounter in a room and can unlock most of the things that you want to achieve. Being a good workshop leader isn't about doing one thing well, it's about doing lots of little things, really well. I hope this book guides you and unlocks the best in the people that you work with, as the people I worked with unlocked the best in me.

Points to Note Before Reading

- The guidance in this book should give you the foundation to work in any workshop environment, regardless of the setting. However, some settings will require more specific adaptations. Some of the key ones are in the relevant chapter from page 151 of this book.
- Not every technique in this book will work for every type of group. Different demographics require different approaches, so make sure that you adjust to your audience.
- While there is some crossover between running a drama workshop and directing a production, be aware that they're different environments. A technique you might use as a workshop facilitator won't necessarily translate to being a director, and vice versa.
- Some sections will have a personal reflection from me at the end. These appear in speech bubbles and will give you an insight into how I came to learn those particular points, or give my own personal take on them.
- To give a broader perspective, several other practitioners have contributed their thoughts and reflections to sections of this book. These are practitioners whose work I know well, who are specialists in their respective areas, and are extremely successful and effective at what they do.
- Other than the contributing practitioners and those in the introduction, all of the names in this book have been remixed to cover people's identities.
- At times I'll refer to the National Youth Theatre courses that I've run. For reference, the National Youth Theatre of Great Britain is the UK's most established and respected youth theatre, with alumni such as Daniel Craig, Dame Helen Mirren and Chiwetel Ejiofor. Thousands of young people audition every year for a chance to be in the

company, and, if successful (at the time of writing this), do either a two-week Junior course (for ages 14–17), a three week Senior course (for ages 18–25), or a four-week Epic Stages course (ages 22–25). These are intensive, six-day-a-week, full-time courses, with the participants coming from all over the country and often staying in halls and living together. Each course has one director, one assistant and thirty course participants. The courses are planned entirely by the director, and must be ensemble-based, with a short, devised performance at the end.

1 Your Workshop

Planning Your Workshop

The Basics

So you're looking to plan a great session? Brilliant. Let's start at the beginning.

When you're given a blank canvas and have a workshop to plan, there are some key elements you should consider for every workshop you do. These are:

- The workshop's overall aim.
- The aim of each exercise.
- The physical transition between each exercise.
- The impact of the exercise on the group's energy.
- Who the group interact with.
- How long each exercise will take.
- Fun!

Nothing in your workshop should be done for the sake of it, so be clear about why you're doing each exercise and how it fits into your overall structure. Let's break down some of those key elements.

The workshop's overall aim

All of your exercises should stem from your workshop's overall aim. You might be given an aim by the company you're working for, but if not, you'll need to set one. Here are some examples of what an overall aim could be:

- To introduce the group to the key themes and characters of a play.
- To explore physicality and movement in relation to acting.
- To explore different stage configurations, e.g. end-on, thrust and traverse.

Having an overall aim will focus your session and allow you to choose exercises that support what you're trying to achieve. It'll also make your workshop easier to plan, because it'll be easier to choose from the handful of exercises or topics that support your aim, rather than the hundreds of drama exercises in existence.

The aim of each exercise

Each exercise needs a purpose. Otherwise, why are you doing it? Time spent on an exercise that doesn't have a purpose could be better spent on an exercise that does. Each exercise should support your workshop's overall aim, so select them with that in mind.

This doesn't mean that every exercise has to be linked to the overall aim in a literal sense, so long as it supports it. For example, if your workshop is about the history of workers' rights in the UK, is a game of Stuck-in-the-Mud related to that? Hell no. But if you're playing it to energise your group and to warm up their teamworking skills for the session, then go for it.

One key exception here is when you're running a full course. The more time you have with a group, the more you can afford to break this rule. But that should be the exception, not the norm.

The physical transition between each exercise

When scene changes would take place in older plays, the play would stop, the lights would dim, and ninja-like humans dressed in black would rearrange the furniture for the next scene. The same *could* happen with the exercise transitions in your session (where an exercise ends, people rearrange themselves, then you start the next exercise...), but we don't want that. We want your transitions to be silky smooth.

Getting your previous exercise to end in the formation that the next one starts in will mean your group won't need to physically rearrange themselves. You can go straight into the next exercise with no fuss. Obviously there'll be times where you have no choice, but reducing the amount of rearranging people need to do will speed up your workshop, make it more efficient, and keep the group's attention.

A workshop with bad exercise transitions

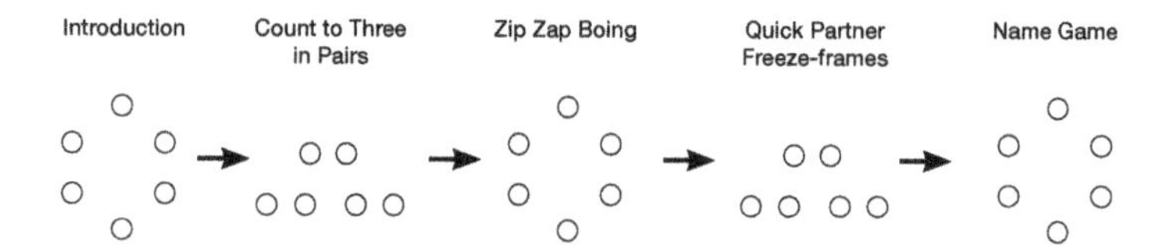

A workshop with good exercise transitions

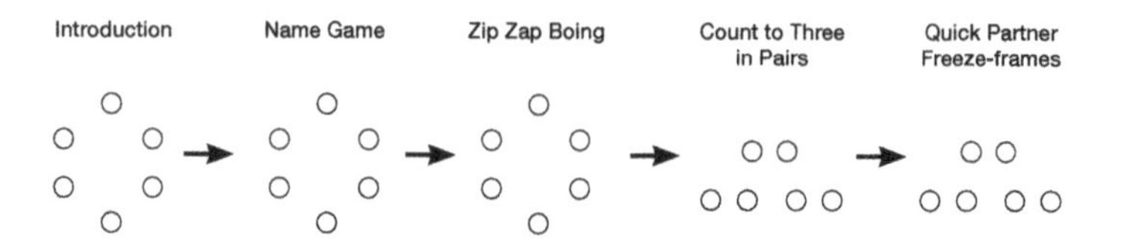

It's not the end of the world if your exercises aren't all seamlessly linked, but it is something to be aware of, particularly with challenging groups. The more you get people to rearrange themselves, the harder it'll be to keep them focused. A disciplined group can rearrange themselves in ten seconds. A group of feral teenagers? In ten minutes.

Doing this will also give more weight to the exercises that aren't so seamless. If your exercise transitions have been silky smooth throughout, breaking this style and having the group form an audience to watch each other's work will mark a gear change in your workshop. It'll then make them take their performances more seriously.

Lastly, it's particularly important to bear this in mind if you're using chairs. It's much better to do all of your chair exercises in one go than it is to set them up, put them back, set them up, put them back, then set them up to put them back again. Do all the chair exercises together, then kiss the chairs goodbye.

The impact of the exercise on the group's energy

You need to be aware of the impact that your exercises will have on your group's energy. Will it energise them? Will it get them focused? Will it get them into a competitive mindset? Each exercise should build on the previous exercise's energy or set the group up for the next one. Sharon might find it harder to stay focused on the current exercise if you've just played a competitive game of Tag, compared to if you do a calm, focused game beforehand.

Who the group interact with

There are two modes of interaction with a group:

- *The facilitator engaging with the group* – when you're actively leading the room.
- *The group engaging with each other* – when the group are working with each other or by themselves.

There are pros and cons to each interaction style, so you need a balance of both. Here are some of the pros and cons of each:

Facilitator to participant	
+	-
• You can actively teach and share knowledge. • It's easier to keep the group on task because you're in control. • You can actively guide the workshop.	• Participants can only listen for so long before they become disengaged. • Participants don't get to actively explore the content themselves. • The loudest students can often get the most direct interaction.

Participant to participant	
	-
• Allows the group to actively engage in the material. • It's much easier to have every participant engaged. • 'Mistakes' are less exposing because they won't be exposed to the whole group. • Allows you some downtime to check in with your plan, assistant, or individuals in the group.	• It's more difficult for the facilitator to share their knowledge to everyone. • Groups can easily go off-task if given too much time or they lack focus.

Bear in mind that you can sometimes alter the interaction style of exercises. This can allow you to balance a workshop more by creating more opportunities for the group to interact with each other, or with you. For example:

Task: Establishing the rules of the room	
Facilitator to participant	**Participant to participant and facilitator to participant**
• The facilitator asks the group for suggestions for rules for the session, which get written on the board.	• The facilitator puts everyone into groups and asks them to come up with a list of rules. • The facilitator asks each group to share some of their rules, before writing them on the board.

How long each exercise will take

You need to have a rough estimate for how long each exercise will be. I say 'rough', because no matter how experienced you get, there's no way you'll be able to plan your timings accurately. And if you can, you've been gifted by the gods. There's no use spending hours meticulously figuring out your timings to the minute because workshops are organic and you'll need to be flexible to your group. All it takes is for Stella to tell you what she thought of an exercise and your timings can fly out the window.

But you do need to have an idea for how long you want each exercise to be, otherwise you run the risk of a five-minute warm-up becoming the entire hour-long session, with only a few minutes left for the core of your workshop.

Fun!

Often forgotten, your sessions need to be enjoyable and engaging. Theatre workshops shouldn't be a chore, and certainly shouldn't feel like punishment. You could have the best workshop plan in the world, but if it's dull and people fall asleep, what's the point? They may as well stay in bed.

Playing games, using a variety of exercises, and choosing engaging, relevant material are all ways to support this. But all in all, be creative. And if something's boring, either make it un-boring or take it out of your workshop and throw it as far as the eye can see.

> " I aim to get the best out of groups by creating an environment where people can build positive relationships. Getting people playing and listening to each other is essential for this. Here they start to develop a sense of fun and respect for one another. It's important to have fun!
>
> Fun is anything that brings joy. It may be joyous to make a mistake and get applauded for it, to receive praise, or to learn something new about someone.
>
> The playing has to be safe and the listening has to be genuine: such as listening to understand rather than listening to reply.

My golden rule is to throw in lots of playful activities that require people to listen, whether it be with their bodies, eyes, ears or anything else.

Ann Ogbomo

Freelance Practitioner and Trainer, *National Theatre*
Actor (*Wonder Woman*, *Justice League*, *The Sandman*, *Krypton*)

How to Plan Your Session

There isn't a definitive manual for 'this is how you plan a workshop'. As with anything creative, planning can often take a mix of different approaches and will vary from workshop to workshop, so this section will give you some strategies to consider. But regardless of your approach, you need to get as much information about the group as you can in advance and be clear about your workshop's objective.

Get as much information as you can

The more information you can get about your group before you start planning, the easier it'll be to design a workshop that's suited to them. You don't need to pull together a ten-page questionnaire for people, but there are some key questions that it's worth having answers to, such as:

- What is the context of the workshop – e.g. is it a school group, a drama-school course, a paid adult class?
- Will the group already know each other or will they be meeting for the first time?
- Will there be any access needs for people in the group – e.g. wheelchair users, learning disabilities, etc.?
- What room will the workshop take place in and what is it like – e.g. how big is it, will the space be empty?
- If the workshop's related to a play, will the group have read the play or have seen it on stage before? Will they be going to see it? What's their level of knowledge?
- How much drama have they done before?

This isn't a complete list of questions to ask, but it's a good place to start. The answers to these questions will inform how you plan and deliver the workshop, so they're important to know from the very beginning. The more information you have, the better, as it'll allow you to avoid any inconvenient surprises and to adapt accordingly.

> I once found out that my workshop on the story of Anne Frank had to take place in a classroom, so movement exercises would be really limited. However, it gave me a chance to plan some drawing/writing/diary activities with the idea for some of these to take place underneath the desks, which created a really evocative cramped space for the students to work in. The teacher was very excited by the kinaesthetic experience of writing diaries in a small space, and the way it enhanced the quality of the children's writing.
>
> **Kate Beales**
> Senior Artist and Practitioner, *National Theatre Learning*
> Associate Artist, *Project Phakama*
> Freelance facilitator, *The Drive Project* and *Bravo 22 Company*

Working backwards from your objective

After you've gathered your information, the next stage of planning your workshop should be to figure out:

- What's the aim of your workshop?

and

- What do you want the group to achieve by the end of the session?

Once you figure these out, you can start gathering ideas for suitable exercises to plan. Here's an example that we'll use throughout this next section:

> **Topic:** Shakespeare
>
> **Aim:** To teach the group how to explore a Shakespearean text and iambic pentameter
>
> **To achieve:** For the group to perform a short extract of a Shakespeare scene at the end of the session

This'll instantly give you something to focus on. Improvisation, movement and break-dancing will likely be out. Voice and Shakespearean text will be in. It's not to say that you can't include movement, etc., but if it doesn't specifically support the aim, it's a no-go. Make sure that you know what you want to cover and what you want your group to go away with. This'll make it much easier to structure and plan.

> "I find it helpful to start by imagining the end of the workshop first. I try not to hold back, ignore all the logistical challenges, and ask myself 'What would be the dream ending to this workshop?' It's important to start from a place of creativity, ambition and excitement. A good workshop plan should have a crescendo, something to build towards that will give participants the feeling of having really achieved something.
>
> **Euan Borland**
> Head of Education and Community, *The Old Vic*

Breaking your plan into sections

So you know your workshop's aims. Noice. Let's look at how you put it all together.

Staring at a blank page knowing that you need a whole session on voice, movement or the complete works of Shakespeare can sometimes be daunting. How on earth do you fill the time? Well, breaking your workshop into sections can be a good place to start. Here's an example:

Whole-day Workshop – Shakespeare
10am – 5pm (7 hours)

We know we'll need some breaks. So let's say we'll have:

A 1-hour lunch
and two 15-minute breaks

Spreading these evenly throughout the day will automatically give us four sections of content:

Whole-day workshop – Shakespeare 10am – 5pm (7 hours)		
Section 1	10am – 11.30am	1 hour 30 minutes
Break	11.30am – 11.45am	15 minutes

Section 2	11.45am – 1.15pm	1 hour 30 minutes
Lunch	1.15pm – 2.15pm	1 hour
Section 3	2.15pm – 3.45pm	1 hour 30 minutes
Break	3.45pm – 4pm	15 minutes
Section 4	4pm – 5pm	1 hour

Broken down like that, the timings we have now are:

Breaks – 1 hour 30 minutes
Work – 5 hours 30 minutes

Automatically that seven-hour workshop becomes 5 hours and 30 minutes, which makes it less intimidating straight away. Now let's break down each section.

Whole-day workshop 10am – 5pm (7 hours)			
Section	**Time**	**Session Duration**	**Activity**
Section 1	10am – 11.30am	1 hour 30 minutes	30 minutes – Intro to the day and ice-breakers / team-building games 1 hour – Introduction to Shakespeare
Break	11.30am – 11.45am	15 minutes	Chillin'
Section 2	11.45am – 1.15pm	1 hour 30 minutes	Shakespearean techniques to unlock the text

<table>
<tr><td>Lunch</td><td>1.15pm – 2.15pm</td><td>1 hour</td><td>Eatin'</td></tr>
<tr><td>Section 3</td><td>2.15pm – 3.45pm</td><td>1 hour 30 minutes</td><td>Rehearsing their Shakespeare scenes</td></tr>
<tr><td>Break</td><td>3.45pm – 4pm</td><td>15 minutes</td><td>Chillin'</td></tr>
<tr><td>Section 4</td><td>4pm – 5pm</td><td>1 hour</td><td>45 minutes – Showing the scenes
15 minutes – Debrief on the day</td></tr>
</table>

Sections 3 and 4 will have the group working by themselves or showing their work, which means that aside from finding their scripts, the content you'd need to plan for would be:

- Up to thirty minutes of ice-breakers/team-building games.
- One hour of an introduction to Shakespeare.
- One hour thirty minutes of Shakespeare content, techniques and exercises.

This means that in a whole day's Shakespeare workshop with a plan such as this, you actually only have to plan two hours and thirty minutes of content once you've found your scripts. It's still two hours and thirty minutes, but that's nowhere near the mammoth seven hours that you started with. And even then, it'll be much easier to crack once you're clear about what the objective of your workshop is.

Breaking your workshop into sections will help with workshops of any length, not just whole-day workshops. Here's an example of a two-hour workshop without breaks.

2-hour workshop – Introduction to acting			
Session	**Time**	**Session Duration**	**Activity**

Section 1	10am – 10.15am	15 minutes	Intro
Section 2	10.15am – 10.30am	15 minutes	Ice-breakers
Section 3	10.30am – 11am	30 minutes	General acting exercises
Section 4	11am – 11.35am	35 minutes	Devising
Section 5	11.35am – 11.50am	15 minutes	Presentation of scenes
Section 6	11.50am – 12pm	10 minutes	Debrief/ closing

Starting from what you want to include

Sometimes there'll be activities or exercises that you know you need to include in your workshop. If you do, it can be helpful to write them down and to include them in your thinking alongside your objective. They can be your starting point when it comes to designing your workshop, or even the entire workshop itself.

For example, here are some ideas that could be included in a Shakespeare workshop:

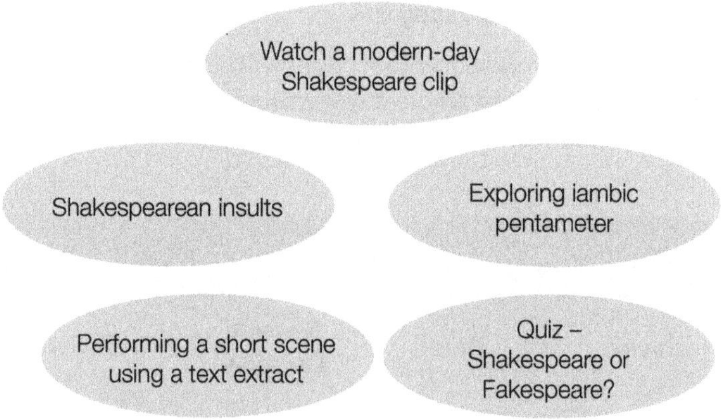

Watch a modern-day Shakespeare clip

Shakespearean insults

Exploring iambic pentameter

Performing a short scene using a text extract

Quiz – Shakespeare or Fakespeare?

With this approach, you know what you want; you just need to build a structure around the content to make it work. You might not have time for everything that you want to include, and some things may not make the final workshop plan, but it can be a good place to start from. Here's a step-by-step of how you might turn these ideas into a workshop:

1. Write down the exercises or activities that you know you want to use.
2. Decide how you want the workshop to end and what you want the group to achieve.
3. Get a rough idea for how long you want to spend on each section. (You'll want to spend more time on the key sections and less on the warm-up/introductory bits.)
4. Figure out a logical order for each section.
5. Figure out if there are any gaps or other exercises that you need to support those activities.

Giving each section a logical progression

Every story has a beginning, middle and end. And so should your workshops. You need to build up to the core of your session – you can't just jump in and have your group performing *Hamlet* straight away. So make sure that your plan takes the group on a journey by warming them up with the foundations of the work first, before getting into the depths of the content.

No matter how short your workshop is, you should always have some sort of warm-up or introduction to the content that you'll be delivering. You'll then want to build on that work, before delivering the crux of your session. Let's take the plan from the previous section. We can break each section down into the following:

Exercise	Outcome	Position in the workshop
Quiz: Shakespeare or Fakespeare? 5 minutes	Introduces Shakespeare in a light-hearted way	Introduction
Watch a modern-day Shakespeare clip 10 minutes	Allows the group to see a modern-day version of Shakespeare, to get rid of any preconceptions	Introduction
Shakespearean insults 15 minutes	Gets them playing with Shakespeare's language in a fun way	Introduction / Middle
Exploring iambic pentameter 30 minutes	Teaches them the fundamentals of verse-speaking	Main
Performing a short scene using a text extract 30 minutes	Gets them actively using the text	Main

With this plan, we lightly introduce the Shakespeare element before getting to the main section. It then builds so that the group explore the language more and more, before setting them off to apply those skills to a scene.

Also remember that while the length of your workshop will impact what you're able to include, as a bare minimum, you should always have an introductory exercise and a main one, with more time dedicated to the main. If you were cooking a meal, you wouldn't bring out a massive starter first, then serve a small main course. That'd be weird. The same applies here.

Here's how we can order those activities based on three different workshop lengths:

Workshop plan		
30 minutes	**1 hour**	**1 hour 30 minutes**
Shakespearean insults Introduction 10 minutes	**Quiz: Shakespeare or Fakespeare?** Introduction 5 minutes	**Quiz: Shakespeare or Fakespeare?** Introduction 5 minutes
Performing a short scene using a text extract Main 20 minutes	**Watch a modern-day Shakespeare clip** Introduction 10 minutes	**Watch a modern-day Shakespeare clip** Introduction 10 minutes
	Shakespearean insults Middle 15 minutes	**Shakespearean insults** Middle 15 minutes
	Performing a short scene using a text extract Main 30 minutes	**Exploring iambic pentameter** Main 30 minutes
		Performing a short scene using a text extract Main 30 minutes

As you can see, each one builds up to the same goal and has a logical progression. The only difference is that the longer workshops have more time to explore the work than the shorter ones do.

Teach – Explore – Create

'Okay, Linden, so what if I want to teach a group a brand-new technique. I can just teach it to them and they'll get it, right?'

Not quite. Theatre is the art of play, so you need to let people actively explore the new techniques you teach them.

So how do you do that? One of the best ways is through the teach – explore – create strategy:

1. **Play a suitable game**
   Warms them up for the session ahead.
2. **Teach them something new**
   Introduces a new technique that you can actively teach.
3. **Give them time to explore**
   Gives the group the opportunity to practise their new learning, while still having your guidance.
4. **Give them time to create**
   Allows them to apply the new techniques creatively. This means they can explore at their own pace and take full creative control of their process, giving them a sense of autonomy.
5. **Sharing of work**
   Presenting the work to the group will give them a sense of achievement and ownership, and it'll allow your group to reflect on the work and the process. It'll also mean you won't need to plan as much, because a chunk of the workshop will be your group creating and presenting, rather than you leading.

Here are two examples using this strategy:

	Shakespeare – How to speak Shakespearean verse	Movement – Laban efforts (*Direct/indirect, heavy/light, sudden/ sustained, bound/ unbound*)
Game	A Shakespeare call-and-response game	A movement game to get their bodies activated
Teach	Iambic pentameter/ verse-speaking techniques	Introducing one pair of the eight Laban efforts
Explore	Individual script work to apply the new techniques, before hearing a selection of them	Giving them time to play with those two efforts, before teaching them another pair, until they've done all eight
Create	Shakespeare duologues for the group to work on	Create a character with the Laban efforts
Sharing of work	The group present their scenes	An improvisation where their character meets somebody else's

The teach – explore – create strategy can give people the time and space they need to fully explore a new technique. It's similar to the 'scaffolding' approach used in teaching (which is the approach of 'I do', 'we do', 'you do'). It can also be scaled up or down depending on the length of your workshop to cover anywhere between half a day and a day – you'd simply give more or less time to each section based on how much time you have.

> "A good plan needs to leave space for participants – you should always be hearing their voices more than your own. You need to leave them space to create. If you've got the structure right, you will have given your participants a toolkit to work with – now you need to trust them to use it.
>
> **Euan Borland**

Drawing from previous exercises

A well-planned workshop will draw on your previous exercises, as well as the skills or learning points they covered. This'll allow your exercises to build on what's come before and will reinforce the work. It doesn't need to be done for every exercise, but the more you can do it, the better. It's a great example of how a well-planned workshop will always be better than a workshop planned at the last minute.

Here's an example:

Activity	Skills used/learning point
Stop/Go The group walk around the room and stop/go on your command. You task them with balancing the space equally amongst the group.	Balance the space.
Yes, Let's In pairs, person A makes a suggestion for something the pair can physically do. Person B says 'Yes, let's!', then they do it.	Accepting your partner's offers.
Counting to Three in Pairs The pair count to three, taking it in turns to say a number each.	Actively listening to your partner.
Sit, Lie, Stand Two/three people do an improvisation or a scene where only one person can be sitting, lying or standing at a time.	Balance the space. Accepting your partner's offers. Actively listening to your partner. Using different physical levels in the scene.
Improvisation Performance Two actors are given a scenario with a brief outline of their characters. They then improvise a scene.	Balance the space. Accepting your partner's offers. Actively listening to your partner. Using different physical levels in the scene.

With this example, you'd be wise to actively remind your group about what they've learnt before and to apply their learning to what they're doing now. Doing this will allow your workshop to be more focused and effective at achieving your learning outcomes.

Games/warm-up activities

Every workshop should include a game or some form of warm-up activity. It's easy to think of games as being a luxury, but don't underestimate their impact. Games can:

- Bring joy to the room and allow the group to have fun.
- Get rid of any nerves and allow the group to relax.
- Get the group more connected to each other through play.
- Warm up the skills they'll need for the session (such as teamwork).
- Lightly introduce or set the foundation for later exercises.
- Set the scene for the workshop's topic or theme.

Some games will be quite neutral in terms of their style, but you can often adapt them to suit the theme of your workshop with a few minor tweaks. For example:

Zip Zap Boing *The group stand in a circle*		
Normal	**Shakespeare**	***Star Wars***
Zip *Sends the energy to the next person in the circle.*	'To be!'	*Lightsabre sound*
Zap *Sends the energy to someone across the circle.*	'Thou villain!'	'I am your father!'

Boing *Deflects a zip back to the person who sent it.*	'Or not to be!'	'The force!'

Even though they're games, don't fall into the trap of thinking you can just choose games willy-nilly. Hell no. You should choose the games that best support your plan. Here are some examples:

Workshop Theme	Game	Why
Improvisation	**Yes, Let's** *Partners take it in turns to suggest an action/activity to do. The other partner responds with 'Yes, let's!', then they do it. The action/activity is carried out until the other partner suggests something else.*	This establishes the foundation of improvisation, which is to accept the offers that the other actor is making in the scene.
Movement	**Hand Hypnosis** *In pairs, person A holds their palm open a few inches away from person B's face. Person B follows their hand wherever they move it, trying to keep their hand the same distance away from their face.*	This gets the group moving their bodies and gets them out of their heads, stopping them from overthinking.

Healthy relationships	**Master and Servant** *Half the group sit on chairs in a circle. These are the 'servants' (one chair remains free). The other half of the group stand with one person behind each chair, the 'masters'. The master with the empty chair must make eye contact with a servant to get them to leave their master and to sit in their chair. When the servant moves to swap chairs, if their master taps them on their shoulder, they have to stay in their seat.*	This can be linked to how difficult it can be for partners to leave an unhealthy relationship.

You could, of course, use Hand Hypnosis in the healthy relationships workshop, or Master and Servant in the improvisation one. Nothing bad will happen; the world won't blow up. But clearly they wouldn't be as suited to those sessions as they are here. Choose games that complement your workshop where you can. It'll be for everybody's benefit.

"Integrated exercises really come into their own later in the workshop if the warm-ups themselves can be used to create scenes. For example, balancing the space or using levels can become vital tools in creating a battle scene in a Shakespeare play. If these exercises have been set up as part of the world of the story, the group will absorb them naturally into their own performance vocabulary, rather than perceiving them as separate to the play itself.

I once worked with a teacher who wanted to work on the wintry world of Narnia. They also wanted to do a warm-up and created a tightrope exercise to develop movement and focusing skills. We agreed that the exercise would work best if applied to the world of the story – so instead of being about a tightrope, it became about walking on ice, or over narrow bridges in the snowy world of the story.

Kate Beales

How to plan a course

Planning a course is an extension of planning a workshop, so just like with an individual session, you need to give your course an overall objective. The key to a great course is to have each day build on the skills or learning points of the previous sessions, so it should be a combination of creativity and logic when planning. Some key questions to ask yourself are:

- What's the overall aim of your course?
- What are the specific learning outcomes?
- Which specific areas of work do you want to cover?
- What do you want your group to be able to do by the end?

Planning a course for the first time may feel like you're having to plan 10,000 hours' worth of content, but once you break things down, you'll often realise that you'll have far less time than you thought, and will probably be wishing for more. So you need to be clear about what you want each day to achieve. Ultimately, the more specific you can be about the outcomes of your course, the more creative you can be with how you design it.

Once the aim of the course is established, it then becomes a question of figuring out which areas you need to cover to support that objective – then everything should go from there. Having several days of content to plan can sometimes feel quite daunting, but, broken down into the areas that you want to cover (e.g. voice, movement), things become far less intimidating. So start with the main aim of your workshop and work from there.

Let's take a look at an example:

6-day workshop
Aim of the week: To learn how to approach a modern text and how to develop a character **Sub-aim:** To learn to stop trying to be interesting

Day	Focus of the Day	Notes
1	Team-building/ getting to know the group	• Gets the group acquainted with each other and with you, creating a coherent team for the week.
2	Body language/ movement	• Teaches the basics of non-verbal communication, essential for character development. • Engages them physically and encourages them to stop overthinking.
3	Improvisation/ voice work	• Teaches them to play their objectives, rather than trying to be interesting. • Looks at vocal technique and how to use their voices effectively to support text.
4	Shakespeare	• Teaches them techniques to approach Shakespearean text and verse, which can then be applied to modern text.
5	Modern text	• Draws on all of the work from the above, to inform their approach to text and character.
6	Scene presentation	• The group perform their modern texts, drawing on: ▪ A strong sense of group cohesion. ▪ Body language skills. ▪ Playing their objectives and vocal technique. ▪ Shakespeare and modern text skills.
7	Off	Off

There's nothing stopping you from having content that's completely separate from your main aim, or having a whole week on one particular form, but the key questions you should always come back to are 'Why are you doing this?' and 'What is the aim of your workshop?' Something such as clowning, for example, might seem completely out of place on a naturalistic acting course, but if you were to link it to an overall aim of finding the truth of your performance, it'd absolutely be relevant. So the actual style or techniques can be wildly different – so long as you have some kind of through-line to tie it all together.

Finally, just as you would for an individual workshop, you need to make sure that you plan your course with your group in mind, in terms of both what they'd enjoy and what would be a logical flow for the course. All the same rules apply. You'll need to build up to your content throughout the course in a similar way to how you would for a one-day workshop. Introduce the work, explore it, then build up to your core content.

'What do you want to do?'

Ask a kid what they want for dinner and their answer will probably be closer to cake and ice cream than it will be fruits and vegetables. What they want won't necessarily be what they need.

Asking groups what they want to do can be helpful as an addition to your course, but it should *inform* your decisions about your plan – it can't *be* the plan.

People don't know what they don't know. Shakespeare, improvisation, singing, dance, Meisner – most of these would never make a group's request list, so basing your plan entirely on what a group wants to do can be limiting. It's always good to bear in mind when you're planning, but you shouldn't be outsourcing the planning of your course to your group. It's your job to make the decisions.

Also, if you're running an intensive course, you're going to need to have some idea of what you want to cover before you start. Workshops take time to plan, so if you haven't done any planning before you start and you're working with a group every single day, you'll have wasted a huge amount of potential prep time. The best approach is to have a general plan or outline before you begin, then to adapt it once you meet your group and know who you have in the room. Plus, it's easier to remove content from your plan a few days in than it is to start from scratch midway through. You won't have the luxury of time that you would if there were days or weeks in-between each session, so make sure you prepare as much as you can. It's also helpful to spend the first session getting to know the group before jumping into any in-depth content on your first day, because you'll have a better idea about who you're planning for.

Finally, if you do want to get the group's views on what they'd like to cover, make sure that everyone gets the chance to input. Break them off into smaller groups to generate ideas, or offer a suggestion pot for people to put ideas into. Asking the group for opinions during a whole group discussion will likely favour those who have the loudest voices, and you probably won't get much input from the quieter people in the room.

Additional Points on Planning

Now that we've covered how to plan a great session, there are some additional points you should bear in mind when you're planning, as they can have a big impact on your delivery.

Doing a session without a plan

'Billy's great, but he never puts the work in. Can you imagine how good he'd be if he actually prepared?'

Doing a session without a plan, otherwise known as 'winging it', should be a last resort. It should never be your default position. You can always chuck a plan away if you don't need it, but you can't make one up on the spot if you don't have one. A well-planned session can save you from most of the challenges you can encounter in a workshop, and your group will get far more out of it. Plus, they'll be able to tell when you haven't put the effort in, so there's no benefit to going into a room without being prepared. Always make sure that you're going in with a plan. Saying you haven't got the time isn't an excuse. Stop being a diva. You're not Beyoncé.

Don't feel the need to reinvent the wheel

You don't need every workshop plan to be revolutionary. If you have new or creative ideas, great, but it's likely that over time you'll figure out a core group of exercises that you can adapt to a range of different groups, which will become your go-to exercises. And that's okay; you don't need to have a thousand games or exercises under your belt. So don't feel that you need to start each workshop from scratch if you've already delivered a workshop successfully in the past that you can draw from.

'Listening mode'

Drama workshops should actively engage your group. They

shouldn't be lectures. So as a general rule, you should try to have as many people actively involved throughout your workshop as possible. The longer people have to sit and listen, the more likely they'll go into 'listening mode' and become passive and disengaged. And that's not what you want – you want Charlie and his friends listening and participating, not dozing off in the background. Listening and observing obviously have their place in a workshop, but the more you can actively engage your group, the more you earn the moments in which they need to listen.

You can help to prevent 'listening mode' by being actively aware of it when you plan. Notice if there are big chunks of your workshop where people will be listening and not engaging, or if there are exercises that you can tweak to have them engaging with each other rather than listening to you. Thirty minutes of you telling your group how to perform Shakespeare should bring up some red flags on your radar, because they'll probably listen for ten minutes at most – the rest of the time could be better spent on something else. So be aware of this in advance, rather than watching your group melt into a slumber while you're delivering.

Make sure your plan is easy to read

Make sure you have a version of your plan that's easy for you to dip into when you're running the workshop. You don't want to be wading through mountains of material to find your plan amongst reams of notes and scribbles. If your plan isn't simple enough for you to look at and get what you need within seconds, write out a clean version of it so that you can. Also, putting the actual time frames for each exercise can often be more helpful than writing how long you expect the exercise to take. Here's an example:

Writing the time frames vs the time each exercise will take

Whole-day workshop – Shakespeare
10am – 5pm (7 hours)

Timeframes			Time each exercise will take	
Intro to the day and ice-breakers/team-building games	10am – 10.30am		**Intro to the day and ice-breakers/team-building games**	30 minutes
Introduction to Shakespeare	10.30am – 11.30am		**Introduction to Shakespeare**	1 hour
Break	11.30am – 11.45am		**Break**	15 minutes
Shakespearean techniques to unlock the text	11.45am – 1.15pm	**or**	**Shakespearean techniques to unlock the text**	1 hour 30 minutes
Lunch	1.15pm – 2.15pm		**Lunch**	1 hour
Rehearsing their Shakespeare scenes	2.15pm – 3.45pm		**Rehearsing their Shakespeare scenes**	1 hour 30 minutes
Break	3.45pm – 4pm		**Break**	15 minutes
Showing the scenes	4pm – 4.45pm		**Showing the scenes**	45 minutes
Debrief on the day	4.45pm – 5pm		**Debrief on the day**	15 minutes

Knowing when you want to start and end each section can make it easier for you to keep track of your workshop in the moment, as you won't need to constantly calculate your timings. But you also have the option of using both:

Time frames	
Intro to the day and ice-breakers/ team-building games	10am – 10.30am (30 minutes)
Introduction to Shakespeare	10.30am – 11.30am (1 hour)
Break	11.30am – 11.45am (15 minutes)

It's also good practice not to refer to your workshop plan while you're delivering. But at the same time, it's not a memory test. You can refer to it if you need to. If you can, it's better to have it as an aid at the side of the room and to refer to it during breaktimes or when you've set the group a task, but if it makes the workshop smoother to have it with you, then go for it. And it's definitely fine to refer to if you're doing something specific, such as putting people into groups that you have written down.

Visually it's better to refer to your notes on a notepad rather than a phone or a tablet. There's something about the single-use function of paper that keeps you present in the room. You'll know that you're not scrolling social media, but your participants won't. So keep it old-school and get a notepad and pen.

Lastly, be mindful of what you write about the people in your group. If you're on the other side of the room and a participant gets a chance to have a peek at your notebook, they will. Who wouldn't? So make sure you don't write anything outrageous that you wouldn't be happy for them to see.

Example Workshops

Opening section of a workshop

This is an example of the first part of a workshop that I often deliver with new groups. It's relatively flexible, and you'll see how each exercise builds on the previous one and how the basics translate into an actual workshop plan.

Exercise	Formation	Energy of the exercise	Interaction
Touch Every... (right knee, elbow, forehead)	Scattered	High	P – P
Stop/Go	Walking around the room	Calm	F – P
Group line in name order	Line	Calm	F – P / P – P
Group line in eye-colour order	Line	Calm	F – P / P – P
Group circle in house-number order	Circle	Calm	F – P / P – P
Name Game	Circle	Focused	F – P
Tell your partner a moment in your life when you felt happy/proud	Partners around the room	Calm	P – P

P – P = Participant to participant
F – P = Facilitator to participant

A pretty straightforward selection of exercises. Now let's break them down to see how each exercise works, and why they've been selected.

<table>
<tr><th>Exercise</th><th>Formation</th><th>Energy of the exercise</th><th>Interaction</th></tr>
<tr><td>Touch Every…</td><td>Scattered</td><td>High</td><td>P – P</td></tr>
<tr><td colspan="4">The exercise – Being the first exercise of the day, this would get everyone to greet each other in seconds and instantly breaks the touch barrier between each person.
Formation – Breaks the circle you had them in to open the workshop and scatters them in the space.
Energy – High. Giving them a 10-second time limit ramps things up. It's a great way to transform the group from being reserved and apprehensive to being energised in under a minute.
Interaction – With each other. It acts as a mild ice-breaker.</td></tr>
<tr><td>Stop/Go</td><td>Walking around the room</td><td>Calm</td><td>F – P</td></tr>
<tr><td colspan="4">The exercise – Gets them physically moving and embodied in the space.
Formation – It can start straight away from the previous exercise, because people will start from wherever they happen to be. They'll also be less able to talk to each other because they'll be walking around.
Energy – Calm, but energised, because the previous exercise will have energised them a bit. Any energy they do have would be relatively controlled with this exercise.
Interaction – Because you'll be actively leading, it'll allow your group to get used to your style of delivery from early on in the workshop.</td></tr>
<tr><td>Line in name order</td><td>Line</td><td>Calm</td><td>F – P / P – P</td></tr>
<tr><td>Line in eye-colour order</td><td>Line</td><td>Calm</td><td>F – P / P – P</td></tr>
</table>

<table>
<tr><td>Circle in house-number order</td><td>Circle</td><td>Calm</td><td>F – P / P – P</td></tr>
<tr><td colspan="4">These exercises would be delivered one at a time, firmly establishing each one before moving on to the next.

The exercise – Serves as an ice-breaker by getting them to engage with each other through an active task.

Formation – The transitions between each exercise are relatively quick, because you can call out each one and get them into each formation in seconds. You can also reintroduce Stop/Go, to combine the two exercises. If you wanted to make smaller groups that aren't friendship groups, you can call out one of the formations, then get them into partners or groups with the people next to them. If you end with a 'house-number order' circle, it automatically puts them in a circle ready for the next exercise.

Energy – Calm, because they'll be focused on their task. Alternatively, they'll be more energised if you give them a time limit to get into each order, e.g. three seconds.

Interaction – You'll be leading the exercise when you're setting up the task or calling out the instructions, but the interaction will be with each other when they need to figure out their relevant orders. This'll allow them to get to know each other.</td></tr>
<tr><td>Name Game</td><td>Circle</td><td>Focused</td><td>F – P</td></tr>
<tr><td colspan="4">The exercise – Gets everyone to share their name to the group in the circle, along with an action. This gets their names into the room from the very beginning.

Formation – Seamlessly leads on from the previous exercise as they're already in a circle.

Energy – Focused, because each person is given their moment to say their name. They're also not able to interact with each other because you're actively leading the session.

Interaction – Allows you to establish your working style as a facilitator and to be able to repeat everyone's names in the space.</td></tr>
</table>

Tell your partner a moment in your life where you felt happy/ proud	Partners around the room	Calm	P – P

The exercise – This gives your group some time to get to know someone else in the group and to share a bit about who they are with that person (not to be shared with the rest of the group).

Formation – They're in a circle from the previous exercise, so you can tell them to get into partners with the person next to them.

Energy – Calm, from the focused Name Game before.

Interaction – With another person in the room. This gives you the opportunity to step back and for them to interact with each other.

Planning process and workshop plan

Here's an example of a workshop I delivered for a drama school using the 'starting from what you want to include' approach that I mentioned in the 'How to plan your session' chapter on page 9.

What I was asked to focus on:

Drama schools/The acting industry

- How do you get into drama school?
- Do you need to go to be successful?
- Which drama schools are good, which are bad?
- How do you deliver a good monologue?
- How to survive in the industry.

Here's what I wanted to include, based around what I'd been asked to focus on:

- **How to carry yourself confidently as an actor** – How actors present themselves is important. From the way they walk into the room to the way they conduct themselves in the interview.
- **How to deliver a good monologue** – The group had monologues prepared, so it was important to work on and improve their performance.
- **Q&A on drama schools** – I knew they'd have questions, so it'd make sense to give them the space to ask them.
- **Q&A on the industry** – Same as the above.
- **Top tips on drama schools** – I had some tips that they probably wouldn't know to ask, so I needed to be able to share these.
- **Top tips on the industry** – Same as the above.

I then decided on the following:

- There had to be a balance between the amount of practical work that they did and the sections where I gave them information. Not necessarily 50/50, but balanced.
- The sections had to be spread out. It couldn't have all the practical work together for an hour, followed by an hour of listening.

This was the final workshop plan:

Drama schools and the industry (2 hours)	
Practical: How to carry yourself confidently	30 minutes
Drama-school advice	15 minutes

Drama school Q&A	15 minutes
Practical: How to deliver a good monologue	30 minutes
Industry advice	15 minutes
Industry Q&A	15 minutes

I then simply had to decide which exercises I wanted to use for the practical tasks and the advice that I wanted to pass on in the Q&A sections.

By being clear about what I wanted to cover and how I wanted the session to be run, planning this workshop was relatively straightforward.

Comedy workshop for a course

This is a real-world example of a comedy workshop by Louise Fitzgerald. She's adapted a typical workshop template and improved it to suit her own needs. There's no right or wrong way to write down your workshop plans, so long as you have enough detail in your workshop when you deliver it, along with clear learning objectives. You need to know what you want your group to have demonstrated by the end.

This plan is for session one of her week-long course, but you'll see that the template could be used for single sessions, or duplicated to cover a whole course. It's a framework that she uses for guidance, but she adapts the timings and tasks as she needs to, and makes written notes of her changes straight after the session.

Week No.	Session Title	Imagination, openness and play
1	**Session Aims**	• Introduction to the course's expectations and the teaching style of the tutor. • Identify students' personal targets and what kind of comedy they like to watch. • Discuss what the students want from the course. • Get students to work together, have fun, play and engage their imagination. • Understand importance of comedy connection with the audience.
	Learning Outcomes	• Play with gesture, body and movement. • Explore the fundamental basics of physical comedy, finding the funny in conflict, desire and failure. • Work with others in devising a physical comedy slow-motion fight scene.

Time	Activity
6pm	**Introduction to session and course expectations** • Outline the course structure, the overall aim of the next six weeks, student/tutor expectations, and the approach to work specifically relating to comedy acting. • Check-in – 'One word/gesture or sound to illustrate feeling.'

6.10pm	**Ice-breakers/focus and warm-up exercises** • Name Game. • Call-and-response movement game. • Introduce their partner to the group. Try to sell them to the group as well as possible. • What are their expectations/desires/wants from the course?
	What makes you laugh?
6.40pm	• In small groups, discuss what you find funny, what you like to watch, who you admire and what you want to achieve from the course. • Tutor to go to each group as they discuss, then to bring the discussions into the wider group.
6.55pm	**An actor's discipline – it's all in the detail** • Physical warm-up – body and facial stretch, chewing a wasp, etc. • In two groups, work together to be an object moving across the room, then all work together to 'move' an imaginary object across the room. Focus, be detailed, be as truthful as possible. • Slow-motion race.
7.15pm	**Universal appeal/physical comedy** • Discuss the universal appeal of physical comedy.

7.25pm	**Create a physical slapstick piece in slow motion** • Put students into pairs (or threes if necessary). Ask them to face opposite each other. There must be distance between the pairs (two lines work well). Play a suitable track to create tension ('Duel of the Fates' works well). • Tell the students they're going to create a fight sequence. They must tell a story, it must be heightened, including failure, pain, triumph, etc. They must not touch each other – even as they move closer together. • At first, they just need to stare each other out. Then they can see what grows out of this as the music continues. Build the reaction each time, but still keep the distance. Have fun. PLAY. • Use these playful 'act and react gestures'/ movements to create a sequence of at least 10 moves. It must also be explored/ presented in slow motion. (Keep the music on in background.) • Other tracks to play with: 'Tequila' / 'Eye of the Tiger' / Theme from *The Good, The Bad and The Ugly* / *Kill Bill* / *Benny Hill* / *Superman* / *Star Wars* / *Indiana Jones* / *Mission Impossible* / *James Bond* / *Rocky* / Brahms – 'Hungarian Dance No.5' / Rossini – 'William Tell Overture'. • Highlight – what each character wants (objective) in order to sharpen the actions.

7.50pm	Perform the piece (choose a soundtrack from above to support the piece): • Always slow and using the same choreography. • The tutor gives notes to improve on the first performance then rehearses them to explore, discover and add layers. • Show the work, do it again, this time include the audience.
	• Maybe add a line of dialogue at the beginning, middle or end: ▪ Add a given circumstance – old, drunk, children, need the toilet, etc. ▪ Become better, bolder and braver each time...
8.15pm	**Feedback, recap and reflect** • What did we enjoy as an audience? • How did body language/facial expression communicate intention? • One 'takeaway' from the session. • Talk about the concept of character for next week and get students to read the handouts.
8.30pm	The End.
Next week	• Look at stock comedy characters. • Create a comedy character. • Explore the background, needs, wants and desires of a character through improvisation. • Introduce comedy monologues.

Scheme of work template

If you're working on an accredited course, you'll be required to submit a Scheme of Work for every session. A Scheme of Work is basically a template that shows your session plan. Some people may find that it takes away from the creative joy of the work, but they can actually be a godsend when you're a freelancer, because they allow you to keep track of what you did, and when, which can sometimes be difficult if you're doing multiple jobs at the same time. It also means that once you plan a session and have it written down, you'll be able to draw on it again in the future, which'll save you from having to start from scratch every time.

This template is one I was given when teaching at a UK drama school, but remember that you can adapt your workshop plans and templates to suit you, just as Louise did with her template in the previous section.

Term and year	Tutor

What are the aims of the course:
Unit: **Course Structure:** Within this section the tutor should outline the teaching pattern, length of module and levels of outside study/work, e.g. line-learning. **Content:** Within this section the tutor should outline the overall content of the module. For example, you may be considering mask work and looking at seven expressive states using tools such as improvisation and learnt techniques from personal and contextualised practices.

Week	Date	The main focus of this class is to:
		Theme: Within this section the tutor should outline the main focus of the class, for example: 'The First Mask – a journey of neutrality.'

1		**Key Task or Exploration:** Within this section the tutor should outline the main task that the learner will explore during the session. This could be something like: 'Learners will explore the process of putting on the neutral mask and turning to face the audience using an anatomical and atmospheric neutrality. Processes for achieving this state and witnessing each other attempting to embody this state will be explored throughout the lesson.' **Development (reading, exercises, references):** Within this section, the tutor can list textbooks that have helped them to prepare for the lesson, and also outline work they expect the student to do outside of class. **Differentiation:** Within this section the tutor will state how they offer techniques for differentiation between learner's needs, such as providing a blue film for dyslexic learners to read scripts.
2		**Theme:** **Key Task or Exploration:** **Development:** **Differentiation:**
3		**Theme:** **Key Task or Exploration:** **Development:** **Differentiation:**
4		**Theme:** **Key Task or Exploration:** **Development:** **Differentiation:**
5	Week off	

Learning Outcomes:
Within this section the tutor will outline the learning outcomes for their course.

Teaching Methods:
Within this section the tutor will outline the teaching methods used for their course.

Assessment:
Within this section the tutor will outline the Formative Assessment agreed with their Head of Department and all Summative Assessments with dates and timings.

Before Your Workshop

So you've got your plan established? Great. This section will cover some key points that you need to bear in mind before you walk into the room. Preparation is key with any workshop, so be sure to take these on board before you begin.

Arrive early

Thirty minutes before. This is as true for life as it is for workshops. I can almost guarantee that something will go wrong before you start, so being early will allow you time to prepare. Here's a snippet of some of the problems I've had in the past when I've arrived at the space:

- I'd planned for a large space. It was tiny.
- They said there'd be a music speaker. There wasn't.
- I was locked out of the venue. With the group and their parents.
- (In London) A leaf fell on a train line. The entire rail network shut down.
- The laptop the school provided to play our opening video wouldn't work. Their alternative laptop did work but it wouldn't connect to the projector because the screws had come out of the socket meaning that when you pushed the cable into the connector the whole socket moved in as well, so it wouldn't connect and therefore nothing worked.
- They asked to see my criminal record check. And to check it on their system. And to photocopy it. And to see every ID I had on me. And to trace my ancestral history.
- The school had two campuses. Fifteen minutes apart. I was in the wrong one.

- Tables and chairs. Tables and chairs everywhere.
- Our room was changed. To the dining hall. After lunch. Before cleaning.

Living far away isn't a justification for being late. Neither is a delayed train or 'being a late person'. Plus, you don't want your first impression to be you bursting through the doorway drenched in sweat. There'll always be something that crops up – either on your journey to the venue or once you enter the room – but arriving early lets you solve the problems with peace, rather than panic. Plus, the great thing about being early is that if you are running late, you're still able to arrive on time.

Don't over-assume

Workshop leaders can sometimes be their own worst enemy when it comes to how they think a group will be. Subconsciously, assumptions give us a sense of comfort because they take away the discomfort of the unknown. But that's what good preparation is for. Your planning and preparation should allow you to adapt to whoever you get in the room.

Here are two real-life examples I've seen from people over-assuming about their group, and what happened:

Group	Facilitator's reaction	What happened
A healthy-relationship workshop in a sixth form, with a group of boys studying game design.	'This will be hard. They're going to be really misogynistic.'	The group were great. An all-round positive workshop.

A workshop on healthy relationships with a mixed sixth-form group.	'They might have anxiety. What if they can't read?' (*The facilitator then did all of the reading and script work for them.*)	I took the lead for the next workshop (the other half of their class). I had them read the scripts and they were great. They took a lot from the session.

Over-assuming will create problems, not solutions. Ultimately, you'll have no idea who your group are or what their capabilities will be until you meet them, regardless of the demographic. Assumptions like the above can massively lower your expectations for the group, and groups will rise to whatever expectations you have for them. So if you go in with low expectations, expect a low-level outcome.

Now, clearly there are some things that are reasonable to assume. If you're delivering a workshop for a special needs group or with young people in an alternative provision setting (such as a pupil referral unit), it's reasonable to assume that you'll need to adjust your plans to make them more accessible. Or if you're working with a school group that's completely new to Shakespeare, you'd be wise not to attempt your long dreamed-of vision of *Hamlet*. But don't assume that they're going to hate it. Sally may have been waiting all her life to do Shakespeare. Over-assuming will limit your ability to work with the group effectively, and will prevent Sally from living her best life.

It's about having a healthy balance and being aware of your assumptions, but not reducing your level of expectation for the group. Be responsive to the actual people in the room, rather than who you think they are or who they might be.

Using music in a workshop

'Oh my gosh I love this song!'

Music is an invaluable tool for any workshop leader. It allows you to instantly set the mood of the room and to completely transform a space. You don't need to have brilliant taste in music, but a few good playlists will go a long way. Having a side hustle as a DJ will also help.

Buy a portable speaker if you're serious about using music. As with all technology, the list of problems you can encounter with music is endless. Including:

- Venues that say they have speakers but don't.
- Venues without connector cables.
- Venues with cables, but the wrong ones.

All these things (and more) will happen at some point if you rely on the equipment you're given. Having your own speaker means you can walk into any space and be confident you can blaze some tunes within minutes. The speaker I have is powerful enough that I could play music in the middle of a field if I needed to, which means I can pretty much play a tune in any circumstance.

A portable speaker also means you can control your music wirelessly from your phone, rather than having a speaker shackled to a plug socket with you constantly walking over to it. Plus, if you're really cool like me, you can even fade the music out to mark the end of an exercise or whenever you're about to speak. All from your pocket. Magic.

Lastly, it's useful to stand at the opposite end of the room to wherever your speaker is. You won't be able to gauge how loud your music is from the group's perspective if it's next to you, so by standing away from it you can adjust the sound to the right level.

Use music intentionally. The more specific you can be about the music you use, the more you can influence the mood of the room. I once ran a course where the group seemed to gravitate towards being gloomy – everything they did leant towards being bleak and melancholic. So what did I do? Put on feel-good music. Whenever I could. Positive vibes only. If I didn't, their mood would've set the tone for the whole course. It helped to lift the weight off their shoulders, which was far more enjoyable than drifting into misery.

Being intentional about music is especially important if an exercise relies on a song. For instance, if you're using music to influence a scene, don't leave it to chance. Plan ahead and be specific. And if you're doing an exercise that needs a particular rhythm, make sure you have a song lined up with a beat that fits. Spotify's decent but it's definitely no DJ.

Before, after, and during breaks. Music can be used to set the mood of your room even when you're not actively working. Your group have never met before and are sitting in silence? Put on some music to break it. Want to set the tone of the room from the minute they walk in? Have a playlist on as they enter. Want to give the breaks more of a vibe? Put on some tunes. The in-between times of your workshop are important because they're when people can relax and get to know each other. So help them along by creating a positive atmosphere.

Set up your playlists before, not during your workshop. It's fine to search for songs and to change tracks during a workshop, but remember that you're a workshop leader. Not a DJ. So keep your eyes on the room.

If you do have to search for songs, searching through playlists that you've already made is far easier than coming up with songs on the fly. Spotify playlists can be helpful, but being thrown wildcards from the eighties that you didn't expect can really throw your exercises off. So make your playlists before your workshop starts. Then it's easier to put it on and leave it be.

Filter any songs that have swearing if you're working with younger groups. Spotify has a setting where you can stop it playing songs that have explicit lyrics – but be aware(!). I've had times where it's still gone ahead and played some hardcore rap, even with this setting on. So at the time of writing, this setting isn't foolproof. There's nothing quite like hearing a 'f***' or a 's***' ping out from your speaker when you're in a primary school and the group are working on a task in silence.

Shazam can be a godsend for workshop music, so if you're out and hear a good song, Shazam it; or use any other similar music recognition app on your phone. There've been tons of times when I've watched a theatre show and I've subtly, absolutely not obviously, Shazammed a music track from my pocket. It's given me some of the number-one hits for my workshops.

I always try to play a wide variety of music on my courses, to give everyone a 'this is my song!' moment. It's a nice touch as it gives people that little nugget of joy. I'll also make a playlist of the songs from the course for the final goodbye session, along with any songs that people referred to as being their favourites. It echoes our time together and is a nice way to make things more personal as we bring things to a close.

Designate a coats and bags area

Much as they might want to, bags and coats should not be participants in your workshop. Keep things organised and keep clutter to a minimum by having an area for people to put them in. Have a quick scan for the best place for this when you arrive at your room. If you tell your group where to put their stuff as soon as they walk in, they'll automatically put them there every day.

Technical equipment

Have your technical equipment preset and ready to go so that you can pull it up instantly. Nobody wants to wait for your computer to boot up, do a virus scan or update, or for you to find the right document or music. So make sure you have everything ready and that you've ironed out any technical issues beforehand.

Resources

'How am I supposed to do the scene? I don't have page three!'
Terry

Make sure you have everything you need prepared in advance. If you have scripts, print them double-sided with page numbers, and stapled. It might seem pedantic, but you'll want to prevent as much confusion and reasons to avoid the work as possible. It's harder for people to lose their place in a script if it has page numbers, and even harder to lose the pages when the sheets are double-sided or stapled. You only need Terry to lose page three of *Macbeth* a handful of times before you realise a few staples and page numbers are a worthy investment.

It's also a good idea to make extra photocopies of scripts. That way you have backups if you need to give out a different scene or if anybody loses one. Printing a few extra copies will save you the time and stress of having to dash around a venue to get another print-out.

Lastly, particularly if you're running a course, it's good to keep in mind any specific adaptations that you'll need to make to your resources. This could include the colour of paper that you print on (for people who are dyslexic) and having the text in an easy-to-read font. Regardless, there are some things that should be standard practice and are helpful for everyone. Size five font will be requested by nobody. Neither will pages crammed full of text. So make sure that your resources are as easy to access as possible for everyone.

Make the space work for you, not against you

Clean the space – Do a quick scan. Remove anything dangerous, disgusting or distracting.

- *Dangerous* – Chairs stacked too high? Split the stack. Sharp items on the floor? Pick them up. Spillage everywhere? Find a mop.
- *Disgusting* – Sweetcorn and broccoli on the floor? Find a broom.
- *Distracting* – Mirrors where they can see themselves? Draw the curtains. Windows where they can wave at their friends? Draw those curtains too. Water machine where they can get water and spill it everywhere which basically stops the workshop because apparently everybody's thirsty now and everybody's doing it? Take the cups.

The vibe – Every room has a vibe. If you have the opportunity to make your room more pleasant, you should, because the vibe of your room will affect your group's energy and mood. Dim, fluorescent lighting can be a drag. Black drama rooms without windows can be bleak. Rooms with no ventilation can get stuffy and make your group sweat rivers during movement work. The room being too hot or too cold can have an impact too. So do what you can to improve the mood of your room.

Where you'll stand – Remember when you were a kid and you'd walk past a room with your friends and you'd all wave at each other? Yeah. Good times.

Not so good when you're running a workshop though.

To avoid your group getting distracted every time somebody walks past, consciously choose your main position in the room. Don't leave it to chance. If there's a doorway or window that people might walk past, don't stand in front of it. Stand on the opposite end of the room. This goes for any other distractions that might be around. It'll save you having to fight for people's attention.

The size of the room – You have thirty people but the room can barely hold ten? Yep, it happens. The size of the room can wreak havoc on your plans if it's not what you expected. This also has an impact on sound. Having twenty people do partner scenes in a small room will be loud and they probably won't be able to hear each other. But having twenty people in four groups of five will mean that fewer people will be talking at the same time, making it less noisy. So bear these in mind for your exercises and planning. Also, depending on the exercises, be mindful of the ceiling...! Far too many times, I've set up a game of keepy-uppy, only to realise that the ceiling was barely higher than the group. Don't be like me. Be better.

Are there breakout rooms? – Sometimes the room you're in just isn't big enough. Are there any other spaces you can use for the group to rehearse in? Even an empty corridor or an outside space can give you more room to work with (weather permitting), so have a quick check before you start so you know what your options are. A note of caution though – make sure that any public areas you send people to won't disturb anybody else. Having your group rehearse their musical finale outside another group's quiet meditation session will likely raise a few eyebrows.

Reset your room after you finish – Speaks for itself. Leave the room as you'd wish to find it. Do unto others as you would have them do to you.

Bonus ways for the group to enter

There's nothing wrong with having your group simply enter the space. Sometimes simplicity is best. But here are three extra ways you can have them enter if you feel it'd be useful.

Some of these options will be more suitable for groups that you only work with once, while some will be better for groups that you're working with over a period of time. You'll also need to consider the flow of people as they enter; for example, a group of thirty manic teenagers arriving at the same time will give you different options to if they're entering one by one over the space of half an hour.

Give the group a task. Having them enter the space with a task can save people from having to wait around when they enter. For example, asking them to look at pictures or quotes that you've placed around the room that are linked to the play that you're doing. This can be especially helpful for groups that haven't met each other yet and might feel awkward, or school groups where you may be waiting for people to stroll in after lunch.

If you're new to a space that's familiar to the group, you can have them leave and then re-enter. This allows you to take control of how they enter, along with the energy that they come in with. It also gives you the opportunity to greet everyone as they come in, which gives you a moment with each person. You could also decide to have them enter individually or in small groups.

You can have a game running when they enter. This can be a good way to get people active as soon as they enter the space. It can also be more forgiving for people who are late. To do this, make sure that the game you're playing is simple enough for people to jump in and pick up quickly. There's no point doing a game that takes ten minutes to explain, because you'll have to constantly stop the game to explain it. If you're with them over more than one session, you could even kill two birds with one stone and do a game like Foursquare, which they could then do during breaktimes themselves.

Foursquare

Setting the game up

- You'll need an inflatable football, the type that's soft and bounces easily.
- Create a formation of four squares on the floor. Make sure that they're equal in size:

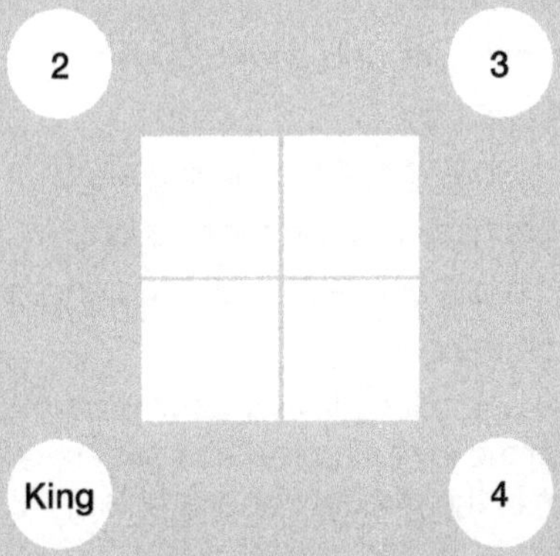

2 3

King 4

- The size of the squares can be as big or as small as you want. It's often played with each square being somewhere between 2x2ft and 5x5ft. Small squares will make the game tighter and more dynamic, while larger squares will make the game more physically active.
- Number the squares from 1 to 4, going round clockwise. Number 1 is the King/Queen (or some other royal dignitary of your choosing).
- Select a King, then give everybody a number. If there are more people than there are squares, the rest of the group will form a queue. The next person in line will be the next person to join the game when somebody goes out.

Playing the game

- The King does the opening serve. They do a short call-and-response, saying 'Foursquare?', to check that everyone's ready. The group then say 'Foursquare' to confirm. The King then serves.
- The game is played with your hands, so you don't need any equipment to hit the ball.
- To serve, the King must drop the ball once into their own square, then bounce the ball into somebody else's square with their hand. They cannot catch the ball. The ball must drop, bounce, then the serve needs to be taken.
- The aim is for each player to bounce the ball into another player's square. The ball needs to bounce once before the player is allowed to hit it.
- The game continues until somebody's out.
- Players are out if:
  - They hit the ball out of the playing area.
  - The ball bounces twice in their square.
  - They hit the ball before it's bounced once in their square.
  - They catch the ball.
- If a player is out, each player below them moves up a square, with the lowest numbered square replaced by the next person in the queue. For example:

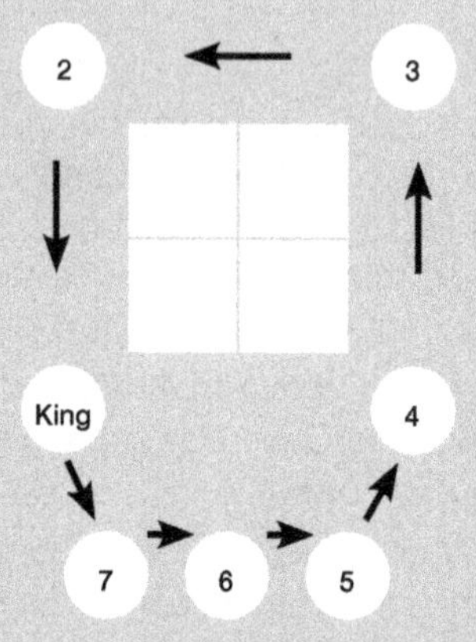

- The winner is whoever's still King when you bring the game to a close

Variations

- The game can also be played with nine squares. In this situation, the King then takes the central square. The squares must be big enough for each player to stand in.

Points to note

- LX tape is usually the best thing to use to mark the squares if you're inside, because it's designed to not leave any stickiness or marks. Chalk can be used if you're outside – just make sure that your venue's okay with it. Either choice is good because they won't move if the ball hits them.
- Make sure that you're allowed to create the squares for the space you're working in. Some rehearsal spaces won't allow you to stick things to the floor, in case it leaves marks.
- Players are free to move inside and outside their square whenever they want, though it's common to stand on your corner at the start of a round.
- You can elect somebody who's not playing to be the referee.
- Players are not allowed to 'smash' the ball, sometimes known as a 'cheeky'. All hits must be underarm or to the side, not downwards.
- Feel free to adjust the rules or create new ones, but make sure that everyone is clear on the rules when you play it.

Number of people: 4+	Standing in the space
Focus Fun Physical	Competitive
Props needed: Inflatable ball the size of a football (one that can bounce)	Suitable for a course

During Your Workshop

There are lots of different things to consider when you're running a workshop, but this chapter will focus on the delivery of the workshop itself. Knowing how to adjust your session and your delivery will give you the power to be more relaxed, more adaptable, and more effective.

What's your workshop about?

Make this clear from the start so your group know what the workshop will be about. You don't need to deliver a PowerPoint presentation about it, just be clear about what the focus is. Your group shouldn't have to find out halfway through a session, or worse – have to work it out for themselves. Knowing what the session is about will put the exercises into context and help to guide their learning.

Start as you mean to go on

How you start your workshop will have an impact on the rest of your session, so make sure that you start as you mean to go on from the very beginning. Trying to establish a way of working halfway through will be much more difficult than if you do it at the start, so make sure you're clear from the get-go.

For example, if you don't want people to talk when you are, you need to be clear about that from the very beginning. In this case, there'd be two ways that you can do this:

Direct – *'Jonathan – no talking when I'm talking thank you.'*

Indirect – **You simply stop talking and wait until he stops**

Another personal example for me is that I always do a countdown from three whenever we're watching back the group's scenes. From the very first time we're about to see a scene, I'll explain that I'll do a countdown and that we'll need everyone's attention, then I'll count down from three to one. That'll then carry through for the rest of the time that I'm with them, and they'll know what to expect every time we do scene work.

You should also bear this in mind when you have an assistant. Assistants are often used to run the warm-ups or games at the start of a session, but having them run the very first exercise with your group can sometimes set up the working environment in a way that isn't in line with how you'd like it to be. This isn't really a concern for a 2-hour workshop or from the second day onwards of a course, but if you're working with people over several days, it's important that you take the lead at the very beginning. You can then let your assistant lead after the break, or from the start of each day from day two. This'll also give them time to observe the group before leading.

> The best example I saw of this was with a workshop leader from Tender Arts. We were running a domestic-abuse workshop in an all-girls school, but because she couldn't make the morning session, she joined after lunch. Normally when I join somebody else's space I tend to take a step back so that the lead practitioner can lead, but this facilitator was different. We started the session and a couple of girls started talking straight away, but she instantly nipped it in the bud, setting the record straight about not talking when somebody else was talking. She wasn't rude – she was calm, assertive and respectful. She then seamlessly carried on the conversation we'd been having as a group before lunch. It was expertly done, and the group respected and warmed to her from that moment, and nobody spoke over us again.

Why are they doing the exercise?

'Sir! Why we doin' this tho?' Charlotte

People need to know why they're doing an exercise. If

Charlotte's doing improvisational dance for four hours and has no idea why, she won't be signing up to do it again.

Explaining the 'why' of an exercise focuses the group's learning. What has an exercise achieved if they don't know why they've done it? You don't need to engrave your aims on slabs of stone and hold them up atop a mountain, but you do need to be clear.

Sometimes it's better to establish the 'why' before you do the exercise, sometimes it's better to establish it after – but the group should always know what the purpose of it was by the time you move on to the next activity. Yes, there are some exercises that will be more abstract or experimental and will be more about the group experiencing the exercise; but even then, that's what you should tell them. So let them know. Plus, people will be far more willing to do a task they don't like when they know there's a reason for doing it.

To note, this applies to exercises rather than games (unless you're specifically doing a game for a purpose that's worth mentioning, such as a game on status if it's related to your workshop). Charlotte doesn't need to be told you're playing Splat for her to have a good time. You can just play it.

Breaking your exercises into stages

'So your instructions are... stop means go and go means stop and clap means jump and jump means clap and head means knee and knee means head... understood?'

'Um...'

This is one of the most powerful tools in your arsenal as a workshop leader, because it gives you immense control and adaptability in how you deliver your exercises. By breaking your exercise into stages, you'll have the control to only progress to the exercise's next stage when the group have completed the stage they're on. The opposite of this would be to give all of the instructions at the same time.

There are a few benefits to doing this:

It allows you to tailor your exercises to smaller groups. This'll stop advanced groups from becoming bored if they finish early, and stop slower groups from getting left behind if they still need more time. A lack of challenge can lead to a group losing interest, whereas work that's too difficult can also make people disengage. So if Miranda's team finish an exercise before the rest, great, give them the next section. David's team still needs more time because they've been talking non-stop? No problem, give them more time.

It allows you to finish exercises earlier if you're running out of time, while still achieving your learning outcome. You can bring the session to a close at any stage of the exercise, rather than feeling like you have to push on at all costs. The group won't know any different because they won't have reached the stages they didn't get to. It'll be an unknown unknown.

It allows you to only move the game or exercise forward when the whole group's ready. This means that you're less likely to be running an exercise or a game with only half the group understanding it, which will save everyone the frustration of you having to re-explain it.

Here are two examples of this technique in action:

Exercise: Devising a scene		
Stage	**With stages** Broken down into stages.	**Without stages** Gives all of the instructions at once.
1	Create a freeze-frame based on a word/ stimulus. (The middle of the story.)	Create a short scene based on the given stimulus. The scene must have a moment of stillness, slow motion and group dance.
2	Create a freeze-frame of something that happens before your first freeze-frame. (The beginning.)	

3	Create a freeze-frame of something that happens after your middle freeze-frame. (The end.)	
4	You have your beginning, middle and end. Now turn it into a scene with dialogue.	
5	Add a moment of slow motion, stillness and group dance.	

Game:
Zip Zap Boing

One of the classic, foundational drama games.
Infinitely versatile.

With the group standing in a circle, the facilitator sends a pulse of energy around the group.

Zip – Sends the energy in one direction (left or right).
Zap – Sends the energy to somebody across the circle.
Boing – Deflects a person's zip to send it back around the other way.

A zip can't be returned to the sender – only a boing can send the zip back from the direction that it came.

You can also choose to have people go out if they make a mistake or are too slow.

Stage	With stages	Without stages

<table>
<tr><td>1</td><td>Establish the zip.</td><td rowspan="5">Teaches the group the zip, zap and boing at the same time, before playing the game.</td></tr>
<tr><td colspan="2">Once it's clear the group have got it...</td></tr>
<tr><td>2</td><td>Add the zap.</td></tr>
<tr><td colspan="2">Once it's clear the group have got it...</td></tr>
<tr><td>3</td><td>Add the boing.</td></tr>
</table>

To be clear, not every exercise can be broken down in this way. But if you're able to, you should. It gives you far more control over your exercises and will be smoother than if you give all the instructions at once.

> "I often layer exercises and games to build the group's confidence and skills. If I'm going to play a game like Zip Zap Boing, I'll begin with a simple game of passing a clap, sound, or movement around the circle at some point during the workshop before I do the actual game. This lets me introduce the key principles of Zip Zap Boing to the group before they play it. I might also use Zip Zap Boing as a lead-in for an ensemble acting exercise, or improvisation exercise – building up the difficulty and complexity in layers.
>
> **Paul Edwards**
> Freelance Practitioner, *National Youth Theatre*, *Almeida Theatre*, *Southwark Playhouse*
> Visiting Lecturer, *Royal Central School of Speech and Drama*, *Brunel University*, *Italia Conti*

The pace of the workshop – know when to move on

This is one of the most important aspects of any workshop. Sticking with an exercise for too long will make your group bored and disengaged, so you need to keep the momentum going and keep the pace of your workshop up. I simply can't stress how important this is. If you feel an exercise has achieved its purpose, or if it feels like it's time to move on or to change the dynamic of the room, do it. This doesn't mean that you need to abandon ship immediately if an exercise drags, but it does mean that you need to push things along as best you can. The key is to be aware of your group and to constantly observe how they respond.

This might mean reducing the amount of time that you give for an exercise, cutting your next exercise completely, only taking a few more comments during a discussion, or doing something different if you know the energy of your next exercise is too similar to what you're currently doing. If you've just had your group sitting and listening for half an hour, don't have them doing the same for the next part of the workshop. Keeping your group engaged should be at the forefront of your mind, because once you start losing your group, it'll be much harder to bring them back again.

This also requires a bit of forethought, because it's easy to set yourself up to fail. Make sure you're not planning activities that are doomed to drag on and you can't get yourself out of, such as asking all one hundred people in the room to say how their day has been. Prevention is always better than cure.

> I was once in a workshop where we had to go round the circle and share what we each had for breakfast, describing each flavour and taste that we experienced. There were thirty of us. And by the time we got to the fifth person, it was clear that, yes, we were going all the way round the circle – because to stop the exercise sooner would be unfair to the other twenty-five people who didn't get their turn. That day, I wished I hadn't had breakfast at all. And I love breakfast.

Always be one step ahead

'Okay, team, time for some script work. Oh, hold up...'

Takes ten minutes to get the scripts

'Okay, let's go!'

If you need to prepare anything for your next exercise, have it ready to go before the current exercise ends, and by the time the next exercise starts. For example, if you're using scripts, have them ready and prepared by your side. It'll save you having to dash over to the opposite end of the room while everybody waits. Get them in place beforehand so you can go straight into it without delay. It'll help to keep up the momentum of your workshop.

Model the energy you wish to see

The energy that you give your exercises as a workshop leader will massively influence the energy that you get from your group. Let's use two examples, using the word 'go' – when you're giving instructions:

- Imagine you're in the army about to storm into enemy lines, and your general shouts 'GO GO GO!' You then storm the barricades.
- Now imagine you're in your weekly Bikram yoga class, and your instructor, signalling the next move, calmly says 'Go...' You then proceed into lotus position.

Same word, two completely different effects.

Running a workshop is the same. Want your group to be energised? Be more energised in your delivery. Want them to be quiet and calm? Bring down your volume and tone. When you're playing something like keepy-uppy and you want your group to be more grounded – holding the ball for a moment, waiting for them to recentre, then calmly saying 'Go' will give you a different result to if you hit the ball and scream 'GO!' This can be done for any word, instruction or exercise. The energy you give will be the energy you get.

Tell people if they're going to share/perform

Make it clear from the start of an activity if you want people to share their work. People will respond differently to an exercise if they know they're sharing back to the group, compared to if they're not. Terry will probably take it easy if he knows his scene won't be seen, but he'll be much more likely to perk up if he knows that Cassie and Tina will be watching.

This is especially important if an exercise is personal or sensitive. Take a game such as the Sixty-Second Life Story, where each person has sixty seconds to tell their life story to their partner before swapping round. Tyrone might be happy to share with his partner that he supports Arsenal, but might be horrified if he has to share that with the group. Being clear from the start allows him to adapt his response appropriately.

You also have the option of checking with the groups beforehand to make sure they're happy to share, which gives you the chance to find out if they're comfortable sharing with an audience.

Everyone performing or only a few?

When you have a group working on a task, you have the choice to have everyone share their work back, or only a few.

The default position should be that everybody does. With school groups in particular, if you give people the option to opt out, they usually will, even if it's something they're perfectly capable of doing. Making things optional means you'll have to negotiate with groups. That's not your job. You're a workshop leader, not a negotiator. Expecting 100% of your group to share and then allowing a last-minute exception will mean 90% will share their work; but setting the expectation that they can opt out may mean you only get 10% to share. It'll be like pulling teeth.

If you're worried that sharing work might be daunting for some – it's only daunting if you make it so. Frame a task as a simple sharing of work rather than as a National Theatre production and people will generally be okay. See the section 'Your reaction shapes their response' on page 229 for more on this.

> “Take care to observe the groups as they work on an exercise or piece of performance, so that you can modify or adjust expectations of the sharing as they develop the work. This can also help you to organise a running order so that a confident and well-drilled piece doesn't come immediately before a group who have found the task a little more challenging.
>
> **Paul Edwards**

Being in control of your instructions

Groups can often get hasty and try to start an exercise before you've even finished explaining it. But it doesn't have to be that way. Having your group wait until you're ready for them to start isn't difficult, you just need to be clear and in control. Some subtle changes here can make a huge impact. For example:

You out of control:

You: 'In groups of three I want you to –'

CARNAGE AS THEY GET INTO THREES

You in control:

'In a minute…(!), I want you to get into groups of three, then I'll explain what to do next.'

or

'When I say "Go", get yourselves into groups of three.'

or

'In a moment you're going to get into threes, then I'll explain what I want you to do…'

Calmly giving these instructions and slowing down your pace will mean they'll likely wait for you to finish, rather than pouncing to get into groups. But if anyone does, calmly but assertively stop them and reiterate that they need to go when you tell them to, rather than straight away. There may be the odd straggler, but reining one person in will be far easier than reining in thirty. Committing to this will mean you'll establish with the group that they don't go until you give the go-ahead. This is particularly helpful to establish early on in the workshop, because it'll then carry on through the rest of it.

Then, to get them into their groups, it's simply a case of being clear when you want them to go, which can be said with:

- 'Okay, go.'
- 'When you're ready...'
- 'Right, get yourself into threes!'

It's also important that you establish the groups before you give out a task. For example, you should create their groups, then only give the instructions once that's done – otherwise the group may still be distracted while you're trying to give them the task. This also applies to when you need people to label themselves A and B.

The clearer you can be as a practitioner, the more your group will know when you want them to start, and the less likely it'll be that you have chaos when you're running your exercises.

Countdowns

'Johnny you've got three seconds to get down these stairs...! Three. Two. One...!'

Poof!* *Johnny's downstairs

There's something about a countdown that sparks people into action. Parents do it all the time.

But they can also be great for workshop leaders. People need time to adjust to instructions. Some practitioners will ask for silence in a room and expect it to happen instantly. Why? Paulette was mid-sentence when you asked for the group's attention. Give her a minute. Even the most well-behaved and focused groups would likely need a few seconds.

You can use a countdown to get people's attention, or just to get them to do a task quicker. Tell a group to get into a circle and they'll probably chill. Tell that same group to get into a circle within five seconds and they'll dart into place like their life depends on it. We all do it. I have no idea why this is. What do we think will happen if we're not in a circle by the end of the fifth count? We'll never know. But it works. So use it.

I started using this from my work in special educational needs schools, where teachers would use it all the time. The children always responded to it well. I then started using it in workshops whenever we'd watch a group's performance, counting from three to one and saying 'Go' for their scene to start. It made things much clearer for the group, rather than having that awkward moment when the actors don't know if they've started yet while some have started and some haven't. It also made it clear for the audience that all conversations needed to end and that it was time to listen.

Time constraints

'But sir! You said one more minute but you gave us five!' No one

Every exercise or task should be given a time constraint. The scientifically proven breakdown of time constraints is as follows:

The time you say they've got	The time you actually end up giving them	How long they'll think they have if you don't give them a time constraint
10 seconds	20 – 30 seconds	Forever
5 minutes	10 minutes	Till infinity
30 minutes	45 minutes	Till death do them part

The actual time you set for a task should be flexible, so don't think you need to give a group exactly five minutes just because you said it. They'll be too engaged in the activity to worry about the time anyway.

It's also helpful to update the group on how much time they have left, which'll help them to pace themselves and to wrap things up. This prevents the situation where you're watching a group perform but still have groups whispering about last-minute changes to their performance. If your vocal projection is good enough, you can announce to the room how much time they have left, or you can go over to each group and tell them one by one.

Failing to give people a deadline will mean that nothing will get done. Or certainly not as quickly. If you wanted to test this, give a group a task without a time constraint and see how relaxed they are. Then tell them they've got one minute left and watch them spring into action.

Visible timers

This is something you can do if you really want your group to work quickly. This works by giving them a timer that they can see, and giving them until the time is up to complete the task. This could be a physical timer or a digital timer on a screen – you can find them online for free with a quick google. A visible timer shows there's no room for negotiation, so your group will have to work efficiently. It's a good technique to use for really quick tasks that you don't want the group to dwell on for too long, or when you really want to be in control of the timings of an exercise.

Get them doing, not thinking

Your group will probably learn better and work quicker by trying things out rather than mulling over their options. If you give a group five minutes to do a task, they'll likely spend four minutes thinking and one minute doing. So encourage them to get up physically in the space and to try things out as soon as possible. It's important to say this as soon as they start working because the sooner you do, the sooner they'll get moving.

You can also tie this in with time constraints (see page 69). If you tell them they only have five minutes to do their task, they'll need to cut the chat and get to work, whereas they won't have that same level of urgency if they don't have some form of deadline.

Side tasks – make them meaningful

Side tasks are when you give people a task during a game or exercise to keep them engaged when they'd otherwise not be doing anything, such as when people go out during a game. They can be a good way to stop people disengaging, and they have their place in a workshop... as long as they're meaningful. Having somebody be a referee, a judge, or to be responsible for keeping track of a score – these are all meaningful activities. Having them do star-jumps is not. Trying to keep people engaged through side tasks can be helpful, but you're better off not giving them at all if they're going to be lame.

As well-intentioned as they might be, side tasks are often better used for specific individuals who may be challenging or who may need to be more actively engaged, because sometimes they respond better when you give them responsibility or something that they can focus on. But even in these cases, side tasks will backfire if they're not meaningful. Ultimately, most people will be fine sitting on the side for a few minutes if they're out in a game or an exercise. Most usually understand and accept it so long as they're not waiting for too long.

> I once saw a facilitator play a game where people went out. To keep them engaged in the session, they had to stand on the side and dance, which was supposed to be fun. And he'd tell them to dance harder because it was fun and they should be enjoying it.
>
> This was not fun, it was cringe.
>
> If a task isn't meaningful, don't do it at all.

Adjust your plan to the group

You need to be flexible with your plan based on who you have in the room. Sometimes that means chucking out exercises that aren't working, sometimes it means switching the order, sometimes it means scrapping the entire workshop plan. Maybe you have too little time left. Maybe the group isn't engaging with the work. Maybe you feel that your plan isn't suited to their needs. There are tons of reasons why you might adjust, but if you feel it's better to change course, do it. Your plan should support you, not restrict you. The only exception here is if the company you're working for has given you a workshop plan to deliver. But even then, most companies won't object if you chuck in an extra game or make some slight adjustments if it makes your group more responsive.

Keeping your eye on the group will allow you to stay responsive. If Phillipe and friends are out of breath, dripping with sweat, then doing that fifth energiser that you'd planned probably isn't the best idea. Send them on a break or do a calming exercise instead. It can sometimes be a bit daunting to adjust and react to who you have in the room, but that's part of the beauty of live theatre and workshops. Each group will be different and will need a slightly different approach. So embrace it.

> " Each group of participants has a different energy, attention span, needs and expectations, and each group has a different dynamic and mix of these factors within it. Workshops can be a complex and charged space where there's potential for life to happen in the most exciting way, and the facilitator is responsible for holding the room and creating a space where creativity can happen. To be that person you need to prepare for the unexpected and commit to your objective for the session; but if all the information you're receiving is telling you it isn't working, be prepared to make the changes that the room is calling for. In the words of Peter Brook, 'Hold on tightly, let go lightly.
>
> **Rachel Ellis**
> Freelance practitioner and Head of Drama,
> *Cambridge School of Visual & Performing Arts*

Managing the timings of your exercises

Being flexible with your plan will mean you'll need to adjust the timings of your workshop to give your exercises the time they need. Sometimes you'll need to speed exercises up or slow them down, so they'll be different to the original timings that you planned. It can be a bit like flying a plane, making constant tweaks and changes to stick the landing, so here are some tips that can help when it comes to adjusting your exercises:

Don't start what you can't finish. This is particularly important for the main content of your workshop. If an exercise needs a solid thirty minutes to deliver it, you need to give it the thirty minutes it deserves. If you've only got fifteen, don't do it. This can sometimes be a challenge because the main part of your workshop will usually be towards the middle or the end, so you often won't know that you're running out of time until it's too late. But prevention is better than cure.

Know what time you need to start an exercise in order to do it justice. If you know you need to start the exercise by 1.30pm, then that's what you need to aim for; though it's always helpful to start a bit sooner if you can. Things usually end up taking longer than you expect.

Don't plan too much content for your session. Quality is always better than quantity, and it's far better to do less, well, than it is to do more, less well. If you do find that you're running out of time and have the choice between speeding through exercises, or doing fewer but doing them justice, you're usually better off with doing less but giving exercises the time that they need.

Be aware of your buffer points. Buffer points are your workshop sections that are flexible, which you can reduce or extend as you need. For example, when it comes to your group rehearsing a scene, you could give them fifteen minutes or thirty, depending on how much time you have. Likewise, having a debrief planned for fifteen minutes at the end of the session can be reduced to five minutes if you need more time on your final exercise.

Take more time on other exercises if you need to. If you have forty-five minutes left but your devising task was planned for thirty, you can simply take your time with it and give them more time for the task than you otherwise would. You can give it the full time it needs.

Play a game in odd gaps. Sometimes you'll end up with a chunk of time that's hard to use. Say, fifteen minutes before a break, which would be too little time to do anything significant but, in some environments, too much time to let your group finish early. In this case you could always play a game rather than starting something substantial.

Adjust who they're interacting with. Setting people a task to work on in groups will usually make the exercise longer than if you led it as a whole group. Adjust the interaction style to lengthen or shorten exercises as you need.

Recalibrate your plan. Breaks are good moments for you to evaluate where you're at with the workshop and to see if you need to make any adjustments. Exercises in which the group are interacting with each other are good for this because they allow the group to carry on working while you recalibrate.

Let go

You're never going to know what'll happen in your workshop, and you'll never be able to control every outcome or be able to prepare for every eventuality. Rather than letting this get to you, let it free you.

If you can let go of needing to be in control of every aspect of your workshop, you'll find it far more enjoyable, and so will your group. Trust that once you've come up with your plan, the rest is for you to figure out as you go.

After Your Workshop

Save your workshop plans

Keep a record of every unique workshop you deliver. It'll save you huge amounts of time in the future. Designing workshops from scratch can take a lot of time, so saving them means you can reuse them and adapt your old workshops easily. You won't need to do this for generic workshops that you can plan in a few minutes, but for anything that requires a big time investment, keep it.

I spent hours designing a body-language workshop once, but I binned the notes. It took me hours to remember it when I needed it a few months later. This happened about four times before I finally decided to take the five seconds to photograph my plan and save it to my computer. It saved me hours in the future when I needed it again.

Store your plans in the cloud and on your phone

Having your workshop plans saved online or on your phone means you can access them from anywhere. The same goes for all the exercises, games or activities that you know. There'll be times when you'll have delivered everything you've planned for but will still have time left; or when an exercise just isn't working, or when you're faced with an accessibility need that you didn't expect. It's much easier to search through the pages of a document than it is to search through your mind.

If you are saving them online, saving documents so they're available offline means you'll be able to access them even if you don't have the internet. I did this with my workshop documents that I stored on Dropbox, and it meant I could run a workshop in the middle of the ocean and still have access to all my resources.

Backup your music playlists

If you're a music lover, you'll know there are plenty of ways that your perfect playlists can be gone in an instant. From upgrading from CDs to iPods to Spotify; computer crashes, new phones or phones getting stolen on holiday – I've had to remake the same music playlists so many times, I've been scarred for life. The simple solution is to simply save them. Back them up.

This might become less important over time since music streaming services such as Spotify have become more popular, but who knows what the future will bring? Creating playlists can take a lot of time, so it's definitely worth backing them up as a file if you can. Having it as a file means you can simply load up the playlist and get going again. You'll thank yourself for it.

Constantly learn, evaluate, improve

The only way you'll improve as a workshop leader is if you analyse and evaluate your delivery. Nobody's going to do it for you. You'll never be able to control exactly what your group do, but you'll always be able to control how you influence and respond, so the only way to become a more effective workshop leader is to improve your delivery. Some key questions to ask yourself when you're reflecting on your work are:

- Did the group achieve your workshop's main outcome?
- What aspects of the workshop didn't go as you expected? Why not?
- Which parts did they engage with and which did they not?
- How could you improve as a facilitator?

If people are struggling in your workshops or on your course, you need to reflect on why. It can be exposing to look at your work honestly, but it's the only way to improve. You'll probably have the best of intentions with what you're doing, but if something isn't working then you need to see what you can change. Sometimes that might mean a slight tweak in the way that you deliver an exercise, other times it might mean a complete rethink about your approach.

This also goes for the positives. Don't get drawn into focusing only on the negatives when there'll be positives that came out of the experience too. Reflect on what you thought worked, and why. Because the positive aspects of the experience can also be huge sources of learning.

There'll always be things that you think can be better. No matter what your skill level, there'll be groups that don't respond in the way you expected, or you'll make a judgement call that, on reflection, you think was the wrong one. Your workshops will never be perfect, nobody's will. But it's by reflecting and improving that you'll grow to deliver the best experience possible for your groups.

Don't stop being a student

Some of the best lessons you'll learn as a workshop leader will come from being a participant. Especially if it's in an area where you're a complete beginner.

Theatre workshops are sometimes for people who are new to theatre, and the only way you can replicate that feeling is by putting yourself in a new environment. You'll be able to see what it's like when a workshop leader pushes forward at a pace you can't keep up with, or when they give an instruction that they think is clear, but makes absolutely no sense to you. But even without that, being a participant in other people's rooms will give you an insight into different ways of working – which can teach you what works, as well as what doesn't.

2 Your Group

An overview

Knowing how to deliver a workshop won't mean much if you don't know how to engage with the people in your group. Knowing how to get people working together effectively and building your relationship with your group is vital. Mastering these aspects won't only help your group, it'll help you. One of the key aspects to behaviour management is that prevention is better than cure, and the better you are with your group, the less likely you'll have behaviour-management issues to contend with. But in this section, we'll look at how you can empower your participants to get the best that they possibly can out of your workshop.

Getting People into Groups

How to get people into groups effectively

Working in smaller groups is an important part of any theatre workshop. With adults or a relatively disciplined bunch, groups should be relatively easy to arrange. You can simply ask them to form groups of X number of people or to find a partner, which should be straightforward. Things become far more complicated when you're working in a school.

It's usually best practice to keep mixing the groups up, so they get to work with different people. This will:

- Help them to work with everyone in the room.
- Help them to form bonds with everyone in the group.
- Make it harder for cliques to form.

It's good to regularly encourage people to work with those they haven't worked with. Sometimes you can be direct with this and simply ask them to: 'Get into groups, ideally with someone/ people you haven't worked with before.' But there are several strategies you can use to group people that will give you more control, or are more creative:

Giving people group numbers – This is probably the most popular method that practitioners use. With this, with your group in a circle, you'd give each person a number between one and (as an example) four, then you set them off to their relevant numbered corners in the room.

However, this has the downside that people can easily get confused about which groups they're in. If you're in a school, this technique will create absolute carnage.

'What number am I again?'

'I'm not a one, I'm a four!'

'There are four groups? But, miss, I'm a six!'

'Sir! We've got two in our group and they've got seven!'

Hell on earth.

To solve this problem, put them into their groups in real-time. For instance, if you're doing four groups, give each corner of the room a number up to four, then give each person in the circle a number and send them off to their corner straight away. Don't give out the next person's number until you see the current one walking. It might take a few seconds longer than giving out the numbers in the previous way, but it's as bulletproof a strategy as it gets.

Shuffle their positions – If you're in a circle, you can simply call out 'Find a new space in the circle and stand next to somebody different!' Repeat this as many times as you like, then put people into pairs/groups with the people next to them.

Five-second groups – If you give school students five seconds to get into groups of three, they'll likely go with their friends. You can then simply call for new groups of three with different people as many times as you like, and stop when you feel they're in groups that're suitable. They thought they were playing an energy game but ohhh no... you've got it all figured out.

'Find someone who...' – An example of this would be 'Find someone in the room who had the same breakfast as you.' This strategy also has the benefit of encouraging the group to speak to each other, which serves as a bit of an ice-breaker. It takes a bit more time and probably isn't ideal for schools because they'll likely go with their friends anyway, but it can be another way you can get people to group up with those who they otherwise wouldn't.

The ideal group size

Five per group is the sweet spot. More than that and quieter individuals will get lost and become bystanders. Fewer than that and the responsibility on each person becomes much greater. Five is usually a good balance.

Being specific with their groups

Sometimes it's useful to be specific about the groups that people are in. For the most part you don't need to worry about who people work with, but if your group are working towards an assessment, or if the outcome of the work is important (such as a performance), it's important that you're specific about their groups, because who they work with will have a big impact. Leaving the groups to chance will never get you the ideal results for these situations. There are three key factors to bear in mind here:

- Ability grouping.
- Mixed-ability grouping.
- Personality grouping.

How much you choose to group people by ability or personality should depend on the individuals and the task at hand, and you'll usually have to consider both to a certain degree. But you'll need to plan in advance if these are things you want to consider.

Similar-ability and mixed-ability groups

You'll always have different ability levels in your room, and it's important that you're aware of people's ability when you're putting them in groups – especially if you're working with them over a period of time. You can choose either to group people by their level of ability, or to have them in mixed-ability groups. There are upsides and downsides to both:

Similar-ability Groups	Mixed-ability Groups
+	+
• Allows people to work at their level, rather than working above or below their capabilities. • Allows you to match the difficulty level of the task to the group's level more accurately, so you can better develop their skills.	• Gives the more capable members of the group the ability to lead. • Gives those with a lower level of ability the opportunity to be supported. • Makes it more difficult for there to be 'good groups' and 'bad groups'.

-	-
• Can run the risk of there being 'good groups' and 'bad groups'. This can lead to unhealthy comparisons if done too much. • Requires you to plan and arrange the groups. They won't just happen by chance.	• Those of a higher ability can sometimes feel like they're being held back, while those of a lower ability can sometimes feel out of their depth or inadequate. • Those of a higher ability can be less challenged and can develop less compared to if they're in a group with people of a similar level.

Both approaches require you to specifically select your groups. Neither of these can be arranged effectively by chance, so you'll need to plan ahead if you want to group people like this. This'll take more time than if you group people up randomly.

When grouping people by ability, bear in mind the ability and skills that relate to the task. Someone may be a brilliant actor, but if you're doing a movement task and they're not good at movement, for that specific task they'd be classed as low ability. Don't fall into the trap of applying a 'halo effect' to people, where you view someone as being good at everything just because they excel in one particular area or in general.

When doing mixed-ability grouping, make sure you have a good balance of different abilities. For example, if you have a group of four, this could mean having one person of a higher ability, two of a medium ability and one who's lower. You need to be aware of this because it'll have an impact on the group dynamic. If you have one person of a high ability and three who are lower, it could put more strain on the higher-ability person, who could end up working harder to carry the group. But it works both ways. Because if you place three higher-level people with one lower-level one, then the lower-level person can often become overshadowed and may not have much of an input.

Ability grouping can be particularly important for adult courses. If you've auditioned all your life to get into RADA or you've paid a heap of dollar for an acting course, but you're spending your time supporting other people's learning, you're going to be pissed.

You won't always be able to cater to people's ability level, but if you're working with people over a period of time or on anything significant, ignoring it will definitely cause frustration amongst your group – so ignore it at your peril. This isn't something you should consciously bring up or talk about with your group, but being aware of these choices will help the group to get far more out of your workshop than if you only ever had mixed groups.

I used to only do mixed-ability grouping when I first started, pairing higher-ability people with those of a lower ability, but I've rejected that view over the years. Being partnered with someone of a lower ability (not necessarily low, just lower by comparison) can leave people frustrated, and there've been times where I've actively seen the irritation in people.

No amount of rationalising with your group is going to make this any different. It's perfectly reasonable to explain that we can't always choose who we work with, but the reality is that nobody wants to feel like they're having to carry another person in a situation where they want to learn themselves. And likewise, nobody wants to feel that they're inadequate or out of their depth.

Personality grouping

Grouping people based on their personalities can bring out the best in people, or the worst. You'll want their personalities to complement each other. If you put all your pessimists together in one group, they'll struggle to see the light, whereas putting them with people who have a more positive approach can bring them out of the depths of despair. Similarly, you may have people in your workshop who are great leaders or really inspire people and bring others together. It might not be a good idea to have them all grouped together because it'll concentrate those qualities in one group, rather than spreading them out.

This can also work for people's performance styles. Grouping people who have an over-the-top acting style may create content that's bouncing off the walls, whereas balancing them out with people who are more grounded and natural might even things out. There isn't a right or wrong with any of this, but it's important to keep in mind because people will work and respond differently based on who they're working with, and their process will vary too. What they learn and the outcome of their work will also vary depending on their groups as well.

It's also important to factor this in for group dynamics, because you'll want to minimise conflict as much as possible. Don't create a group of four with three loud, brash best friends and one quieter person who's never met any of them. The quieter person will get swallowed up. And if you know you have an important task for your groups, create them based on who you think will have the best working dynamics. It'll be a recipe for disaster if you put people together who don't like each other; or people who have so much fun that they don't do any work.

How to Get the Best Out of Your Group

Learn the names you think you'll need

The chatterbox, the lively kid, the one with their hands in their pants? Probably best to prioritise their names first.

Unless you're superhuman, you'll probably only be able to learn a handful of names per workshop, so if you're only with a group once, prioritise the names you think you'll need. This is especially important for people you think may be a challenge in the session. If John is setting the room on fire, using 'Hey!', 'Excuse me!', 'Oi!' or 'You there!' is the last thing you want to do. You're going to want to call him by his name. But if you haven't attempted to learn it, he'll burn the building down in no time.

Prioritising the names you think you'll need will allow you to get a person's attention directly and instantly. This isn't about prejudging people or having it impact the way that you treat them in the room; the reality of a one-off workshop is that you won't have the time to get to know people or to learn everybody's names, so your only option is to go off first impressions. Here are some tips to learn their names if you're with a group for a one-off session (there are some extra tips for learning names on a course on page 154):

Quick name circle – With everyone in a circle, go round and have everyone say their name to the group. I usually do it twice. Once normally, and a second time even faster and louder to make it seem more like a game than an exercise. I'll then make a mental note of the names I think I'll need.

Write their names down – Writing their names down will give you something to refer to. Writing little descriptions can help too. e.g. Grant – red top and glasses; Rachel – red hair and braces; John – Northern, backflips.

Asking for their names after a contribution – You can request somebody's name whenever you need to validate their contribution. This allows you to learn their name and to positively reinforce them at the same time. For example, if Fiona makes a great point, you could say:

'What's your name, sorry?'

'Fiona.'

'Fiona made a great point!'

Make an active effort to learn them – If somebody says their name and you make no effort to remember it, your brain will make no effort either and you'll forget it. So make sure you repeat it a few times in your head, and that you at least try to remember it.

I once did an immersive show for Punchdrunk where a kid in my group dashed off into the distance for no reason.

'Gary!' I called.

He leapt into the air and spun 180 degrees to face me.

'How did you know my name!?'

He'd only said it once, during our quick name circle at the start.

As surprising to him as it was effective for me.

Giving groups feedback

When you're watching small groups share their work, it's a good idea to spread your feedback across the groups as best you can. Spreading out the feedback will give people more reason to pay attention because each feedback session will benefit everybody, rather than your group simply switching off because they feel like it's irrelevant to them.

This can take a bit of thinking ahead. For instance, one group might be able to improve on balancing the stage, increasing their volume and having more energy. But if you know that the feedback would apply to the other groups too, you'd be better off giving one of those points per group, but being more detailed with each. You can often get an idea of the type of feedback they'll need by observing them as they're working, so make sure you keep your eye on the room.

Feedback session – Without spreading the notes	Feedback session – Spreading them out
Group 1 • Balance the stage. • Speak loud enough that we can hear you. • Give it more energy.	**Group 1** • Balance the stage.
Group 2 • No notes…?	**Group 2** • Speak loud enough that we can hear you.
Group 3 • No notes…!	**Group 3** • Give it more energy.

This means you'll be giving less feedback to each group, but it'll be of a higher quality, while still allowing them to learn from your feedback to the other groups. It's also helpful because it means you won't bombard people with a list of critiques that'll make them feel rubbish. By spreading out your constructive feedback, you give everybody the same package of guidance but in a way that's easier for them to process.

It's also good to direct your feedback to everybody, even if you're commenting on a specific group. People can often learn just as much from watching as they can by doing, so alternating your eyeline between the group that have performed and everybody else can help to make the feedback relevant for everyone.

Constructive criticism

'He gave me a line-reading: "It's not 'To be or not to be", it's "To BE or not to be." Can you imagine? He's spear carrier number one!'

We often say there's no right or wrong in theatre. This is only partly true. An actor giving another actor performance advice is about as wrong as you can get.

It's the same for your group in a workshop. Yes, your group need to be able to look at work critically, but there can be problems with asking the group to give feedback after watching each other's work. The feedback they give can sometimes be unhelpful or misjudged, and it can cause them to irritate each other. Here's a better approach:

You: Give the constructive criticism
• Allows you to give constructive feedback sensitively. • Allows the group to get high-quality feedback from the professional (that's you). • You can make sure that any critique is focused on the specific points you want to address – there may be several points worthy of a discussion, but you may only want to highlight one of them. • Saves you from having to correct poor feedback from the group.
Your group: Say what they like or what they think worked
• Gives the group the responsibility to support each other (which should extend into their general group dynamic). • Encourages them to see the positives in each other's work, rather than the problems.

Setting this up is simple, you just need to establish it early on. When a group has just performed a scene for the first time, you can simply say:

'Okay, hands up, what did you like, or what do you think worked? Don't worry, I'll handle the constructive feedback.'

This isn't about creating a room without criticism – it's about making sure you're the one delivering it. Otherwise, John might say something completely uncalled-for about Sonya's scene and open a Pandora's box of problems, putting you in a world of pain.

Embrace mistakes

'There's no right or wrong.'

Drama workshops aren't maths or science (thank the heavens), so embrace the idea of it being okay to make mistakes. The more relaxed you can make people feel about making mistakes, the more comfortable your group will be. Perfection and 'getting it right' can be one of the most paralysing things ever. Mistakes offer you the chance to learn what works and what doesn't, and actors spend weeks in rehearsals getting things wrong to learn what works.

If you're going to encourage this, you need to be fully committed to it, because saying that you welcome mistakes and then looking down on people when they make them will create a huge level of bitterness within your group. So make sure you practise what you preach.

Don't have unrealistic expectations for their reactions

Your group will naturally want to respond to certain exercises in certain ways, which is important to bear in mind when delivering them. Asking them to respond differently to what would reasonably be expected can really frustrate your group. For example:

- Having the group do a task where they'd naturally want to talk... without talking.
- Having the group play a tiring game... then wondering why they're tired.
- Asking the group to play a game that will make them laugh... without laughing.
- Setting up an exercise where the group would rightfully want to debate... then not allowing a debate.

Expecting them to respond in a way that's unnatural will only irritate your group. Which will irritate you. Which will irritate them. Which will be irritating.

This isn't to say that you should allow a group's reaction or behaviour to become uncontrollable or unacceptable. Not at all. It's more that you shouldn't be shocked when people respond to exercises in the natural way that would be expected – and you certainly shouldn't demand the opposite.

I often see this when practitioners ask groups who have just met to get into a line of alphabetical name order without talking, before telling them off when they start doing charades and all sorts of physical theatre to try to communicate non-verbally, and bursting into flames in rage if anyone so much as whispers.

What's the point? It goes against the whole aim of the game – which is for the group to interact and to find out each other's names. And it sets them up to fail. There are games you can do if you want people to work in silence, and if that's your aim, pick an exercise that already supports that, not one that doesn't. Placing a request or an expectation on people that's unreasonable is just that – unreasonable.

Reading the room

It's easy to set a task for the group and then to switch off into your own world – but it's always important to observe your group. You can learn so much about them from how they respond, and the more in-tune you are with your group, the more you can adjust to them.

How a group responds (or doesn't) can tell you a lot, and everything they do (or don't do) can give you valuable information. For example:

- How quickly or slowly do they get through the tasks that you give?

- How quickly do they adjust to notes and feedback?
- Is their acting over-the-top, or is it more grounded and realistic?
- Do they discuss the work a lot before making scenes or do they jump in and try things?
- Do they voice their opinion? Do they not?
- How agreeable are they? Are they willing to disagree?
- Are they confident or more reserved?
- Are they a strong presence in the room, or are they easily forgettable?
- Do they volunteer for tasks? Do they not at all?
- How productive or unproductive are they with other individuals?

You'll have a choice about how you adjust to your group depending on the answers to these types of questions. If a group are getting through your tasks too easily, maybe you need to give them more challenging content. If their acting's over-the-top, you might want to teach them how to find the truth in acting. If they spend all of their rehearsal time talking, it might be that you give them less time to work, to encourage them to work faster and to try things out quicker.

How people behave and what they do will tell you more than asking them ever could. Also, what a group don't do can often tell you just as much as what they do. So make sure that you keep your eyes on the room, because the more you can gauge who people are, the better you can adjust your work to suit their needs.

I always use the first day of my courses to figure out my group, because it informs how I approach the rest of the course. I'll do a short devising task to gauge people's rough ability level, and I almost always play Grandmother's Footsteps – because it can tell you a lot about the individuals in the room. Who are the daredevils that charge towards Grandma? Who are the ones that are more cautious? Who are the ones that don't listen to instructions? Who are the real team players? Being aware of who the members of the group are and how they respond means I can cater to who they are and what they need.

Stand in different parts of the room

You'll likely have an area in the room that'll be like your home base, which is probably where you'll stand when you're not actively leading, and where you keep your belongings. It's important that you move around to different parts of the room so that you don't spend your whole workshop in that position, because where you stand will affect who you can see, and you could end up not seeing some people at all if you don't actively move around the space.

Doing this means you'll be able to see everyone in the group, rather than simply whoever's closest to you. You'll be able to make sure that everyone's working well and to spot any problems before they happen. Definitely bear this in mind if you're working in a big space where the people at the other end of the room will be even further away than usual. It's also particularly important if you're running a workshop audition, because the people that are closest to you will naturally have an unfair advantage if you stay in the same place.

Competition

There's a healthy and an unhealthy side to competition.

Healthy competition can be energising. Nobody likes to lose, so competitive games can energise people, which can be particularly helpful at the start of the day or after lunch. Play a game where everyone's a winner and Jenny will take it easy. Play that same game where she'll be out if she's too slow and she'll soon perk up. If you as the facilitator say with humorous conviction that you're going to win the game you're playing, the group will usually work ten times harder to try to get you out.

Healthy competition can also be productive if your group are supportive, as it pushes people to strive to be better.

Unhealthy competition would be when you're pitting individuals or groups against each other, and it becomes more about the people than the task. This can sometimes happen in drama schools and is something to actively fight against. We all naturally compare ourselves to others, but you'll want to dial this down and encourage them to be cooperative first and foremost. This can also happen if a group's identity is built in relation to another group, for example, 'We're the best course and all the others are rubbish', which wouldn't be productive at all.

So all in all, make sure that the competition within your room is healthy, rather than toxic.

Domino effect

The way that people in your group react can have a knock-on effect on everybody else, and it can quickly lock people into unhelpful behaviours if you're not careful. You need to be aware of this because you'll have to adjust quite quickly if you want to stop this from happening, otherwise it can be difficult to change the group's reaction.

Here's an example. Let's say that you're working with a shy group and you ask them a question. If you don't get a response the first time you ask and you don't make the right adjustments, this might be how the interaction plays out:

Question attempts	You	The response
1	'What did you like about the play?'	*Silence*
2	'What did you like about the play?'	*Tumbleweed*

3	'Come on, guys, what did you like about the play?'	*Crickets*
4	'So nobody liked anything about the play then?'	*Paint dries*

By the second time you've asked the question, the domino effect is kicking in. The fact that nobody's responded will mean that nobody will want to respond – because nobody's responded. When you ask a third time, it's even less likely that you'll get a response, and from that point on you'll be lucky to get a response at all. This can be particularly challenging because by the time you become aware of it, it's probably already too late. But the key is to not let it get to that stage in the first place.

What you need to do is to change your approach as soon as you see it's not working, because sticking with the same tactic will likely get you the same reaction. By adjusting, it reboots their response to allow them to respond in a different way. With the above scenario, rephrasing the question into a closed question would be more likely to get you a response because it's much easier for them to answer, which will reset the interaction. For example:

You	The response
'What did you like about the play?'	*Silence*
'What did you like about the play?'	*Tumbleweed*
'Did you enjoy the play?'	'Yes.'
'What do you remember the most about it?'	'The bit with the dog.'

The key here is if you're getting a response that isn't what you'd like, adjust your approach as soon as you can, because sticking with the same strategy will only make things worse.

Volunteers

You have two strategies for how you get volunteers for an exercise, both with their upsides and downsides. These strategies are:

- You choose who the volunteer will be.
- You ask the group for a volunteer.

Choosing someone – This is where you select someone without asking them, which is quicker than asking for a volunteer. With this, you need to make sure that you pick someone who's capable of doing the task, and who you know wouldn't mind doing it. If you're working with a group that's chosen to be there – such as on a course that people have paid for – then the person you pick probably won't object to being chosen. But you might get some resistance in other settings, such as in a school.

Be aware of the domino effect if you're choosing a volunteer and you're with a group who might not want to, because one person refusing may inspire the rest to do the same. If this happens, your chances of getting a volunteer will reduce each time you get a no from someone, so pick a person who you're sure will step up or will at least be open to persuasion. It's far easier to persuade the first person you choose than it is to persuade the fourth – who by that point could make a pretty strong case to be let off, given that you've let off another three people before them.

Asking for a volunteer – You can say that you'll take the first person who jumps up, or you can have people put their hands up and you choose. Having the first person to jump up is more suited for exercises where you're not concerned about the outcome, or if everyone will be doing the exercise afterwards anyway. Having people put their hands up will let you choose those who are more suited to the task, because not everyone who's willing will be suitable.

~~'No, that's wrong'~~ 'Not quite...'

Sometimes participants will give you a wrong answer. But if you respond with an outright 'no', or 'you're wrong', you may make them think twice about contributing again, given how blunt it can be. So take the edge off by being a little less direct. Some examples of this would be:

- *'Not quite.'*
- *'Nearly.'*

Or:

- *'Yes, but...'*

It's a softer approach and is less blunt. It won't feel as harsh. Though obviously use these sensibly. There's no use saying 'nearly' if Neville's answer to what comes after four is five hundred.

This isn't about removing the word 'no' from your vocabulary, and it certainly isn't helpful to say yes to everything as if every idea or contribution is correct. It's about being considerate about how you knock back people's answers.

Be mindful what you encourage

What you encourage can shape your group for better or for worse. You should encourage the behaviours that you want to see, but it's easy to encourage unproductive behaviours without being aware that you're doing it. This can be through:

Not addressing behaviours that should be addressed – For example, if Johnny starts talking over you and you don't nip it in the bud, you're essentially giving everyone permission to do the same, which can quickly spiral and become a real challenge. It's easy to think that mild behaviour issues aren't worth addressing, but if you're working with a group over a period of time, dealing with problems when they're small is much easier than trying to address them when they're out of control. This may be less of a concern if you're only with a group for an hour, but the principle still applies.

Positively encouraging behaviours that are unproductive – Perhaps Barry isn't feeling too well and wants to step out. It's a perfectly reasonable thing to allow – but if you bring out the palm leaves, serenading music, snacks on-demand, and cater to his every whim, you're going to encourage him to opt out and to self-select when he participates. In this instance, it'd be better to check in with him once, then to leave him be and let him return in his own time – so the incentive is to participate rather than to be an audience member. But this goes for anything. Don't allow your care for the group or your desire to be nice allow you to encourage behaviours that are unhelpful.

Invite their input

It's easy to run a workshop where you're the one doing all the talking, giving all the ideas, and giving all the direction about how things will be. But you should look to empower your group, not to dictate to them. One of the ways to do this is to allow your group input into the workshop. There are broadly two ways to achieve this:

- By giving them opportunities to share their opinions and ideas, such as:
  - Asking for their thoughts, feelings or opinions after an exercise or piece of work.
  - Check-ins/check-outs, to have an open space to share their views (see the section on 'Check-ins/check-outs' on page 114).
- By giving them opportunities to have a creative input, such as:
  - Giving them a stimulus or a task and allowing them to create something independently without you directing.
  - Asking for and using their ideas for a final performance.

Getting the group's input will make them feel a sense of ownership in the work, otherwise they won't feel that they have a voice. Some directors are more hesitant about opening their rehearsal process to the group's ideas, which is a directorial choice – but you're then making a trade-off between the group feeling invested in the work and you being able to chase your artistic vision. And it won't necessarily be for the better. Anyone is capable of a good idea, so using your group's ideas doesn't necessarily mean that the work will suffer for it.

Giving your group a degree of choice (where you can) can be helpful too, such as giving people the option between a male or female Shakespeare script, rather than a single text. Just be careful not to give too many options. We all like a degree of autonomy, but giving a group five scenes to choose from will be paralysing, and giving them the complete works of Shakespeare would be sheer madness.

Lastly, the only thing worse than not asking for input is to say that you welcome the group's input... then not to. You can't say that you value their input then knock it back every time. It'll only create resentment. So if you're saying that you value their input, mean it.

'That's not how you play it!'

'But sir! I played this once in my drama club and the way you play it is that it's actually Zip Zap Zop, where the zip goes left and the zap goes right and the zop goes across and there's actually no boing and if you're too slow you're out. So that's how you play it.'

The number of drama games that exist is endless, and so is the number of variations of them. This means that some people may find your exercise to be 'wrong', because you're not doing it in the way that they expect.

But nope. No thank you. It's your room, your rules. Yes, they may have played the game differently with Miss Bagley last year. But that was last year. And you're not Miss Bagley.

Sure, you can have a discussion about alternative versions, but this is not the time to negotiate. Time spent in trade negotiations on the rules of a game is time taken away from playing it; and it slows down the pace of the workshop. Plus, it gives your power away to whoever you're negotiating with.

There may be times where you play by other rules or hand over the reins to somebody else, but this needs to be an active decision by you, rather than you being pushed into it.

Don't micromanage. Let people get on with it...!

If you set a group off to do a task, it's easy to swoop in to micromanage the group and to constantly give them corrections – or worse, to do the work for them. But this takes away the benefit of self-exploration. Let them get on with it...! Learn to take a step back and allow your group to play, experiment, and work things out themselves, without your input. People are often far more capable than you think, and letting them work things out themselves will help them to be independent and self-sufficient. If things don't work out, or go wrong – great; it'll give you more to discuss at the end of the exercise and there'll be more to learn.

Saying that, it can sometimes be good to check in with each group while they're working to make sure they're on track or to offer specific guidance. But it should be just that – a check-in. It shouldn't be you managing the output of their work or doing it for them. Plus, if your feedback is something that the whole group can benefit from, you're much better off addressing it to the whole group when they show the work back so that everybody can learn from it, rather than only giving that feedback to that one group.

Affirmations

Affirmations are a fantastic way of recognising and acknowledging people in your group, and can be an absolute game-changer if you're working with young people on projects over a few days or weeks. I learnt this from Lucy Shaljian, who is a master at engaging with even the toughest groups.

Affirmations at their most basic are when you give a specific, direct compliment to somebody in your group, and they're done in front of everyone. The upside to giving them when you're working on a project over a period of time is that it'll become a positive ritual for your group – though it does still work if you're only with them for a few sessions.

We'll look at this one as if you're with a group of young people, which is where it's probably most effective. The way it works is that with your group in a circle, you:

- Choose a young person that you want to affirm.
- Turn to face them, look at them directly and say their name.
- Speak to them and give them your affirmation.

An example of an affirmation could be:

'Gerald. I want to affirm you for the way you spoke in today's session. I really appreciated your contribution and I thought that what you said in the group discussion about truthfulness was fantastic.'

Or:

'Daisy. I want to give you an affirmation. I think you've got a really confident voice that supports the group brilliantly, and I want to affirm you for that.'

You can then ask any other colleagues you have in the room if there's anybody who they'd like to affirm. This is especially powerful if teachers can take part too, because it's rare that a teacher would acknowledge a student so directly in this way. This has the added bonus that it can support the bond they have with their students in a positive way, which will last beyond your time with your group.

Once you've given an affirmation, everyone should give a round of applause, before you move on to the next part of the workshop. It's usually best to do them either at the end of a workshop or just before lunch – though you can do both if you have full-day workshops. You can probably give a maximum of two affirmations per person in one go (so if you have yourself and a teacher, a maximum of four affirmations at once). If you do have somebody else who can give them, it's sometimes helpful to discuss who you're thinking to give them to, to make sure you're giving people the recognition they deserve and that you're not planning on doing it to the same people.

Make sure that you actively set this up and explain how it works the first time you do it, so that they know what to expect. You can't just deliver an affirmation without setting it up because it'd be a bit weird. Also, make sure that your affirmations are specific, genuine, and that you make eye contact with the person and say it directly to them. So you want to be saying: 'Lola, I want to give you an affirmation...', rather than: 'I'm giving Lola an affirmation because she...' When you say it directly to them and really acknowledge the great work that people are doing, it can be a really powerful technique.

Lastly, be mindful of who you give affirmations to. Make a note of them if it's helpful. You don't want to get into a situation where you've given an affirmation to the same person three times, or you give one to everyone but leave one person in the room out.

" I think affirmations are one of the most effective ways of working with young people. For me, it's a way to build relationships, to get young people on side and to raise their self-esteem. I always start each session or each project with affirmations in mind.

It only works if it's authentic. It can't be done in a way where you're trying to ingratiate yourself, because young people will sniff that out. They'll know if you're doing it just to score points. So it's about being really authentic. But I guess it's about creating the culture of affirmations.

By the end of the project, you might want to do an affirmation circle, where you affirm yourself for something you've done well, then you affirm the person next to you for something they've done well. You can make sure that you have people sitting in certain positions so that the adults aren't affirming adults, etc.... or sometimes that's okay and it just happens organically.

I use affirmations all the time because I know it's one of the best ways to work with young people, and leaves them feeling so much better about themselves.

Lucy Shaljian

Freelance practitioner and consultant, *Leap Confronting Conflict*, *Playing On Theatre Company*, *Tender Education and Arts*

How to Build a Positive Relationship with Your Group

The power of praise

Never underestimate the power of praise. Praise is one of the key ways to build a strong bond with your group, and it'll help to create a positive atmosphere. People will react far better to praise than to being constantly criticised, so you should lead from a place of positivity, focusing on what the group are doing right and reinforcing what you want to see, rather than focusing on the negatives. Also, if you create a positive atmosphere along with strong boundaries and consequences, your group will have far more reason to stay away from bad behaviour. Just be mindful that praise *has* to be deserved.

The key here is to be authentic. Praise is done best when it's specific and sincere, because we can all tell fake praise a mile off. Don't be a beg-friend. If you're praising everyone, for everything, for every minute of every day, your praise will become meaningless. So it has to be genuine.

There's a range of things that you can praise a group about. These include:

- Ability/quality of work – Somebody does something to a high standard.
- Effort – Somebody puts in a level of effort worth recognising.
- Development goal – Somebody achieves a specific goal that was set for them.
- Improvement – Somebody improves in a specific area.
- Specific action – Somebody does something specific that's worthy of recognition.

Praising effort is possibly the most effective because it isn't linked to a particular outcome. Everybody's capable of putting in effort, and if that's what you encourage in your group then it gives them more of an incentive to participate; which can then lead to them behaving in a way that'll be worthy of praise in those other areas. Praise in general can also be great for difficult young people in schools because they'll probably be more used to being told off than being praised.

Also be mindful that you have the choice about how you praise people. You can do it in front of the group or you can do it privately. I'd encourage a mix of both. Praising people in front of the group can give them the recognition they deserve, and it'll feel particularly great if the rest of the group is in strong agreement and reinforces it. Some are of the view that praising people publicly runs the risk of embarrassing them (which can happen), but I don't think it's a bad thing to be embarrassed when you're being recognised for something good. Giving somebody individual praise can also be hugely effective because it makes it much more personal, and it's almost as if you've gone out of your way to do it. Being specific, authentic, unapologetic and direct when it comes to praising somebody one-on-one can sometimes be enough to turn a renegade child into your star pupil.

The power of humour and fun

'This is too much fun. I don't like it!' No one

All workshops should be fun. Otherwise you may as well be teaching Pythagoras' theorem.

Your group need to be able to enjoy themselves, so make sure that you design and deliver your workshops in a way that people will enjoy. This doesn't mean everything needs to be a comedy... but it can't be a Shakespearean tragedy either. You can have the greatest workshop and the best of intentions, but if your sessions aren't enjoyable, people won't pay attention. Theatre is the art of play, not the art of over-seriousness.

Games can be one of the best ways to achieve this. It's easy to overlook games once you get into the depths of your work or it hits crunch time, but games keep the joy and camaraderie in the room and keep people together. So don't ever feel that playing games is at the expense of the work, it only enhances it.

Investing in the relationships in your room is just as important as the investment you put into the work.

It's also good if you as the workshop leader can jump into games from time to time. Competitive games instantly become more fun when you get involved because they become about getting you out. And it shows that you're willing to get stuck in and have a good time with your group – bringing yourself on to their level. But, ultimately, give yourself permission to have a good time as well. Because if you enjoy your workshop, they will too.

“Don't underestimate how brilliant a little bit of humour can be and how good it is for bonding. By making a few jokes about yourself or the subject it allows a group to see that you don't take yourself too seriously, while also establishing that you're confident enough to make light of yourself and your subject. Be careful not to make jokes about the participants before you know them a little bit, but this can also be a hugely effective way of allowing a group to be silly and playful.

We relax when we laugh, and a relaxed room will give your participants the opportunity to be themselves. If you don't think of yourself as a 'funny person', find some clips or footage that's exaggerated or silly and bring them in for your group. Laughter really is the best medicine for most things.

Tara Boland
Freelance practitioner, *Punchdrunk Enrichment*, *The Free Association*, *Mountview*

How to motivate your group

It's useful to be aware of the different ways that you can motivate people, because there isn't one method of motivation that will universally work for everyone. The more flexible you can be, the more effective you'll be. Strategies include:

- Positive reinforcement.
- Tough love.
- Being told what to do.
- Being given a goal and the freedom to achieve it.

It's not that helpful to ask people what the most effective strategy will be for them because they probably won't know. But if you only ever use one method and ignore the others, you probably won't be motivating people as effectively as you can, because different situations and different people require different approaches. You might have a personal preference about which one works for you, but it's not you you're motivating, it's them.

Also bear in mind that different situations will call for different approaches. If you've got time on your hands, you might set them a task and give them the freedom to work things out. If they're generally doing a good job, it might be positive reinforcement. If positive reinforcement isn't working and they're letting themselves down, it might be tough love. And if you've got an hour before your show and the world's crumbling before your eyes, it might be that you just tell them what to do. In that scenario, if you stick to being soft and using positive reinforcement... there's a high chance there won't be a show at all.

All of these approaches are valid, and all of them have their place in your toolkit depending on the circumstances. This isn't something you should overthink, but they're useful to be aware of as you reflect on your practice, to make sure that you're not limiting yourself with how you engage your group.

Be patient

It's easy to get frustrated when a group aren't where you want them to be, either in their abilities or their behaviour. But don't take for granted how much you know about a subject and your own development journey. What might seem easy to you may be a huge leap for somebody else, and some people may not have done drama at all. Be patient and non-judgemental with where people are at on their journey, and understand that just because you've told somebody how to do something, it doesn't mean they'll grasp it instantly. So be patient. You're not Gordon Ramsay.

This also goes for doing exercises. If you teach a group an exercise and they still don't get it, it's your responsibility to make sure that they do.

I'll repeat that. If you teach a group an exercise and they don't get it, it's your responsibility to make sure that they do.

It's not on them. *You* need to adjust. Don't get frustrated, don't get angry, and certainly don't tease your group or mock them for not understanding. Losing your patience with a group will be the quickest way to lose them. So make sure you give them the time that they need with respect.

I was at a salsa class once where we were being taught a new dance sequence. It started off with the salsa move 'the hammerlock'. If you've no idea what a hammerlock is, don't worry. Neither did I.

My first attempt at the move was a shambles. As was my second. My third was a mild improvement but still nowhere near good enough to qualify me for a second dance with my partner. To add to the frustration, the teacher carried on teaching the rest of the dance sequence, which I clearly wasn't ready for, but the horror and disgust on his face made me feel far worse:

(His face) 'Why on earth can you not do this? I just taught you. Are you a child?'

Of course I couldn't. He'd been doing the move for years. I'd barely been doing it for five minutes. I'd have to be a professional salsa dancer to get it that quickly. And if I were, I wouldn't be there in the first place.

See everyone!

One of the most basic things that you can and should do with your group is to see them. It sounds obvious, but I've been in countless workshops before where it's felt like the facilitator hasn't ever looked at me unless I've put my hand up to say something. Be better. You need to make sure that you actively see everyone in your group. It's easy to end up looking at some people in the room but not others, but whenever this happens, it makes the people that you don't see feel invisible. It might not seem like a big deal, but having people in your room feel insignificant because you don't see them is no small thing.

This is something that you'll need to be consciously aware of, because you should try to spread your attention as evenly across the room as possible. It also means being aware of your natural blind spots. For example, most of us will tend to look at people on one side of the circle more than the other when we're speaking, or we sometimes don't look at those who are directly either side of us in a circle. But those people still exist, so you need to make the effort to see them too. You don't need to do anything revolutionary here, you just need to make sure you've made the effort to look at everybody. This is about our basic need to be seen.

> “I make a point of both seeing and hearing everyone at the start of the session – even if it's just hearing people's names or doing a short check-in. This has a dual function: allowing each participant to get their voice out there and to feel the group's attention on them for a brief moment, and allowing me to get a sense from the outset of each individual's energy levels, nerves and maybe even relationships to others in the group.
>
> I sometimes imagine there's an extra participant in the room who is a friend or relative of mine who I know would find the situation daunting or uncomfortable. Visualising how that person would be behaving sharpens my attention on anyone that's not finding it easy to participate. It also helps me to connect and empathise with all the participants as individuals, rather than as a solid group, making the room feel less like 'me and them' and more like 'us'.
>
> **Josie Daxter**
>
> Freelance Director and Facilitator, *National Youth Theatre*, *The PappyShow*, *Complicité*

Notice the new people

'Was I even there...?'

If somebody's late or is new to your workshop or your course, make sure that you acknowledge them. If you don't, it can make people feel like they're not even there, as if their presence has had no impact on you or the space in any way. When it should. They're not invisible. You should also introduce yourself so they know your name. Everyone else may know you, but they won't. Plus, it can be a good opportunity for you to ask their name too.

It's also good to take a few moments to bring them up to speed with what's going on in the workshop if you can. Even if you simply tell them: 'Don't worry, you haven't missed much', or 'We were just talking about what we thought of the play.' It's subtle, but it brings them into the space far more than if you simply ignore them.

If you've just given the group an instruction for an exercise when they enter, or are about to set people off to do group work, you don't need to repeat the instructions again in front of the whole group – you could either tell them that their group will catch them up, or you can tell them you'll come over and explain what they need to do. Either way, it's good to go over to them during group work and to give a quick sixty-second rundown of what they've missed, along with a quick introduction to yourself. If they've entered and you're in the middle of running a game, you can either give them a super-quick explanation of how to play it, or if it's simple enough, reassure them that they'll pick it up in no time and that it doesn't need explaining. Either way, the simple act of you doing these things will instantly bring them into the group.

Celebrate progress, not perfection

You should encourage your group to progress, not to chase perfection. Nobody will ever be perfect, so pushing your group to try to get everything right will likely leave them demotivated. They'll be much more free and far more encouraged if you focus more on their progress. It's something that everyone's capable of achieving.

Anybody can make progress if they work hard enough and have the right guidance, which means that everyone in your room can be positively supported in your workshop because it's something that everyone's capable of doing. So make sure that you focus on their steps forward, no matter how small. Though this doesn't mean that you should accept anything below standard...

Have standards

It's important to have standards for your group. Having low standards or accepting behaviour or work that isn't good will tell your group that you don't think they're capable of achieving – and there's nothing more disempowering than that. They'll be able to tell if you're lowering the bar for them, and if you're not there to help them grow, then why are you there?

Clearly, your standards for people need to be relative to the people you're working with. A high standard for Janine who struggles to attend a session may just be standard procedure for Davina. It's all subjective. The key is to have standards that are achievable but which require a degree of effort.

You can have standards for anything. Behaviour, effort, quality of work, verbal contributions, you name it. Some examples could be:

- Expecting your group to be on time.
- Expecting their work not to be below a standard that they're capable of.
- Expecting everyone to give the session a go.

Don't accept contributions that are below what they're capable of, and if you know they're capable of more, don't settle for less – find a sensitive way to acknowledge it.

Have high expectations

Coach Carter, *The Karate Kid*, *Ted Lasso*... All these involve a teacher or coach who believed in their student(s) and pushed them to be better than they ever dreamt. Can you imagine these stories if they did the opposite?

'Hey everyone. You're never going to amount to anything and the odds are stacked against you, so let's do some drawing instead.'

That's not a show I'd want to see. Or a workshop I'd want to be in.

You need to believe in the people you're working with, and the expectations you set will massively impact how they respond in the room and the level of effort that they put in. You shouldn't expect them to win Oscars overnight, but you do need to believe that they're capable, and that with a bit of commitment and hard work, they can become something greater.

People will rise to whatever expectations you set for them, so don't think that by setting the bar low you're somehow doing them a favour or being nice. You're not. Just remember that the tasks you set need to be achievable and within reach – so while you'll want to have high expectations, make sure that they're achievable.

This is why I never, ever accept a participant telling me that they can't do something or that they're not good enough. It's their job to give it a go, it's my job to get them there. That way when they achieve what they didn't think was possible, that sense of achievement opens up all sorts of possibilities for who they can be in life.

“Amen to this! The power of belief is so strong! This is paramount for me. The attitude that you have when you walk into the room will establish the dynamic that you want to achieve.

'I believe in you.'

Let it be your mantra. With this foundation underpinning everything you do, you really can't go wrong. This doesn't mean that you expect perfection, it means you expect the group to respect themselves. In turn this means respecting yourself and your group, which in turn will make the group respect you too.

Think big. Someone believing in you can literally change your life. I'm not saying you can do that in a two-hour workshop, but you can let a light shine for a period of time that might ignite a spark and give someone a glimpse of a part of themselves that they didn't know existed. Go into all workshops with that feeling and be excited about who and what you might find. 'I believe in you.'

Tara Boland

Discussing the Work

An overview

Discussing the work is a key part of any workshop because it allows you to:

- Explore the work more deeply.
- Check the group's understanding.
- Make sure the group are achieving their learning outcomes.

Discussions about the work mainly happen for exercises rather than games. You don't need a roundtable discussion on a game if it was purely for fun, though it's perfectly reasonable to discuss it if it links to your learning objective, or if there's a key point of learning you want to highlight by playing it. But discussing exercises is important, as you'll want to reflect on the work and support the group's learning.

You need to find the balance between discussing the work and keeping up the pace of your workshop. For example, let's take an exercise that has four stages to it, such as teaching your group the eight Laban efforts for how to move in a space (direct/indirect, sudden/sustained, heavy/light, bound/unbound). If you were to do a pair at a time, it might be better to have a few quick comments after each pair with a proper discussion at the end, rather than having in-depth discussions each time.

So, have discussions about the work where you see fit, but always be mindful of the pace of your workshop.

Keep the key learning point in mind

It's standard practice to discuss exercises after they've finished, but the key with any discussion is for you to be clear on the key points of the exercise and for you to keep them in focus. As much as you'll want the group to openly discuss what they've done, you don't want a discussion just for the sake of it, or for it to stray off into corners of the universe that just aren't relevant. Allow the discussion to be fluid, but make sure that the questions you ask guide the group towards the learning outcome. It's your responsibility to make sure that it stays in focus.

Check-ins/check-outs

Check-ins and check-outs allow the group to talk about the work, the process or how they're currently feeling – either at the beginning of a session or at the end. It's a good way to get a flavour for where the group are at, or their reflections on how things are going.

Some examples would be to have the group in a circle, and for each of them to say:

- One word about how they're feeling.
- One word to say what they thought of the workshop.
- One sentence to say how they're feeling.
- One sentence to say what they enjoyed or what challenged them the most.
- Any comments or reflections on the work.

Just be mindful of time. If you ask every person for their views in a room of thirty, you'll be there all day, which will definitely have your group check-out mentally. Check-ins in particular should never be longer than five minutes, or ten at the absolute most. It should be a pre-task to see how people are doing, not a core chunk of your workshop.

Another option is that you can ask everyone to close their eyes and have them do either a thumbs-up or down, or have them show a number on a scale of 1 to 10 on their fingers to show

how they're feeling. This'd be anonymous because only you as the workshop leader would get to see people's responses.

I personally don't find morning check-ins that useful. Ask people how they feel in the morning and most will say they're 'tired' or 'okay'. Even if they give more than that, there's not actually much you can do with that information. So to me it always felt like I was just doing them for the sake of it. Besides, it's my job to get the group in a good place regardless of where they're at.

Check-outs I'm more in favour of. If it's a two-hour or a day workshop, I might ask people for one thing they learnt from the workshop. But only if I feel it's useful. On a course I'd usually have a more open forum where anyone can put their hand up and say what their reflections were on the work or the day, as it allows for an open discussion.

Use their names

Using people's names when you're discussing work is a subtle way to make people feel seen. Addressing people with their names might not seem like a big deal, but it shows you have a real care, consideration and respect for the people you're working with. So don't underestimate its power.

See the sections 'Learn the names you think you'll need' on page 87 and 'Learn their names...!' on page 154 for strategies to help you learn them both in one-off workshops and on courses.

Be genuinely interested

You need to take a genuine interest in what people have to say. It's easy to simply nod, smile and pretend to acknowledge people's contributions without really paying attention, but we can always tell when someone's really listening to us and when they're not. This doesn't mean you need to treat everything that people say as if it's the best thing in the world, or that you need to acknowledge or validate people's every last word, but it does mean that you need to listen with intent.

Curiosity is the key here, which is especially helpful when it comes to people's contributions and opinions. Anyone can have an opinion, but sometimes it's the *why* behind what they say that can really open up a conversation. It makes them think. If you ask somebody 'Why?', it invites both them and you to explore their thoughts further, because sometimes we form an opinion about things without ever having thought about why. So if you feel that somebody's said something that you want to explore a bit more, feel free to stick with that person for a bit longer to ask them more about their thoughts before moving on to the next person.

> I'll often defer to the person speaking with: 'Tell me a bit more about that.' That's the line I use a lot. 'Say a bit more about that.' 'I'm really interested to know a bit more about that.' Often if you say that to a young person... it's not something they hear a lot. Not many teachers will say that to a young person. 'Oh, that's interesting. Say a bit more about that.' If you say that to a young person in front of their peers, they feel really good about themselves. Then they can start to say a bit more about it and articulate themselves and they find their voice.
>
> **Lucy Shaljian**

Having the last word in a discussion

You have the power as a workshop leader to draw a line under a discussion and to bring it to a close. This is important for when you need to move the discussion on because of time, but also for when discussions head off in directions you don't want them to. Only you have the power to move the workshop on, so don't be afraid to do it if you feel that it's time to do so.

This also gives you the power to bring an end to difficult conversations where there've been disagreements. If you're bringing a difficult conversation to a close, it's important that you round it off in a dignified way, so that you still respect the people in your group regardless of what was said. An example of this could be:

'This is a difficult topic, and some valid points have been made. I think we can all agree that it's hard to come to an agreement, but we need to move on to the next exercise because of time.'

This is productive because it brings closure before moving on, rather than saying: 'Right, that's it, let's move on.' There's no use pretending that a conversation was easy when it wasn't, so it's worth acknowledging the reality of it rather than sweeping it under the rug.

One thing to be mindful of is that just because you have the last word, it doesn't mean that it's going to change people's minds. For example, if two people had different ideas about whether a play was good or bad, rounding off the conversation with:

'Marjorie, it was a really good play. That's the end of it. Okay, so let's move on.'

...is only going to make Marjorie dislike you, and it'll make it harder for her and anyone who agrees with her to engage with you. It'll leave a bitter taste because you'd be moving the workshop on without acknowledging her perspective, and you'd stop her from having a response. None of this is to say that you need to agree with everyone and everything when you're closing a discussion. There may well be a right or a wrong with the topic, and you can and should still challenge thoughts or ideas that you need to. It's about how you do it. Here are both a good and bad example of how you could close a discussion:

Bad practice	Good practice
'Marjorie, it was a really good play. That's the end of it. Okay, so let's move on.'	'Well clearly we have different opinions about whether the play was good or bad. I personally thought it was good, but I hear your points Marjorie. And that's the joy of theatre and art in general. We can all see the same thing but have a different opinion about it.'

Ultimately, at the very least, you need to acknowledge the different viewpoints and bring things to a respectful summary or conclusion, rather than using your power as the facilitator to shut people down.

Red herrings

'Sir, why did Shakespeare write so many plays?
Sir, who were Shakespeare's grandchildren?
Sir, where did Shakespeare go on holiday?' Bertie

Red herrings are questions or comments that can distract or divert the discussion from its main focus. Sometimes people can do this deliberately, sometimes not, but it's important to be mindful of them. In this case, if you're working in a school, answering Bertie's questions will quickly derail your workshop and put him in charge, and the rest of the group will soon see that they can get out of work pretty easily by simply asking unnecessary questions.

Red herrings don't need to be outlandish either – they can be perfectly reasonable questions or contributions. But if they lead you down a path that isn't productive to the workshop or doesn't support the workshop's objective, resist the temptation to be drawn into them. Either state that it's something you can answer at another time, or give a short, snappy response and move on.

It's your job to mediate disagreements

You're bound to get disagreements in your room at some stage. The reality is, the wider the range of people you have in the room, the more likely that disagreements will arise. There's less room for people to disagree if people all think the same.

However, regardless of the topic or your own opinion, it's your job to make sure that discussions stay civil and respectful. You're responsible for making sure that things don't get out of hand. This can sometimes mean bringing out both sides of an argument, encouraging different ideas to be explored, or highlighting blind spots that haven't been discussed.

Mediating disagreements can sometimes be easier if you don't give your own opinion, or if you do, by making sure that your input is relatively mild. Holding the centre ground makes it much easier to manage disagreements because your voice isn't giving weight to any particular side. This isn't to say that you won't or shouldn't have an opinion, but you need to accept that as a workshop leader, it's your job to hold a group together and to facilitate a well-meaning, respectful room. And the stronger a stance you take on a position, the more difficult that becomes.

This also ties in with the fact that under no circumstances should you ever get into an argument with a participant or lock horns with them. You can disagree, of course, but you need to be diplomatic and grounded at all times. As soon as you become the enemy of the people in your group, you've lost.

Another key here is to make sure that disagreements remain about the subject, not the person. Under no circumstances should a discussion or anyone's views lead to them being disrespected, demeaned or called names – it doesn't matter what the disagreement is about. There is no exception. As soon as this is allowed to happen, any team cohesion that you've built will disintegrate.

If there are disagreements in the room, it can sometimes be better to ask questions about people's position, rather than to try to provide counter-answers. Questions get people thinking, answers don't. Asking the right questions can be a far better way to open up people's thinking and can create a more effective learning experience for the group.

How to Use Questions and Answers for Maximum Impact

Types of questions

Questions are a vital aspect of any workshop. The more specific your question, the more specific the answer. Here are some examples of the different types of questions you can use in the space:

Retrieval questions Collect information and facts, e.g. 'Who does Tybalt kill in the play?'	**Open questions** Require a longer answer and can't be answered with a simple yes or no, e.g. 'Why do you think the Capulets and Montagues hate each other?'
Prediction questions Ask for a prediction about what will happen, e.g. 'What do you think Juliet will do?'	**Curious questions** Encourage thinking, e.g. 'What if Romeo and Juliet were adults?'
Challenging questions Encourage debate and consider alternative views, e.g. 'What if the Friar refused to wed Romeo and Juliet?'	**Closed questions** Give the listener a limited number of responses to choose from, e.g. 'Did Romeo kill Tybalt?' (Yes/No)
Why? Ask why, e.g. 'Why?'	

By using a range of different questions, you'll be able to talk much more deeply about the work, and your discussions will be much more engaging. Not everything needs to be discussed in great detail, but the more comfortable you are in using different types of questions, the more you can get out of your participants and your workshops.

Closed questions

'Hey, Caroline. Nice to meet you. So tell me about your life?'

'Um...?'

Closed questions are sometimes labelled as being 'bad', while open questions are sometimes labelled as 'good'. For workshop leaders, this is simply not so. Open questions can often be intimidating and too broad for people, especially for those with learning difficulties. But it's something we can all relate to when you think about it. Most of us will have faced the worst open question of all time – 'So, tell me about yourself' – and felt completely adrift at sea about how to answer. Closed questions are much more straightforward and can be highly effective when used correctly.

They allow you to do two things:

- Focus the participants' response.
- Make an otherwise daunting question or topic easier and more focused.

With a group that's reluctant to speak, a closed question might get you a response when an open question may have gotten you silence, so using a closed question can sometimes make your group more responsive. They can also be paired with open questions, for example:

You (Closed question)	*'Did you think the use of silence was effective? Yes or no?'*
Them	*'Yes.'*

You (Open question)	*'What was it about the silence that made it effective?'*
Them	*'It built a sense of suspense.'*

Using closed questions can help you focus the discussion before opening it up for a more open response. Learning to master both open and closed questions is key to getting the best from your group in a discussion.

Inferring answers vs giving facts

While you can tell your group a bunch of facts, that doesn't get them to use their brains. You can use inference to ask your group questions which prompt them to make educated guesses as to the answer, rather than simply give it to them. Here's an example:

To give the facts	To have them infer
You: A dog is a domesticated wolf. It usually takes thousands of years to domesticate an animal.	**You:** What wild animal do you think dogs came from? **Them:** Huskies. **You:** Huskies? You're close. But do huskies live in the wild? What animal can you think of that's similar to a dog that lives in the wild? **Them:** A wolf. **You:** A wolf, absolutely. So how long do you think it'd take to tame wolves? Could you do it in a day? **Them:** No. It'd take a long time. **You:** Exactly. It'd actually take thousands of years.

To have your group infer the answers is to give them the facts at the end, not at the start. It'll also help to involve those who aren't actively speaking, because even though they might not be contributing verbally, they can still be thinking of the answers to your questions in their head.

Expanding your group's thinking – Socratic questioning

'Never underestimate the power of a good question.'

While inferring answers uses questions to guide people to an answer, here we'll look at how questions can broaden people's thinking. Once you master how to ask questions, your discussions will be far more intellectually stimulating and will sharpen people's minds.

There's a lot that can be learnt here from Socrates, the Greek philosopher. His skill of asking questions could delve much deeper into people's views, and he was able to expose the contradictions in people's thinking. He was effective. Perhaps a bit too effective, because it led to his death. And while I certainly don't want the same outcome for you, there's a lot we can learn from his approach when it comes to running workshops.

Let's look at some Socratic questions taken from Wikipedia, with some additional questions related to *Romeo and Juliet*:

'Are Romeo and Juliet in love?'		
	General example	*Romeo and Juliet* example
Getting students to clarify their thinking and explore the origin of their thinking	'Why do you say that?', 'Could you explain further?'	'So you think Romeo and Juliet are right for each other? Could you explain a bit more?'

Challenging students about (their) assumptions	'Is this always the case?', 'Why do you think that this assumption holds here?'	'Are your feelings always right?' 'Have you ever had a feeling about something and been wrong?'
Providing evidence as a basis for arguments	'Why do you say that?', 'Is there reason to doubt this evidence?'	'What's your evidence to suggest that it's love, and not infatuation?'
Discovering alternative viewpoints and perspectives, and conflicts between contentions	'What is the counter-argument?', 'Can/did anyone see this another way?'	'How long do you need to know someone to fall in love with them?'
Exploring implications and consequences	'But if...happened, what else would result?', 'How does... affect...?'	'But what if Romeo had met Juliet in Asda? Would they have fallen in love then?'
Questioning the question	'Why do you think that I asked that question?', 'Why was that question important?'	'Which of your questions turned out to be the most useful?'

Using questions like these will allow you to dig much deeper into ideas and will allow your group to think more inquisitively. This isn't about trying to be Socrates or trying to have deep conversations for the sake of it, but it can open up topics in a way that wouldn't happen if you just took somebody's comment and said, 'Yep, great opinion, Saskia', and carried on with the workshop. You're often able to probe into people's responses more than you think. But ultimately, this approach allows you to:

- Explore complex ideas.
- Find the truth of a subject.
- Open up problems.
- Challenge people's thinking.
- Analyse big concepts.
- Actively engage your group in a discussion.
- Unravel people's assumptions.
- Separate out what you know from what you don't.
- Figure out the logical consequence of a decision.

> "The disciplined practice of thoughtful questioning enables the scholar/student to examine ideas and be able to determine the validity of those ideas.
>
> **Socrates**

There are a few final things to consider when it comes to using Socratic questions. You'll need to:

- Know your subject well.
- Be genuinely curious about people's opinions and contributions.
- Not bully your group. This isn't about showing off your knowledge/intellect.
- Stay as far away as possible from playing devil's advocate or deliberately trying to catch people out.
- Affirm every contribution. The only way to fully explore an idea is to allow everything to be on the table.

So if you have the time and you feel it'd help, use the power of questions to delve into topics further. Your group will become far more inquisitive if you do.

'Asking-for-it' questions

'Am I talking to myself!?'

'Does it look like I've got all day!?'

'Do you think I was born yesterday!?'

Asking-for-it questions will leave you wide open to an answer that you won't find helpful. A challenging group will have the time of their life with these. They're such open goals that even the most well-behaved person will be tempted to take a shot.

These are usually used as a response to unwanted behaviour, but they're an indirect way of responding to the behaviour that you want to address. It's more effective to directly address the behaviour that needs to be changed, communicating clearly what you want to change. Otherwise, using one of these will leave you wide open to an unhelpful response that'll only make things worse.

Drilling/retrieval questions/rephrasing

Here are some additional pointers that can help when it comes to managing discussions, particularly if you're trying to teach something in your workshop.

Drilling – Sometimes known as 'parroting', this can be helpful if you want people to remember certain words, particularly words that are difficult to pronounce. For example, if you were teaching a group how to say the word 'haemoglobin' (hee-ma-glow-bin), you could say, 'Repeat after me, haemoglobin', then have them repeat it. It's often best to do this three times. Usually only a handful of people will repeat it the first time, but then more will on the second, and even more on the third; and with more enthusiasm and confidence each time. Third time's the charm.

Retrieval questions – You can use retrieval questions to draw on any previous learning that you've done in the session, which can further embed what you've taught them. To do this, you simply ask your group to answer a question that you asked earlier. You can also pair this with:

Asking the group to rephrase – If you're trying to establish new learning or new words, and a group gives you an answer that's technically correct but not the word you're trying to teach them, you can get them to rephrase it, and can often pair it with a retrieval question. For example:

Deontay: I liked how the audience were on both sides of the stage, it made us feel closer to the actors.

You: Great, and what did we call that before? When the audience are on both sides of the stage?

Deontay: Traverse staging.

You: Fab!

Bringing in quieter people/pre-loading

'Nigel! You haven't said a word all day. Clearly you're not paying attention are you!?'

Getting quieter people to contribute in discussions can sometimes feel like a challenge. How do you get people to speak up without putting them under pressure?

The first thing to say is that just because somebody's quiet, doesn't mean they're disengaged. If they're falling asleep then maybe they are... But a person not speaking doesn't mean they're not listening or following. So don't think that you're doing a bad job if people aren't actively speaking up.

Nevertheless, it's only right that we create a space where people can contribute when they're ready to, while making sure that the room isn't dominated by the same voices all the time.

One technique you can use to help with this is called 'pre-loading'.

Pre-loading allows people to come up with a response for your question before you ask them to respond, which can level the playing field and makes things less daunting. For example, when you ask a question, you can:

- Give everyone ten seconds to think in silence before you ask for the answer.
- Have them discuss the answer in small groups or with the person next to them.
- Have them write down their answer individually or in groups.

You'd then be able to ask any person in the room for a response because they'll already have thought about or discussed the answer. All they'll need to do is to share what they were discussing. This can be particularly helpful if you want to hear from someone who hasn't spoken yet and otherwise wouldn't have put their hand up.

> One way that I manage voices in a discussion is by being mindful of the airspace, and I usually raise it when I do a group agreement at the start of a session.
>
> I'll usually ask, 'Hands up if you like to talk a lot', and I'll always put my hand up.
>
> 'Right, so we can see the people in here that like to talk a lot. Hands up if you don't like to talk so much, if you like to listen. Okay, so it's an opportunity now for us to speak a bit more or speak a bit less. To create a nice balance of voices in the room.'
>
> And that way, quieter people feel like they're being invited to speak, but only if they've really got something they want to say. So it's not pressure, it's an opportunity. I frame conversations as an opportunity to speak, where people can be heard, not just listen.
>
> Also, sometimes I might say, 'So is there anything for you?' You know, if I'm facilitating the discussion and there's somebody that hasn't spoken, I might directly ask that person: 'Anything you want to add?' Or 'I've heard so much from you and it's fantastic, and I love your contribution, but I'd really like to hear from somebody else.' Just to generate a more equal discussion.
>
> **Lucy Shaljian**

Catching people by surprise

Them: What do you think some of the key challenges will be for the restructuring of our team and how do you think we can implement the best possible changes for maximum impact. Dan?

Dan: Um...?

Throw a ball at someone when they're not expecting it and there's not much chance that they'll catch it. And, depending on your aim, you might even knock them out. The same goes for people when you're asking them a question.

Questions can often put people on the back foot when they come as a surprise. Most people will either trying to blag it and end up giving you a poor answer, or they'll say they don't have one, which runs the risk of having a domino effect on the rest of the group where all of a sudden they won't have an answer either.

It's far better to give people a heads up by letting them know who you'll be asking. For example:

'George, I'm going to come to you first, then to Julie. George, what do you think the main theme of the play was?'

This'll make people feel more comfortable about answering your questions and it'll be more likely that you'll get a good response.

Hands up

When asking the group for answers or thoughts, your default position should be to have people put their hands up and to invite them to speak. Not having the hands-up system (essentially a free-for-all where people can 'just jump in' with their thoughts) creates a no man's land where only the loudest voices get heard. There are a few benefits to the hands-up approach:

It allows you to bring the quieter people into discussions. Speaking from experience as the quietest person in the room growing up, there's simply no way that those with less confidence will be bold enough to get themselves heard in a free-for-all. Over the span of a course, this could easily mean that some people never speak at all. Some might argue that the onus is on the individual to speak up, but I'd say the onus should be on the facilitator to allow everyone the opportunity to be heard.

It allows you to reinforce people's names and to be clear on who's speaking next. For example, if there are three hands up, you could say:

'Let's have James, Lindsay and then Doris. James?'

This reinforces people's names for the group, lets people know who'll be answering next, and is specific. There's none of the ambiguity that comes with gesturing to someone in a general part of the room with people thinking, 'Who, me?'

It allows you to actively facilitate discussions. You can fully explore any interesting points, prioritise those who haven't been heard, and you can manage the session's timing and pace – all of which would be more difficult with the free-for-all. The free-for-all could also mean that you're ignoring a wealth of talent and good opinions. Just because people aren't bold enough to speak up and share their views, it doesn't mean they don't have good ideas.

The only time I might call an exception to having hands up is when working with adults. Depending on the group, it might seem slightly patronising to do the hands-up system. But you need to be aware that the problems with the free-for-all still apply with adults, so it's important to keep them in mind. Also, this is one area where there's a clear distinction between being a director and a workshop leader. It'd be weird to have the hands-up system if you were a director with a group of four professionals. But as a facilitator, especially with large groups of young people, it's essential. So write down the free-for-all approach, scrunch it up into a ball and throw it as far as your arm can chuck it.

You don't need to hear from every person with their hand up

'Okay, what were your thoughts on the actor's use of...'

Thirty hands go up

An hour later

'Thank you all for your thoughts, some really valid contributions. That's all we've got time for unfortunately. See you all next week!'

Having a group that's engaged is great because it allows you to have in-depth discussions about the work and to hear different opinions. But don't fall into the trap of thinking that you need to honour every person who puts their hand up.

As with all aspects of leading a workshop, the key is to make sure that you keep up the pace, and in this case that means moving the conversation on when enough contributions have been made or once you've covered the learning point. A subtle way to manage this is to let the group know when you're only going to take a few more contributions before moving on. For example, if there are twenty hands up in the room, you could say:

'Okay, we'll take two more points then we're going to move on.'

You can also say who the next people will be by saying their names or gesturing to the two people, so they know who they are. This allows the other eighteen people to put their hands down because they'll know who's next in line to speak. Their arms will thank you for it.

Repeating answers/paraphrasing

When somebody makes a comment in a discussion, it can sometimes be useful to repeat back or paraphrase what people have said. This has a few benefits. It:

- Shows the speaker that you were listening.
- Reinforces what was said for everybody else in the room.
- Allows you to make sure that everyone heard the comment (which is particularly helpful if the speaker was quiet).

Paraphrasing is an alternative to repeating somebody's comment because it means you can take the core messages of what people say without repeating the whole thing. It allows you to condense what's being said. Here's an example:

'I felt like the play was boring *because* ***Hannah didn't really engage with the text*** *and just wandered around a bit aimlessly and it was kind of like she didn't even want to be there, so the next time she has a moment to herself, I think she needs to question whether or not she actually wants to be an actor and if she doesn't, I dunno, maybe she should go and work in McDonald's or something.* ***She just wasn't believable.'*** Jonah

There's more that you could highlight from this if you wanted to, but you'd only want to repeat or paraphrase the points that you think are worth bringing out, or that are useful to focus on. You'd have the choice of repeating back all three highlighted points, or even just one if you wanted to. You could also choose to then follow up any of these points with a question. Here are three of the points you could draw out, and some questions that you could choose to follow up with:

You repeating the statement	Your follow-up question
'You felt the play was boring –'	'Was there anything else about the production that made you think it was boring? Or was it all because of Hannah?'
'– that Hannah didn't engage with the text –'	'What was it about what she was doing that made it seem like she wasn't engaging with the text?'
'– and that she just wasn't believable.'	'What could she have done to make her acting more believable?'

If you are going to repeat or paraphrase what people have said, you don't need to do it for everything they say. If you do, it'll get really tiring for your group and will massively slow down the pace of your workshop. So make sure that you find a balance, or that you only do it for the key contributions that you want to reinforce.

Behaviour Management

An overview

Managing behaviour is a key skill for all workshop leaders to have. When it comes to behaviour management, as with most things, prevention is better than cure. Having a suitable, well-planned workshop, a good relationship with your group, and being self-assured can all be big factors to prevent behaviours becoming an issue in the first place, and are all things that are within your control. However, it's naive to believe that this'll always be enough. Regardless of how experienced you are, all of us will face challenging behaviours from time to time, so this chapter will cover some options for you when you need that little bit more.

It's important to note that challenging behaviours can come in a range of varieties and flavours, and aren't necessarily what you'd typically class as 'bad behaviour'. The range of challenges you could face include people who:

- Are exhibiting general bad behaviour, such as if Travis were to hurl abuse at people or throw chairs across the room.
- Are overly dominating or a negative influence in the room.
- Don't want to be there and are actively disengaged.
- Are there just to have an overly (immature) good time.
- Have a negative response/attitude to the work you're doing.
- Have conflicts or drama with others in the group, such as Susan used to go out with Danny but Danny cheated on her and now Danny and his friends won't work with Susan's friends and there's no way you could've known this beforehand but you're here now so you have to make do.

It's also important not to beat yourself up if things don't go the way you planned. You can't force anyone to do anything, and there may be some groups or individuals who simply won't want to engage. However, they'll be situations that you can learn from. And if you do have a particularly challenging time, make sure that you disconnect and do whatever you need to do to de-stress. See a friend. Have a brew. Get something stronger if you really need to.

It's also worth noting that managing behaviour can sometimes be a case of trial and error, because people will respond differently depending on the group, the individual, and the setting that you're working in – which means you'll need to be flexible and responsive to who you have in the room. So not everything in this chapter will work with every group every time, but they're all good additions to your toolbox.

Lastly, I'll be using the terms 'bad behaviour' and 'challenging behaviour' throughout this chapter. There's often a debate about what terminology we should use – 'bad behaviour', 'challenging behaviour', 'problematic student behaviour', 'disruptive behaviour', 'disengaged'... there may be more by the time you read this. But for the purposes of this book, I'm less concerned with what it should be called, and more interested in what you can do about it.

Boundaries

Boundaries are important for all groups, even those without challenging behaviour. Boundaries can sometimes be seen in a negative way, as if they're restrictive – but boundaries are hugely positive because they allow you to be clear about what the expectations are in the room and allow everybody to play by the same rulebook. This means that if any boundaries are crossed that impact on the rest of the group, you're able to address the behaviour, with the group's best interest in mind.

No workshop can succeed without healthy boundaries. So if your idea of workshop utopia is for everyone to roam free with no boundaries or restrictions and for people to do whatever they want, you'll find yourself getting run over by bad behaviour in no time. Or retiring early. Or both.

The key to setting boundaries is to be clear on:

- What your expectations are.
- What isn't acceptable.
- What the consequences are if the boundaries are crossed.

Setting boundaries within a workshop is essential because we all like to know what the limits and expectations are. Children in particular love boundaries because they make them feel more secure, so don't feel like you're doing them a favour by letting them do whatever they want. Sure, they'll protest about boundaries from time to time and they'll often test them, but removing them altogether is an invitation for carnage. And the irony is that rules and boundaries give us more freedom, not less, because they mean we're clear on our limitations. To not have boundaries is to give your group free rein of the room, and will put them in control, not you.

Establishing a group contract can be a good way to establish the rules and expectations at the start of the session so that everybody's on the same page. At its most basic, it's a set of rules that you want for your room, but it can also include the things that you want to encourage. You should ask for the group's input too, which will give them a sense of buy-in and agreement. Just be mindful that doing this won't solve all your problems, and it's often more useful for groups that you're with for a period of time. Also, if you've only got an hour-long workshop, spending ten minutes on the rules of the session could unhelpfully become a good chunk of the workshop itself, unless you do it quickly; so be conscious of time.

Boundaries don't always need to be said. They can be set subtly. For example, stopping to wait for silence when people are talking shows that you won't talk unless people are listening. It doesn't need a monologue about the importance of listening, the mere fact that you've stopped because the boundary's been crossed is enough to get the message across.

Make sure you maintain any boundaries that you set, otherwise they become meaningless. So make sure that once you're clear on what a boundary is, you uphold it. Even and especially if it's challenged. Each time you give in to a boundary being crossed, you're essentially encouraging them to be broken.

Boundaries aren't set *to* your group; they're set *for* your group. So make sure that you're clear on what your boundaries are. And don't ever be apologetic about them. They're for the benefit of everyone.

I had an example of a boundary being crossed during a Battersea Arts Centre performance. It was an immersive production, where each actor would take a group on a journey through different performances around the building. I asked my group what we could do to cheer up the main character who was upset, to which Travis said:

'We could grab him and throw him to the floor and stab him and set him on fire.'

Say what? Hell no.

I called him over to the side and told him sternly that that kind of contribution was unacceptable, and if he were to carry on I'd remove him from the show.

I kid you not, Travis became one of the best members of my group for the entire production. He became the politest person in that group – he was the star player. But that only happened because I put my foot down. And by doing so, he knew where the line was, to everybody's benefit.

Work with the energy of your group

'Oh my goodness, they won't stop talking... :(

...about the work!' :)

Use the energy that your group gives you. An energetic group isn't challenging if they're channelling that energy into an exercise. A talkative group becomes productive when you give them tasks that require discussion. Channelling a group's energy rather than fighting against it can bring benefits for everybody.

This isn't to say that you can't ever work against it or that you shouldn't encourage a group to control their energy. Clearly, you should absolutely encourage a hyperactive group to learn to focus, and a talkative group to listen. Just be sure to make the conscious decision about when you want to work with their energy and when you don't.

I saw this first-hand when I worked for a day in a London primary school as a teaching assistant. They scheduled five-minute breaks for the children to go outside to do laps around the playground to get their energy out. It gave them the opportunity to burn their energy off in a constructive way, rather than to stifle it.

Have them actively engaged as much as possible

The more your group are actively engaged in a task, the less you'll need them to listen to you – which means you won't need to spend as much energy trying to hold their attention. So if your group is highly energised or they struggle to listen, plan for fewer exercises that are facilitator-led and more that allow them to engage with each other. And when you do need to actively engage with them as a group, make sure it's not for longer than it needs to be.

The group's physical configuration

How a group are arranged physically can have a huge impact on their attention, so you can use their physical configuration to your advantage. At its most basic, you can have people either sitting or standing, both of which have their upsides and downsides:

Standing	Sitting
+	+
• Gets/keeps the group physically alert. • It's easier to transition from one exercise to the next.	• Allows the group to relax more. • It's more difficult for people to start conversations with those who aren't immediately next to them.
-	-
• Standing for too long will make groups restless and fidgety. • It's easier for them to move around and talk to other people, or to distract others.	• Sitting for too long will get them too comfortable and potentially disengaged. • It can take more effort for them to get into the next exercise if they're too comfortable.

Because of these advantages and disadvantages, adjusting the physical configuration of your group can often have a big impact on how they behave. Some key points on this are:

- If your group are too energised, sit them down. Sitting them down will bring their energy down too, and it'll make it harder for them to engage with the people around them.
- If your group are getting too comfortable or too lethargic sitting down, have them stand up. It'll give them more energy.

You don't need to have people up and down every few minutes, but it's something to be aware of. Make sure you use the configuration that best suits the circumstance.

Individuals who are challenging

When you're dealing with somebody who's behaving badly, it's useful to try to get to the root cause of the problem. People don't usually behave badly for no reason, so by understanding the *why* behind somebody's behaviour, you can often address the issue that's causing the behaviour in the first place.

This isn't always easy. There's a ton of possible reasons why people behave badly. However, treating Odessa like the naughty child will make everybody's life worse, not better. It might not be that she's a bad kid. It might be that she isn't engaged in the work, or that the task you've given might not match her ability. And for one thing, treating her that way will only make her live up to that expectation because that's the role you've given her.

If you do have somebody whose behaviour is particularly tricky, here are some quick techniques that might help:

- Give them something to do. Having a responsibility can sometimes help people to engage in a positive way. But make it meaningful, such as having them be your assistant for a particular task.
- Keep them engaged by asking questions. This can stop them from switching off. Just make sure you're genuine and aren't doing it for the sake of it.
- Make sure that you address any behaviour that isn't acceptable. Don't ignore it. Ignoring it will only encourage it to get worse.

But as always, prevention is better than cure, and one of the best ways to do that is through consequences.

" I like to engage the 'casting director' in me in a workshop. Not everyone wants to be an actor, and that's okay! You might come across a participant who on the surface comes across as 'disobedient' or craving attention. If the group is influenced by this individual, then actually what you have in front of you is a potential leader – a director! So cast them. Give them that role. Find an opportunity for them to lead, to fulfil their vision. You can do the same with quieter, more subtle participants too.

Whenever I'm in a session and can feel a struggle for power, I bring out a chair beside me. The observation chair. When we're devising creative work, it is always key to get an outside eye during the development of the work, because you can't always see the work objectively when you are in the midst of it.

So once you've established the principle of the chair to the whole group, each group could have an observational chair. This empowers the groups to be responsible for themselves and the work.

You could have some potential costume designers, producers, stage managers or sound designers in your group. Cast them! Tell them what you can see, hand them back their superpower, and tell them you celebrate it in them, you *see* them. And then… find a way for them to use their superpower!

Chetna Pandya
Actor (*Netflix*, *Channel 4*, *ITV*, *Royal Court*, *Complicité*, *Royal Shakespeare Company*)
Freelance facilitator, *Barbican*, *Complicité*, *Royal Central School of Speech & Drama*, *Generation Arts*, *Guildhall School of Music & Drama*
Artistic & Quality Assessor, *Arts Council England*
Board Member, *Complicité*

Consequences

Having consequences for unwanted behaviour can be one of the best ways to prevent it. But you can't go in all guns blazing. Suspending Lamilton from school for looking at you funny will likely get you a backlash, and it'll give you nowhere to go if the behaviour gets worse. By having stepped consequences, you give the person or your group the opportunity to mend their ways, and you can scale the consequence in line with their behaviour.

Robert Plevin outlines some of the key foundations of delivering consequences in his book *Take Control of the Noisy Class: Chaos to Calm in 15 Seconds.*

Stage	Consequence	Your response
1	Warning	'Kevin, you need to stop poking Cassandra. If you carry on I'll have to separate you.'
2	Separation	'Kevin, move to the other side of the room.'

3	Time-out	'Kevin, go and sit on the side for ten minutes.'
4	The ultimatum	*Call in Miss for reinforcements*

The process between each stage would be to:

- Be clear about the behaviour that's unacceptable.
- Be clear about the consequence if the person continues that behaviour.
- Give them a chance and a warning if they continue.
- Following that, escalate to the next stage.

The aim shouldn't be to ramp up through the stages as quickly as possible; you should look to support people as best as you can so that you don't need to escalate in the first place. You also don't need to outline your four-step plan for all to see and to announce it to the room, but you do need to be clear on what the consequence will be if they continue their behaviour. So make sure you give Kevin a warning or two before moving on to the next stage.

There are a few other factors you should bear in mind when it comes to stepped consequences:

Keep calm. Your consequences can do the work for you, so you don't have to. No need to raise your voice; no need to get aggravated or angry. If you've set the boundary and laid out the consequence, but the line is still crossed, they get the consequence. Simple as.

Firm but fair – the consequence must fit the crime. 'Callum, you're the first one to speak after I just told you all to work in silence. Go to the headmaster's office now! You're being suspended!'

Not cool. The consequence needs to be proportionate to the action. You wouldn't send somebody home for the day for being a minute late, but nor should you just have a few words with someone if they pull the fire alarm to get out of an exercise.

Bad actions need meaningful consequences. There's no point telling somebody who's rude, disrespectful and entitled that their behaviour will result in five minutes off their lunch. It won't do anything. The repercussions to bad actions need to be meaningful. So if Ernest is deliberately trying to win the worst-behaved-person-of-all-time award but wants to play Joseph in the nativity – don't let him. If he already is playing Joseph, give it to David instead. It might sound harsh, but if people feel that their actions can't and won't have any impact on them, they'll do whatever they want. Which'll have a huge impact on the rest of your group.

Be consistent – always follow through. Being inconsistent will be the death of behaviour management in your room. If you've given Kevin his warning but you don't follow through with the consequence, you're essentially showing the group that your warnings are meaningless and that they can do whatever they like. This also means that you shouldn't lay out any consequences that you don't have the power to follow through with – so don't tell Kevin that he'll be in detention if you'll never see him again. He'll laugh at you.

Your ultimatum should be your last resort. The only way you should jump straight to stage four is if someone really has done something out of the ordinary that warrants it. It should be an ultimatum for a reason.

In front of the group or privately? The path of least disruption

'That's it, stop the rehearsal. William just talked during Whitney's death scene. Everybody in a circle. Now we're all going to have to talk about William's shocking behaviour.'

Your interventions should provide as little disruption to the room as possible. You'll want to reduce the level of disruption in the room, not to make it worse. You should look to get back to your workshop as quickly as you can. This means that when you're addressing bad behaviour, get to the point, and only say as much as you need to. Be as efficient as possible. This is not the time to become an actor and to go into a *Hamlet*-length monologue about people's behaviour.

You'll also usually have a choice about whether you address bad behaviour in front of the group, or privately. There are times for both:

In front of the group – This can be important because it allows you to make your boundaries clear to everyone in the room. If several people are late, for example, it makes sense to address it as a group so that everyone's on the same page (though if people had a more specific reason then you might want to speak to them privately). Doing it as a group can also reinforce your boundaries and make it clear what is and what isn't acceptable, and while it might single people out, it does make it clear to everyone that unwanted behaviour has repercussions and that you'll call it out when necessary.

Privately – Sometimes it's more effective to address behaviour privately. If somebody really is crossing a boundary or you want to make it more impactful, speaking to somebody one-on-one will often give your message more weight, because you're going out of your way to do it. The fact that you're having the one-on-one conversation is enough for a lot of people to take it more seriously. Speaking to people privately will also almost always be the option to go for if an issue is more sensitive, private or specific.

There may also be times when it's more appropriate for you to hold off addressing something until you set people off to work on group tasks. It can often be easier to deal with unwanted behaviour when people are in smaller groups than it is when they're in big ones, so it might be the case that you need to set people off on a task and then speak to the individual while everyone's working in their groups. Speaking to people privately allows the rest of your group to carry on working, without being disrupted.

If you are speaking to people individually, make sure that it's not private to the point of you being alone in a room with them. See the relevant section on 'Don't be alone with participants' on page 267 for more information.

I had an instance once where I set a group off in small groups to brainstorm ideas for a scene. In one group of three, two boys and a girl, the two boys laughed and joked as they brainstormed:

'It can be about a girl who lost her virginity.'

'It can be about a grandmother who lost her virginity.'

'It can be about a cat who lost her virginity.'

Facepalm

You get the idea.

They thought it was hilarious. I didn't. And neither did the girl in their group, who ended up leaving the room in tears.

The rest of the room were still working in groups so it would've been an active decision to address the behaviour publicly. But it was the perfect example of a situation that needed to be handled directly with the individuals.

Separating people/sending people out of the room

Sometimes people just won't work well together and will need to be separated, or an individual will become so disruptive that you'll need to send them out of the room entirely. Both options are reasonable consequences if people's behaviour isn't improving. Here are some pointers on both:

Split people up if necessary. If people aren't working well together or are constantly talking, split them up. This can apply to two individuals who need separating, or a whole group that are working on a task. Giving them a warning beforehand will give them an incentive to behave better, but if they still can't manage it, split them.

As with all behaviour management, you should look to do this with as little disruption as possible. This means that, as an example, if you know there's only one person who's messing about in a small group, it might be that you remove that individual from the group rather than splitting them all up, because to do that would be a bit extreme if you knew the others were working productively. Also, make sure you think ahead. If you have people working in smaller groups and the people you want to split are quite vocal, it might be an idea to separate them while they're working on a task, rather than in front of the whole group. It'll reduce the impact on the rest of the group.

Don't be afraid to send people out of the room. This should be a last resort, but you should have it as an option. If somebody's behaviour is significantly impacting the rest of the group and you've exhausted all other options, send them to the side. If their behaviour still isn't suitable after that, send them out of the room.

You should try everything in your power to keep as many people involved and engaged in your work as possible, but not at everybody else's expense. Newer practitioners sometimes wrongly assume they're being nice by refusing to send people out of the session. But if their behaviour is disrupting everybody else's experience, that's not exactly being nice to the rest of your group. You have to say no to someone. And not saying no to the disruptive person is to say no to the rest of the group who want to learn. You want to provide a great experience for as many people as possible.

At the end of the day, there needs to be an ultimatum for bad behaviour. You don't necessarily need to send them out of the session and banish them forever – it could be that you send them out, have a word with them, then bring them back in again if they agree to improve – but you need to have this as an option. Plus, once the rest of the group see that you mean business and that you're willing to make this decision, they'll often improve their behaviour.

Remain calm

You need to remain calm when you're faced with challenging behaviour. Shouting or getting emotionally invested will show that you're not in control, so no matter how challenging a situation is, you need to stay calm, poised and composed.

You'll want to have as little of an emotional reaction as possible when dealing with challenging behaviour, so it's important to remind yourself to breathe and to stay grounded. The more you can maintain your self-control, the easier it'll be to manage the situation and your workshop.

This is also important because you'll give your power away to challenging group members if they know they can easily knock you off-centre. If Jeremy knows that a bit of lip or a bit of backchat will get you triggered, he'll have the time of his life by giving you lip all day, just to get a reaction. Don't give Jeremy the pleasure.

Your attitude

The style in which you manage people's behaviour will have a huge impact on your room. Being respectful and understanding will get you a much better response than being a dictator, no matter how bad someone's behaviour is.

Take these three responses to Stella being late (again), where there's a company policy that members of the group have to go to the office whenever they're late:

1. (Angrily) *'Stella, this is the third time. Why are you late again? Go to the office to explain yourself right now!'*
2. **Ignores it**
3. *'Morning, Stella. Good to see you, but you're going to have to go to the office unfortunately. Those are the rules.'*

This isn't even so much about what you say, it's about your attitude. Treating people with respect is always more effective than if you don't, and it'll make your group engage with you far better. We don't like to disappoint the people we respect, so by treating your group with dignity, even when their behaviour may be off, you'll give them a reason to want to behave, rather than to find reasons not to.

“ I learnt some really magical transferable skills whilst assisting in special educational needs and disability (SEND) settings. Some children were on the autistic spectrum, some verbal, some non-verbal, all with varying physical needs. Some children expressed themselves physically and would pinch or scratch, while others might hit when they were feeling overstimulated or overwhelmed.

I quickly learnt that our reactions to a behaviour can be an addictive stimulus. If I had a big reaction to unwanted behaviour, it would make the children want to do that behaviour more. It's kind of like the thrill of a jack-in-the-box: the anticipation of what's coming, the exhilaration when the box pops open, and the security of experiencing the 'expected' reaction. We want to see the jack-in-the-box again and again.

By remaining neutral in response to unwanted behaviour, being economical with my words, and clearly stating what was expected to happen next, I was removing all the unnecessary stimulus that required complex processing. This allowed them to focus quicker on the task at hand. If the child upped their game and tried harder, the reaction would be the same. Kids get bored quickly if something doesn't work. Acknowledging positive behaviour was just as important – 'Thank you for listening', 'I really respect the way you handled that situation and pulled yourself back.' We all want to be respected and acknowledged.

As a creative practitioner, I was able to transfer these key learning points from the SEND settings into my workshop settings, with transformative results.

Chetna Pandya

Joke comments

Joke comments can sometimes happen in schools and can feel like a lose-lose situation. Ignore them and you send the message that there are no repercussions for silly contributions. But to address them is to give that person the attention they crave. Telling them off will also probably only make things worse. So what do you do?

One technique that can sometimes work is to treat the comments as a genuine response that's worth exploring. Ignore the joke aspect, treat it as a valid contribution, and keep asking genuine questions until you get to a response that you can positively reinforce. Praising them for the positive outcome of the contribution will end the interaction on a positive note – one that they didn't expect.

By doing this, you give zero airtime to the joke itself, while reinforcing the part of the contribution that you want to see. It also signals to the group that throwing out jokes isn't without consequence – they'll be treated the same as putting your hand up to answer a question – which will make people think twice. Even if you don't get to a good learning point by asking questions, you'll still be sending the right signals. They'll be getting the attention they want, yes, but in the opposite way to how they want it. This won't work with everyone that gives you a silly comment, but it's effective when it does.

Me: What other things might we want in a positive relationship?

Moses: Dank memes!

Everyone bursts out laughing

Me: Ah okay, dank memes. What do you mean by that?

*Moses: Well, dank memes are like when you go on the internet and download a meme that's bare jokes and you send it to your friends and they send it to their friends and it's just so funny, fam! *More laughter**

Me: Yes, I know what memes are. But what do you mean by that? Why are memes good in a healthy relationship?

*Moses: Oh, um... *a moment of silence* Because they make you laugh.*

Me: Great. And why is laughing important in a healthy friendship?

*Moses: *A pause* Well, because you want to be able to laugh with the people you're friends with.*

Me: Great! Brilliant, Moses! It's so important that we're able to laugh with our friends because it's a huge part of what connects us to people. And that can come through anything – through humour, jokes, dank memes, you name it. Great work, Moses.

Simple breathing exercise/simple stretch/counting game

These simple, straightforward exercises can sometimes be a huge help to handle difficult groups. There's no set-up required at all, which means you can do them whenever you need. They can allow you to massively slow down the pace of your workshop or your group and to get them refocused quickly, especially when their energy is too high.

- *Simple breathing exercise* – Sit the group down either where they are or in a circle and have them close their eyes, breathing in through the nose and out through the mouth.
- *Simple stretch* – Have the group do some simple stretches which you lead, with them copying.
- *Counting to ten* – Have them count to ten as a group with their eyes closed, starting again if two or more people say the same number at the same time.

Having the group close their eyes can be particularly helpful because it'll naturally calm them and stop them from being able to engage with or distract each other. You might get the odd giggler, but that'll be much easier to manage than a group of thirty going haywire. The key with all of these is for you also to slow down your delivery and pace, and to be calm yourself. It'll encourage your group to do the same.

You can also make these a feature of your workshop by establishing them at set points, such as every time you all come back after lunch. This can be particularly helpful if you know your group will be tough. For example, doing a simple breathing exercise at the start of your workshop or before you set them off for a break can become a group ritual, which'd make it a feature of your workshop rather than an add-on, and would be something that they'd come to expect.

Call-and-response/signals

A call-and-response is an easy way to get people's attention. At its simplest, you can do a short, basic clapping rhythm which the rest of the group copies – repeating it until you've got the whole group's attention. You can keep changing the rhythm or keep it the same – both work, because they just need to copy what you're doing. A clapping call-and-response is probably the most widely used, but do whatever works for you. Just make sure that you set it up at the beginning of your workshop so that everyone's on the same page. This works best with younger participants.

Another option is a physical signal. You'll probably recognise this in schools where the teacher puts their hand up and everyone has to do the same in silence. These are usually pretty straightforward once you establish them, and it saves you having to shout over people.

Just be aware of your audience though. If a call-and-response or signal feel like they're too teacher-y and wouldn't suit your group, don't do it. You'd likely get some eyebrows raised if you put your fingers on your lips and waited for silence with a group of adults.

Don't let people become invisible

There's one final point to bear in mind when it comes to behaviour management. It's easy for your attention to be taken up by either the most challenging people, or those of the highest ability. Don't forget the ones in-between. It shouldn't be the case that the everyday person gets forgotten about because they're not at either extreme – especially because by forgetting them, you actually give people an incentive to engage in extreme behaviour to get attention.

3 Specific Workshops

An overview

All of the tips and techniques that I've covered so far will apply to pretty much any workshop you deliver. After you've mastered them, you'll have a solid foundation to walk into any room and deliver a good workshop.

However, some areas of work are quite unique and will need quite specific adjustments, some of which we'll cover in this chapter. This isn't the complete range of areas that you can work in, but it should cover most of the ones that you'll need to consider.

Running a Course

An overview

Running a course is the next step once you're experienced at leading individual workshops. The types of courses you can find yourself running can massively vary – from intensive acting courses that last for a few weeks, to weekly adult courses lasting a few hours in the evening, to being in a drama school for anything from a term up to a year. Each setting will have its own unique challenges and demands, but the foundation for running a course will be more or less the same across the board.

But delivering a course goes beyond the actual delivery of the workshops because you'll be spending more time with your group, so you'll have the added element of building a relationship with your participants, and they with each other. You might be able to get away with not investing in your group in a two-hour session, but you won't get away with that on a course. Similarly, you may get away with not being able to manage a tough group of teenagers for an hour, but if you have that group for an entire week or more, you'll be praying for a career change.

So while the fundamentals of running a course are largely the same as with individual workshops, there are some factors that you need to bear in mind when it comes to running one. If you're looking to plan a course, see the relevant chapter on 'How to plan a course' on page 25.

Have a positive relationship with your group

People will be more responsive to you if they trust and like you as a person, so make sure you put the effort in and go the extra mile where you can. How you do this is up to you, but a group who know that you care, have their back, and whose respect you earn will be far more responsive than if you're cold and indifferent.

This isn't to say that you should be a pushover or that you should give up your role as the workshop leader and become their friend, but you do need to have a positive connection with them. Your relationship with the group will have a massive impact on their experience, so make sure you invest in it.

> "In his book on improvisation, Keith Johnstone talks about 'Getting the Right Relationship'. I found his words really impactful when considering the tutor/student dynamic in my sessions. He wrote... 'I'll explain that if the students fail, they're to blame me.' As a tutor, I do the same, I tell my class it's my job to make them feel safe to explore. I take ownership for facilitating their space. If things are unclear, even a simple set of instructions, it's my job to reframe the exercise and guide them (if necessary) until they understand. I explain it's not the student misunderstanding – it's me not setting the task clearly, so I'll try again in another way.
>
> My honesty at not always getting it right the first time relaxes them and takes away their need to be perfect. I say there are no errors, only insights to be had. It's my responsibility to ensure my group feel free to make bold choices and ask questions when they're unsure, rather than hold back.
>
> I tell my class in my introduction that I care about their experience, how they feel and what they discover. It matters to me. A tutor said it to a class I was in once – and it really stayed with me.
>
> **Louise Fitzgerald** PGCE
> Freelance Acting Facilitator and Life Skills Coach

Learn their names...!

If you're working with the same group for any more than a few days, you need to learn their names. Doing this will show that you care and are invested in them as people. Saying you're 'bad with names' is no excuse. There are things you can do to help with learning them, but, ultimately, learning names is about putting in the effort. If you don't put in the effort, you can guarantee that nobody else will either.

Here are some tips to help. Some of these points were covered in 'Learn the names you think you'll need' on page 87, but some of the following are more specific to a course rather than a one-off session:

Set the example by making the effort. Actively trying to learn people's names and being open to making mistakes will go a long way, and it'll encourage everyone else to do the same. Plus, we can all relate to not knowing somebody's name but it feeling too late to ask them again. Take the lead and continue to ask people, even (and especially) if it feels like it's past the point of being able to ask. You'll give everyone else permission to do the same.

Say them as often as possible. Especially for names you find difficult. The less you say them, the harder they'll be to learn. A few subtle ways you can do this are to use people's names when you're inviting them to answer a question; when you're commenting on somebody's work; or when you want somebody's attention.

Set a deadline for when you want the group to have learnt everyone's names by. Placing a deadline will give everyone (yourself included) far more motivation than if you don't.

Play regular name games at the start. Learning names doesn't have to be algebra. Make it fun. There are tons of name games out there that'll allow you and your group to enjoy the process so much more. Doing these at the start of the day or directly after a break can be a brilliant way to get people's names more embedded within the group during the first few sessions of your course. It also allows people to present their name as they'd like it to be spoken (for its pronunciation, or if they shorten their name).

When you ask for somebody's name, repeat it back as soon as they've said it to you. This'll make sure you've got it right. Don't worry if you mispronounce it, have them correct you until it's right. It sometimes seems like a faff and a bit embarrassing to keep trying and to keep getting it wrong, but the alternative is to say that you've got it when you haven't, then to avoid saying that person's name because you're scared of getting it wrong or mispronouncing it. I always explain that to them too. People appreciate the effort.

Write down the groups that they work in. For example, if they're working in small groups to devise a scene, writing their names down will mean you have something to refer back to – both in the session and outside of it. It'll also help you to organise groups for the next session.

Write down any distinguishing features about the people in your group. For example, you could write 'Chloe, blue top' or 'David, red hair'. You can also do this for memorable things that people do, such as 'Mavis, jumped on top of Randall during Stuck-in-the-Mud', or 'Philippa, had a bacon roll for breakfast.' These would be descriptions for your use only, so write whatever works for you. Just remember to be respectful and to only write what you'd be happy for them to see, in case they happen to have a peek. There's nothing more tempting than a workshop leader's open notebook.

Test yourself after the session. Running through people's names to yourself in-between sessions can be a huge help. Test yourself. Combining this with having them written down means you can even do it when you're commuting in.

Don't avoid saying names that are hard to pronounce. We all do this from time to time. We come across a name that has far more syllables than we're used to or with sound combinations that we're not familiar with, and rather than actually giving it a go, we simply avoid it. Even when we see it in writing, we often skip over the name and use a mental placeholder. As soon as you spot yourself doing this, make the effort to conquer it. The longer it takes for you to put the effort in, the longer it'll take for you to learn them.

Get them to share their names whenever they can. After mixing up the groups or putting them in new partners, I'll usually say, 'Shake hands with the person next to you and swap names.' It gives people permission to exchange names, and removes any awkwardness they might have if they asked for someone's name themselves.

If two people have the same name, ask them how they want to differentiate. Ask this in front of the group so that everyone's clear. This'll be a massive help if you have three Joes or five Isabellas, and it'll get the whole group on the same page at the same time.

Don't shorten people's names unless they do. If Thomas introduces himself as Thomas, call him Thomas, not Tom.

Same goes for Deborah. Elizabeth. Joseph. Maximilian. Adedayo. Victoria. Mohammed. I know a few Rebeccas who'll hunt you down if you call them Becca. You can ask if they're okay with it being shortened, but don't assume it. And clarifying their name in front of the group saves them from correcting each person individually. Ultimately, the best approach is to go with whatever name the person says when you ask their name.

> "My feeling is you should learn names, whatever it takes, within the first ten to fifteen minutes of working with a group. As soon as you address people by their name they feel seen. I'd go as far as to say that learning people's names and saying them out loud, and saying them often, is one of the single most important (and potentially challenging) roles of a facilitator. It allows everyone else to learn everyone's names as well. I make a point of saying I'm going to learn their names, and why, during the first exercise. It's one of the main positive comments I get back from people when I teach. If the group is too large – then have name labels. But even then, learn their names.
>
> **Louise Fitzgerald PGCE**

Breaks

Breaks are not a luxury, they're essential. By law, human beings are required to have breaks within the working day. So if your workshop is more than a few hours long, unless your workshop is intergalactic or you're working in a country in dire need of a worker's revolution, you'll need some breaks.

The benefits of breaks far outweigh the time that you lose from them, so they're far from an inconvenience. Their benefits include:

- They allow friendship groups to be created and strengthened (especially if the group are new to each other).
- People can go to the toilet or fill up their water bottles, so they won't need to during the session.
- People can write notes on the work and the process.

So don't ever feel that you're giving a group less of an experience by giving them breaks, because the work will have less of an impact if it's a great workshop but their brains are fried. Here are some other factors to bear in mind:

Tell the group at the start of your first day when the breaks will be, as well as how long they'll last. This way people can pace their energy levels throughout the day. But be flexible. If you think a break should be slightly earlier because they look tired, or that it'd be better to break a bit earlier to run the next chunk of the workshop in one go – go for it. Aim for the scheduled time that you planned your breaks for, but don't be tied to it. Also, if you call for a break but then keep talking for another five minutes, you've taken five minutes of their time. Give it back. Add five minutes on to whatever time you said.

Give them something to bond over. Give the group something to do. Even leaving a ball in the space can work wonders. Or teach your group a ball game and the group will do the rest. The game Foursquare can be good for this (see page 55). Having an activity they can engage in is a much better way for people to connect than just leaving them to talk or to sit on their phones, especially for those who may not be great conversationalists. Musical instruments are also great. A piano or guitar in the space can bring out your John Legends, Ed Sheerans and Mariah Careys in no time.

Breaks are a great time for you to think and recalibrate. They can serve as pit-stops which allow you to re-evaluate your workshop plan, make any changes you need, check in with your assistant/co-facilitator, and remind yourself of your plan. Sometimes I call for a break when I've hit a creative brick wall, and I usually return with solutions that I'd struggle to come up with if I tried to push on through. But it's important to remember that *you* need a break from the work too. Workshop leading is intense work, so you need to take care of yourself.

Be aware of the energy you're sending the group into a break with. You want them going into a break on a high, not a low. In one of my workshops, I came across as super-strict when I did our ground rules and slightly terrified my group. Rather than sending them on a break as I'd originally planned, I played a couple of quick fun games first, so they went off into the break with joy rather than terror. Another example is that sometimes on the first day of a course, I'll put people into pairs and have them share a moment in their life when they felt proud. Having a break directly after allows them to start the break with a sense of connection and trust with that person, and gives them someone to talk to as soon as the break starts. Breaks don't always need that level of strategy, but you should be mindful of the mindset you're setting them off with.

I usually do an hour's lunch and two twenty-minute breaks for a full day's workshop – with one halfway through the morning and another halfway through the afternoon. Fifteen minutes is often the standard, but the problem with that is that by the time your group's got their stuff and left the room, they've only got ten minutes left. Twenty minutes gives them enough time to do what they need to do without being rushed.

Opening/closing rituals

Rituals create a sense of consistency and predictability in your workshops, so it's good to have some form of ritual throughout your course. Not as in a religious ritual – just something that you do as a group every day. This can be starting and finishing your sessions with a check-in/check-out (see page 114), doing a group debrief at the end of the day, or doing a game after every lunchbreak. Beginning and ending your days in the same way will help to bring your group together and create a sense of stability.

Give content to match their level/ability

Work that's too challenging will make people feel inadequate, but work that's too easy will make them feel bored or disengaged. Let's say that half your room are established actors while the other half are completely new to theatre. Giving them all a Hamlet monologue might be straightforward for the actors, but it'll be a challenge for those that aren't.

Giving people content to match their ability is the most effective way for them to learn and develop. It's rewarding to do because you'll see your group working to their potential, and they'll usually be more fulfilled by working on content that suits them than content that doesn't. It's easier to achieve this by putting people into ability groups or giving them individual tasks so you can make your material more specific, because the bigger your group and the wider the range of abilities within it, the less suited a task will be to the needs of each individual.

Here are two ways that you can give content that matches their ability:

- Choose their groups and give them specific scenes (you can also do this for individuals with monologues).
- Give the group a choice of two or more texts of different difficulties and let them choose one that's suitable.

This approach isn't always possible and will definitely take more time than choosing a single text for everyone to work on, but it'll develop them far more effectively because you'll be able to cater to their specific needs – and it's your duty to supply the material that allows your group to learn best. It's above and beyond what most practitioners would do, though it's standard practice in teaching – and your group will certainly appreciate it. This also means being able to accurately gauge people's abilities and know how to address their needs.

Also remember that you have the option of adjusting a text or task to better suit your group. For example, cutting a script down to make it more accessible, or having them approach a text in an alternative way – such as paraphrasing the text or improvising it. So feel free to get creative in how you adjust your content.

To be clear, there are definitely benefits to having everybody work on the same text or task, so I'm not suggesting that you don't ever do that. But the more you want to develop the people in your group, the more specific you'll need to be with their individual learning objectives and the content that you're giving them.

The only downside to giving people specific content is that it can create problems if you've planned for people who are then absent on the day. This isn't an issue if you know your whole group will definitely be attending, but it can quickly fall apart if you have several people off. One solution to this is interchangeable scenes.

When I'd run courses for the National Youth Theatre, I'd always give specific scenes for my groups to work on, based on their casting and development needs. It'd take whole evenings to plan, but it gave a real sense of achievement for the group because each person was working on something that was specific to what they needed. Plus, it made all the scene presentations fresh and interesting, because most of the scenes were different. At the very least, the fact that I'd gone to the effort to do it generated a great deal of respect, which made the courses more enjoyable.

Interchangeable scenes

One of the biggest challenges of running a course is doing script work with a group whose attendance varies from session to session. Let's say you've allocated specific scenes to your group, with each scene being unique and perfectly suiting each person... then Moses doesn't turn up. Or the week after, Sandra and Rebecca have dropped out of the course. All of a sudden you have groups that don't work because they're missing a person, or they were working on a scene with someone last week who isn't in this week. It can create pure drama. And not the kind of drama you want.

One way around this is to have scenes that are interchangeable in terms of their casting, which aren't specific about their age, race or gender. This gives you more options: if someone's away, it's less of a problem to recast them because you're still able to place them in a scene, and there can always be a plus-one to a group if there's a spare person. Likewise, scripts that don't have a lot of context or background information can allow groups to have different interpretations of the same text. The trade-off here is that you won't be able to be as specific with the material that you're giving, but interchangeable scenes will be the more reliable approach if you can't guarantee people's attendance.

This is a challenge that'll usually come with courses that are spread over a period of time, such as an adult acting course over two months. You're less likely to get it on an intensive course, where you'd probably have more freedom to be specific about who does what, because it's more likely that you can guarantee people's attendance. All in all, it might be that you strike the balance between having the scenes be interchangeable, while still matching their ability as best as you can, so you get the best of both.

Have multiple versions of the same scene (but not too many)

Every actor will have a different interpretation of a text, so giving multiple groups the same scene can be useful because it'll show the range of approaches that can be taken with a script, which everybody can learn from. It'll allow for interesting discussions about the different approaches. But it'll also mean less work for you, because rather than having to find four duologues for a group of eight, you could find two scenes instead, which will make your life easier.

However, it's important to stay away from unhealthy comparisons or there being a sense of 'good' interpretations and 'bad' interpretations, as it can make your group feel like there's a right or wrong way to do a scene. Of course, you can (and should) have a discussion about what choices are more effective or interesting, as that's all part of the reflection process of creating art.

Just be mindful that there's a limit to how many times you can use the same scene. If you have a group of sixteen, having eight of the same duologues will be tiring for everyone to watch back. It'll be too much. So ideally you'd only want to use the same scene twice with the same group, or three times at the most.

Build up a bank of scripts

Finding scripts and scenes for your group when you're in the middle of a course can be a painful experience. You'll have limited time, and will often end up trawling through texts for hours or doing call-outs on social media for suggestions. Save yourself the hassle by building a bank of scripts that you can call on when you need them. These can be from plays that you've seen, scripts you've worked on before, workshops you've attended or plays that you've been given. This goes for both Shakespeare and modern texts. Doing this means that when the course starts, you'll be able to draw on other texts in an instant, rather than being in panic mode to find content.

Do a proper handover if another tutor's covering you

It's important that you do a handover if somebody else is covering a session for you. You don't need to do it over a five-course meal; a phone call will do. You need to make sure that they can pick up from where you've left off. This is essential. The words 'I don't have time' should never come out of your mouth when it comes to this; it's part of your job. You're not Beyoncé.

The key things you need to cover in your handover are:

- What your overall plan for the course is and how the session fits into it.
- What you want them to cover in the session. You can either give them a workshop plan, or give them your objectives and let them plan themselves.
- The exercises/activities that you've done with the group before (so they're not repeating exercises).
- What the group are like in general. Are they loud, boisterous, etc.?
- Anything that you know the group do or don't respond well to.
- Any specific needs within the group, e.g., mobility, dyslexia.

These are also important to find out if you're covering another tutor. Doing a proper handover means the course will have the least disruption possible. It can also benefit the group by giving them an alternative perspective on the work, or a different approach to what you've been doing so far.

Adults will expect their money's worth, so everybody needs a shot

If a group are paying for a course, they'll usually want value for money. While they'll understand that not everyone can be performing all the time, they will expect to participate as much as they reasonably can – so try to minimise the amount of time that people are sitting around and maximise the time that they're actively involved.

This expectation also applies to performances. If one person has a lead role while others only have a couple of lines, expect there to be some anger within the group, because they'll all be paying an equal amount, while getting an unequal result. This can definitely be a challenge, but you need to make it work as best you can so that everyone comes away satisfied.

You can be more honest with an advanced adult class

Adults will often be paying for their course for a reason, so if you're running an advanced adult course, you'll probably have more room for honest feedback than you might think. If you're in doubt, ask them what they'd like. Criticism should always be constructive and delivered sensitively, but don't fall into the trap of thinking that you can't be honest because you want to be nice. You can do both.

Finished early? Finish early!*

(*for full-day, intensive courses lasting a minimum of a week)

Out-of-work-actor: I've been out of work for months. Please, God, give me a job!

In-work actor: I've been working all day. Please, God, give me some time off!

Many of us will have worked at jobs where all the work is finished and you're perfectly able to go home, but your boss has you stay until the very last second that you're paid for. I once had it with a director who had us sitting around doing nothing from 2pm til 5pm, when there was genuinely no need for us to stay.

I'm not saying that you should finish early for the sake of it, but sometimes when you're running an intensive course with full days, if the day's work is done and there's not much time left, finish early. You'll gain far more in goodwill than anything you could gain from an extra ten minutes of a session. You won't want to do this when your sessions are only a few hours long or with adult acting courses (they're paying customers so they'll want their money's worth), but don't feel that every single minute has to be used at all costs if you're running an intensive course or you're directing a show.

And certainly, don't ever finish late. People have lives outside the room and it's important that you respect people's time. If you're constantly finishing late then take a look at your plan and consider doing less, or adjust your plan partway through the session to make sure you're keeping to time. Scheduling a check-out or a closing ritual can help with this because you'd need to finish slightly earlier anyway to do them, and they can often be shortened or lengthened as you need. But do aim to give these parts of the workshop the time they need, because they're still important.

A course is a journey

'They don't know how to listen!'

'They're talking too much!'

'They have zero focus!'

If you're running a course, it can be easy to get frustrated that your group isn't meeting your expectations early on. You need to keep in mind that the start of a course is just that. The start. And it's easy to take for granted just how much you know compared to the group. So don't get frustrated that they're not where you'd like them to be when you first start. It's your job to take them from where they are to where they need to be.

Bring people together through what they have in common

> When my brothers try to draw a circle to exclude me, I shall draw a larger circle to include them.
>
> **Pauli Murray**

This is for if you're running an intensive course where people are spending a lot of time with each other, especially if it's a residential course where they're living with each other. On these types of courses, group cohesion and the relationships within your group are more important than ever because of the amount of time they'll be spending together. So it's vital that you support your group as best you can to come together as one group, and get rid of anything that doesn't support that.

Running a workshop is a great way to bring people together for a common purpose and to turn strangers into friends. This is something that's in your direct control as a workshop leader. It can be one of the best things about the arts. The flip-side to this, however, is that you can end up causing divisions in your group if you don't know what you're doing. And while no practitioner would actively look to do that, it's easy to create divisions without even realising it.

It's important to remember that human beings are tribal by nature. We all want to be part of a group. It's natural. And so we all have a range of different group identities that can pretty much be based on anything. Family, religion, location or postcode, political orientation, sports teams, music tastes, favourite video-game console – the list is endless. However, while some of these group affiliations can be relatively harmless, others can be extremely damaging the more that you amplify them.

For example, a group of strangers will enter the room as individuals:

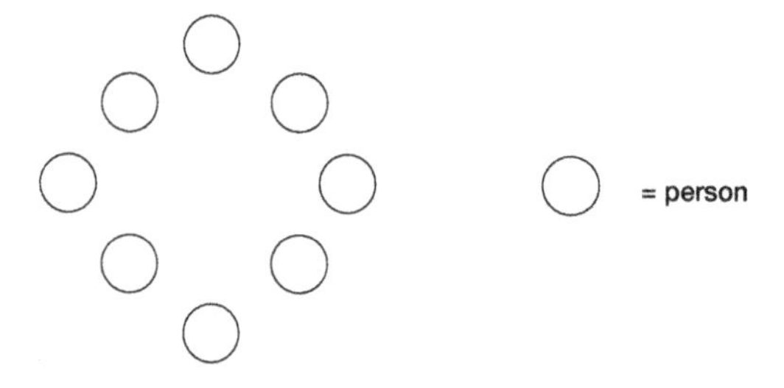

And this is what happens when people start to form groups based on different characteristics:

Favourite football team

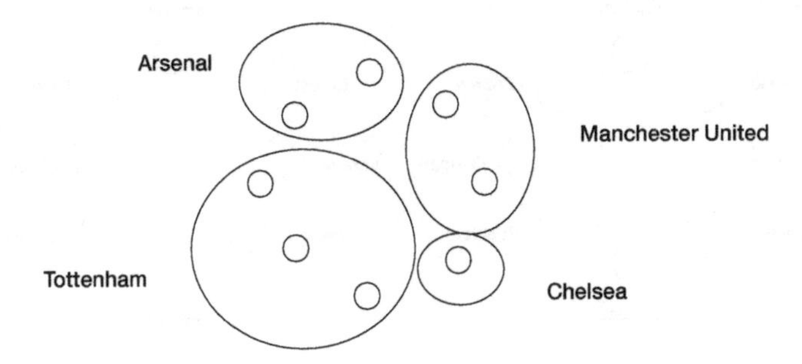

From London / From the north

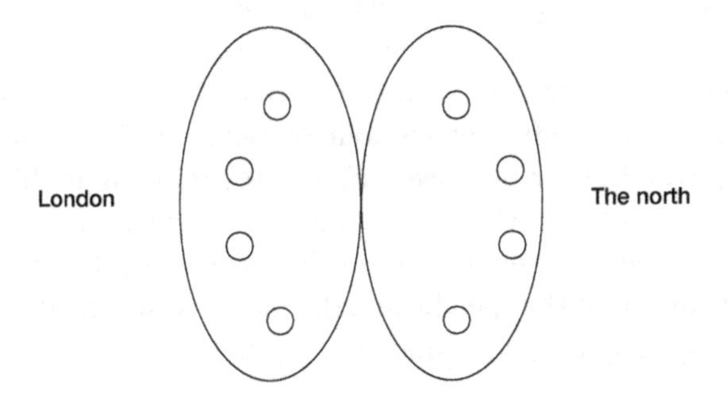

Seems pretty light-hearted right? But now replace those groups with political parties, gender or racial differences, or the different sides of a controversial topic, and the fault lines in your group will create a huge issue for group cohesion. And the more emotive the subject or the group identity, the more toxic those fault lines and your room will become.

This also applies to people on an individual level, because the more you fragment how people view themselves or highlight people's differences without bringing them together, the more isolated they'll feel. The more you encourage people to focus on what makes them different, the less of a connection they'll feel with the rest of the group and the more 'othered' they'll become.

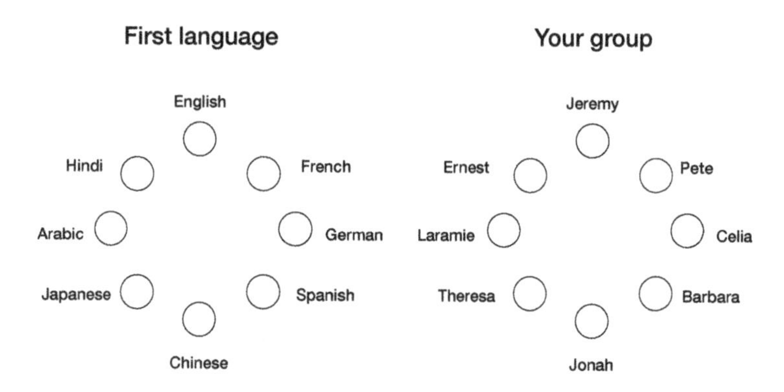

Your role as a facilitator should be to hold the group together and to draw everyone into as big a circle as possible, by encouraging them to find the commonalities with each other and by supporting what they have in common. While this might seem like a contradiction or a challenge to celebrating people's differences, it isn't. You can still do that, but focusing on what makes people different without bringing them together is a recipe for disaster, because you'll create a room of (in this case) eight individuals, when what you want to do is to create one group in which people can be themselves. And in fact, the more different that people are, the harder you'll need to work to bring people together and to bring out those commonalities.

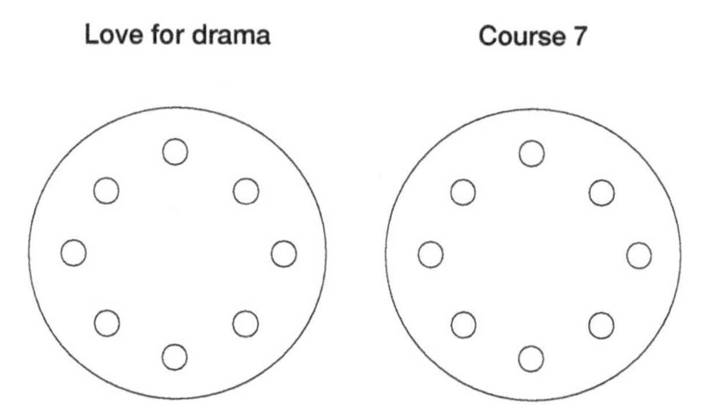

I'm not saying that you need to stop people forming groups or that everyone has to be friends with everyone. People are always going to gravitate towards some people more than others. But you do need to make sure that you as the workshop leader aren't actively encouraging factions within your group or amplifying differences that'll fragment them. So if you're running an intensive course where the group have a lot of contact time, constantly mix up the groups they work in; do activities that celebrate them as a group and encourage them to come together; and emphasise what they have in common rather than what makes them different. Friendships are formed from what people have in common. Focus on these things, and your group will be better for it.

Bonus Activities for Courses

While the previous chapter gave you the foundation for how to run most courses you might encounter, this section has some of the bonus activities that I learnt which allowed me to take my courses to the next level. A lot of them I learnt from my time delivering acting courses for the National Youth Theatre, but because those courses are quite unique, these activities won't necessarily be suitable for all of the courses you encounter. So these are all bonuses, rather than essentials. But nevertheless, they'll make a huge difference to your group's experience if you're able to use them, so they're useful to have in your toolkit.

Guardian Angels

This is a brilliant exercise that will run through your whole course, and it's one that I always do on my intensive National Youth Theatre acting courses. It's particularly brilliant for residential courses and with young people.

Guardian Angels works by giving each person the responsibility to look after one person in the room – without them knowing. It means that everyone will have someone who's actively looking out for them, but in secret. It allows the group to support each other, which is especially helpful if your group are living together, because it continues the support even when you're not working with them. As a workshop leader, there's a lot you can do to bring people together, but this is a great one to empower your group to do that with each other.

To set this up:

- On the first day, get write everyone to write their name on a small piece of paper.*
- Collect the names in.
- Give each person in the group one of the names, making sure they don't get their own name.

- The name they get is the person they're responsible for looking after throughout the course (but they need to keep it a secret).
- Go round the group and get everyone to say their own name to the group. Because it'll be the first day, this'll give them the chance to put a face to the name, which is vital for this.

  * If there are two or more people with the same name, establish what name each person will be called, to distinguish themselves from each other. Do this in front of the whole group so that everyone's on the same page, and make it clear that the name they write down on their sheet of paper needs to be the name they've just agreed on. This'll make sure that there aren't any mix-ups; otherwise Ricky may end with two Guardian Angels while Rikki will end up without one.

It's entirely up to the individual how they look after their person, but it doesn't have to be extravagant. It can be as simple as having a conversation with them when they're feeling down, bringing them in to sit with them at lunchtime, or writing anonymous notes of support throughout the course. Short, simple notes and messages can be particularly powerful because we sometimes struggle to give or receive verbal praise – but there's something great about receiving a note from someone, even if it's only small.

The great thing about Guardian Angels is that because it's anonymous, people will naturally extend their feelings of goodwill to everybody, and they'll be forced to assume the best in everyone because their Guardian Angel could be anybody. I don't think it'd work with every type of group or course out there, but it's a good one to use if you can. The first time I encountered this exercise was when I was assisting on some National Youth Theatre courses, where one of our team would constantly leave a Ferrero Rocher outside the doors of our rooms in halls. It was always a huge morale boost after a bad day, and constantly brought good vibes.

It's also helpful to remind everyone about it every few days, especially if they've had a hard day or if people make some great achievements or progress. Encouraging everyone to show some love or appreciation for the great work of their person is a great way to encourage good feeling within your group. We all have a natural desire to reciprocate, so the only way they can pay people back is by paying it forward with their own person.

Actively encourage them to do so. It'll work wonders for your room.

Lastly, make sure you give them an opportunity to reveal themselves to their person on the final day. I usually encourage this in the final hour of my courses. When I set up the Compliment Game (see page 179), I tell them that at the end of the exercise, they'll be free to reveal themselves to the person they've looked after. This means that once they're thanking each other for their compliments, they also find out their Guardian Angels, which makes them even more emotional. You don't have to do the same, but make sure that you're clear about how you'll bring closure to the exercise, so they can thank each other and show some appreciation.

At the end of one of my courses, one of the guys made a closing comment for the course, reflecting on the exercise, saying:

'The surreal thing with the Guardian Angels is that – I remember somebody did something nice for me, so I said to them:

"You're my Guardian Angel aren't you?"

"No."

"Yeah you are. You're my Guardian Angel!"

"No, I'm not!"

"You are! You're my Guardian Angel!"

"No! No I'm not, honestly. It's not fair for me to take the credit for that when I'm not."

"What, you mean you're just being nice?"

"Yeah."

In everyday life we sometimes react to people with suspicion when they do something nice for us. But the Guardian Angel system encourages people to assume the best in others. Which is a far more healthy and positive way for your room to be.

Ten-Minute Slot

> "I feel like I know more about everyone here than I do my entire class at school.
>
> **National Youth Theatre member, 2017**

The Ten-Minute Slot is an exercise that allows people to share who they are and things about their lives with the rest of the group. It's not often that we get to open up about ourselves or are truly listened to in life, so this can be a brilliant way for your group to get to know each other and to build a strong sense of trust.

It works by having three people at the end of each day talk about themselves and their lives for ten minutes, completely uninterrupted. And that's it. It's a really simple premise – the key is in how it's established.

On the first day of my National Youth Theatre courses, I give each person in the group a piece of A3 paper, put on some music, and get them to write down their life: who they are, their passions, interests, what their journey has been up until that point. I then collect everyone's pieces of paper, which I keep safe for the duration of the course. Then at the end of each day, we form an audience, I pick one of the pieces of paper at random (doing a total of three per day), and with a whoop and a cheer from the room, I hand it to that chosen person, who then takes a seat in front of us all. They then have ten minutes to talk about their life or anything they choose, uninterrupted, and we listen. It's as simple as that.

People are always a bit hesitant about this exercise at first, but after a few turns it quickly becomes one of the most cherished parts of my courses, with other courses often begging their directors to do the same. People always say that it's rare that they get the chance to talk about their life or tell people who they are, and that they end up knowing the people in the room far more than they know the other people in their lives.

'Almost half of Britons admit nobody knows the 'real' them – including friends, family and even their own partner.'[*]

---

* Lucy Brimble: www.independent.co.uk/life-style/britons-real-personality-poll-b1834413.html

Some tips to set this up are:

It's helpful if you lead by example and do it first, along with your assistant, if you have one. People will feel more comfortable from day two onwards, so it's a great way to lead by example if you do it on day one.

The people that go first will likely set the tone for the rest. The group will usually be influenced by the first few speakers. One of my assistants mentioned her age in her Ten-Minute Slot, then every person on the course did it too. One of the girls mentioned she had a boyfriend, then most of the girls mentioned whether they had boyfriends or not. There's no reason why this should happen, but it does. This means that going first gives you the opportunity to set the tone of the exercise, which also means you should be mindful about the tone that you set. So be careful not to say things that might influence your group in a negative way. Or you may want to handpick the first few people to have them set a positive tone for the rest of the group.

Be very clear that the people speaking should be shown the utmost respect, so be bullish on any mini-conversations or distractions that happen. It's an exposing task, so people need to be respected, and these sessions need to be kept sacred. Also, people are okay to laugh and react, but it's important not to have it turn into a Q&A session. One of the joys of the exercise is to have it led by the speaker, rather than the audience. If there are things that people want to ask more about, they can do it afterwards, which will give them something to talk about in their downtime.

Keep them to ten minutes. You can be flexible and allow a bit of leeway, but you should absolutely watch their time and give them a two-minute warning when they're nearing their end, and give them a polite signal if they really are going over. I've known some directors who've done this without honouring the time limit, and the Ten-Minute Slots quickly become thirty minutes. Each. You want a snippet of people's lives, not a documentary.

They don't need to use the whole ten minutes. The time is theirs. They can use as much or as little of it as possible. So there's no pressure. If they get to the end of five minutes and say that's all they have to say, then great. That's that.

If you want the group to do it, everybody should. It shouldn't be optional. If you make it optional there's a good chance that people will opt out, and one of the unifying aspects of this exercise is that everyone takes part. It's balanced because everybody listens, and, in turn, everybody gives (a part of themselves). Remember that they already have full rein to get up and talk about whatever they feel. And failing that, they can just read what they've written on their sheet of paper.

They can use their sheet of paper to refer to if they want. The reason you get them to write down their life on the first day is so they can use it to support them. It'd be tough to get up and just talk about your life otherwise, so if it's their turn and they don't know what to say, encourage them just to tell the group what they've written down.

Whatever they say in the room, stays in the room. This is so important because it'd be a huge breach of trust to have people share their lives, then to have it broadcast to people outside of the room. It'd be completely unacceptable. So make sure you tell your group that whatever they say in the room needs to stay in the room. The only exception to this is if there's a disclosure, which you need to be clear on from the moment you set the exercise up. A disclosure is when somebody says something that suggests that abuse is taking place, which you'd have a duty to report to the designated safeguarding lead. (See the section on disclosures on page 264.) But hopefully that shouldn't happen, so long as you set things up right.

It should be exclusively between you and your group, not with any outside directors. You will have built a relationship with your group and should have a level of trust with them, which a guest tutor won't have. So only have the exercise take place if you're leading it.

Be clear that this isn't therapy. I can't stress the importance of this point enough. Be very upfront that while they can talk about whatever they want and that not everything they say has to be rosy, it isn't therapy, and it's not the space to be airing problems or to be going into deep, dark places. You shouldn't really comment on what people say as a rule of thumb, but if people do veer too close to this or cross the line on it, you should definitely bring it up with your group, because you don't want it to snowball into therapy.

Remind them that they don't need to be interesting. A common comment you may hear is that their lives are boring or that they don't have anything interesting to say. Reassure them that this isn't the goal of the exercise. The aim is to share who they are with the group. That's it. If it's interesting it's interesting, if it isn't, it isn't. Regardless, you'll find that people almost always are. For one thing, if you've grown up as an only child and someone else has grown up with five siblings, automatically that's interesting because it's different, so even the little things shouldn't be underestimated. This is also important to stress alongside the point that it isn't therapy, because young people can sometimes feel that to have had a dark or challenging life is to be interesting, which is absolutely not the case. And you don't want the exercise to become a competition about who's lived the bleakest life, or to become the oppression Olympics.

Stress that it isn't a performance. It's got nothing to do with acting and isn't to be done as a performance or to be analysed in that way. Nevertheless, it's interesting that you can sit quite easily and listen to people's lives for ten minutes, but a poorly delivered monologue can lose you in seconds.

There's no right or wrong in what they say. The time is theirs. If they want to take you on a *Lord of the Rings* – Extended Edition journey of their life, so long as it's no longer than ten minutes, go for it. But if they want to use the time to talk about their pet dog Pete – then go for it. The time is theirs to use as they please and there's no judgement either way.

Choose people at random, but also give them the option of going sooner or later if they'd prefer. Somebody once asked me if they could go at the very end so that it was in line with their birthday. Another person wanted to do theirs at a particular time when they felt they were ready. It's good to keep it random, but allow the flexibility within that.

Be disciplined in seeing some every day. Do the maths. If you have ten days with your group and fifteen people, and you don't do any on the first and final day, you'll have eight days to do fifteen, which is about two per day. If you miss a day, that means you have to do three or four on another day to catch up – and the more days you miss, the more it'll have an impact. So make sure that you calculate how many you need to do ahead of time and stick to your plan as best you can, because you'll need to get through everyone.

Try to get them all done before your final day. Doing a Ten-Minute Slot on the final day isn't the end of the world, but ideally you want them done before your last day so that people feel like they've shared who they are during the course, rather than as you're ending it.

It can be good to have them reflect on the exercise part-way through. Once you've done a few days of it, ask your group what they think about the exercise. Not about the content of what people have said, just ask them what their reflections on it are. It's good for all of you to reflect on its impact, particularly compared to how they might have felt at the very start.

This exercise takes a lot of time, but if you're able to do it, it's well worth the investment. If you have thirty people, that's a total of five hours. It's a lot of time but it's absolutely worth it because the team-bonding and trust it can create will be invaluable. But for the same reasons, I'd only suggest using this if you're running a course where you have enough time to do it. I always do it on my National Youth Theatre courses because they're usually full time for two or three weeks, with the young people often staying in halls with one another, so it supports them outside the room too. However, I wouldn't consider doing it on an adult course that's a few hours each week, because the priority there should be more on the content, given that's what they're paying for.

I came up with this while running an after-school club at an all-boys school, where the boys didn't have much of an outlet to express themselves or to be heard in life. One day a couple of them had asked for a few minutes to share a comedy skit at the end of the session, which I let them do. They all really enjoyed it, so I continued it as an idea for the rest of our time together, but as an open Ten-Minute Slot where they could do what they wanted, which they had to request in advance.

I saw everything. One of them gave us his new stand-up routine, another did their audition monologue for the school play, while another sat and told us about his grandma who was in hospital, which he was really sad about. It became a real outlet for the boys who otherwise didn't get much of an opportunity to be listened to in their day-to-day lives. It quickly became one of their favourite and most requested parts of our after-school group.

I then adapted it to my two- and three-week National Youth Theatre courses, where I'd use the slots to have each person tell us about their life. I had everyone do it – it wasn't optional, but it was always entirely on their terms.

I varied it slightly for a week-long NYT course because of the time constraints, doing a Five-Minute Slot instead – fifteen minutes before lunch and fifteen minutes at the end of the day. Surprisingly, it was just as effective, because people adjust to whatever time frame they're given. I would've preferred the standard ten minutes, but it was a good compromise given the time we had. Plus, they didn't know any different.

It became an essential part of the day for my courses. We'd spend the day working hard, then take the last hour of the session as a campfire moment to get to know each other, before a debrief of the day to finish. It was easily one of the most cherished parts of the courses.

Sometimes it's the little things in life that make it worth it.

Skill share

This is an opportunity to give your group some ownership in teaching each other. It's a variation of the Ten-Minute Slot, but in this instance, you can give a person ten minutes (or a similar time frame) to teach the group something. It doesn't have to be extreme – backflips or fire eating – it can be as simple as some basic origami or rolling your tongue, or a teach-in on a subject they're passionate about. Ultimately, it's about handing over the reins to your group.

I'd personally want some advance notice of what people were doing for this one. I'd be pretty open to most things, but I wouldn't want them to teach something that may be in conflict with something else that I'm doing or which I'd later have to undo. I wouldn't allow anything political, for example, for all the reasons that I lay out in the 'Leave your politics at the door' section on page 236. But otherwise, it's a great way to have the group use and show off their skills, and to empower them to share them with others.

Compliment Game

I always use the Compliment Game as the final exercise on my National Youth Theatre courses. The way it works is either to give each person an A3 sheet of paper or to ask them to bring in an empty notebook specifically for the task. I then get everyone to write their name in the centre of their paper (or on a sheet of paper to the side of their notebook), so that everyone can see whose is whose. The task is then to go around the room and to write compliments to each person on their piece of paper or notepad, which they can then take home with them.

I usually plan for this to be an hour, but I start by giving them thirty minutes (which is never long enough), and then extend it to forty-five or maybe fifty minutes. They'll need another ten minutes to read their compliments and to spend time with each other afterwards (they usually end up in tears as they don't want to go home or say goodbye to each other). I'll then do a check-out for the final time, before sending them on their way.

Some additional tips for this are:

Be mindful of how much time they have. If you have a group of thirty, half an hour for this exercise gives them one minute per compliment per person – even less when you factor in the time it takes to go from paper to paper. Make sure you tell them this, because you don't want them spending twenty-five minutes on Connor's piece of paper, only to realise that they've got five minutes left for the other twenty-nine. It's also important that you give them regular time checks, so let them know when they have fifteen minutes left, etc. When you do, you'll probably get a response of 'Noooooo, give us more time!', which you should – because they have good reason to want more. Giving them a time check will also likely make them speed up too. Feel free to extend the exercise as you need to, but be mindful that if it becomes a ten-hour exercise then it'll probably lose its appeal, so find the balance. And if they don't manage to get to all the people that they wanted, you can encourage them to compliment the person directly or to write to them once the exercise is over.

Put on some music while they do it. I usually put on a playlist which has some of the memorable or key songs that I played during the course. Also, if there are any songs or artists that people have mentioned casually that they like, I'll usually throw some of those songs in too.

Get them to be specific with their compliments. 'Luke, you're really cool, man', won't be anywhere near as impactful as a genuine and meaningful compliment, so encourage them to be specific.

They can either sign their names or be anonymous. Making the compliments anonymous will mean they'll feel warmer about the whole group, because they won't know who to direct their thanks to. On the other hand, having the compliment-giver write their name will strengthen the connection between the two people. It's a choice for you to make, just let them know which one you want them to do.

If you have an assistant, make sure they get one too. It's important to include them, because the group will probably want to show their appreciation for your assistant as well. And so they should.

You can also do this halfway through the course. If you do, it'll serve as a good pick-me-up and will likely boost your group's morale, but only do it if your course is long enough. Doing it at the halfway point might make your group request to do it more, but resist the temptation. I'd suggest doing it no more than twice in total, regardless of how much people like it. Doing it more than twice will make it less special. The upside of doing it halfway through is that if you do want to do it a second time, they'll probably store up some compliments ready for the next time and will come prepared for how they want to appreciate each other.

By a clear mile, this was the most emotional exercise of all of my courses. Every time I did it with my National Youth Theatre courses, the group would end up in floods of (good) tears, no matter how thick-skinned they were.

There was always something special about doing it as the final exercise of a course, watching the group cheerily fill out everybody's sheets with compliments, then watching the room descend into a stunned silence as they read their own... and then slowly melt into a blubbering mess of gratitude. The mixture of joy, appreciation and gratefulness just before their final goodbyes would always send them over the edge.

I also had two other brilliant moments. The first was towards the end of my first NYT course, where we'd all walked into the rehearsal room one morning to find that an anonymous person in the group had covered the wall in Post-it notes, with a compliment note dedicated to each person in the group (the one I received is in the 'Thank-yous from the Past' section on page 271, though I can't you tell which). And on a separate course, one of my participants had missed the day that we played the Compliment Game at the halfway point of the course, but we went ahead and filled an A3 sheet of paper with compliments for him anyway. He returned the favour by spending five minutes of his Ten-Minute Slot going through a written list of individual compliments that he'd written for every person in the group. He wanted to return the favour and to give back what he'd received.

The thing about this exercise is that you can't force it. The closer your group are, the bigger the pay-off, but you can't manufacture good vibes in your group. Success with this one has to be earned, otherwise they'll be forcing their appreciation for each other, which is worse than not doing it at all. But when you're able to do it and it works, it can be the most rewarding exercise ever.

Open talent show

One good way of finding the hidden talents in your room is to create an open space for the group to show them. They'll probably have skills that you won't get to see unless you actively give them the opportunity.

The way this works is simple. Set a date and a time, and tell them that there'll be an open session where people can show off any and all the skills that they have. Dancing, singing, acrobatics, magic tricks, artwork, you name it. Anything goes. It's helpful to get a rough idea in advance of how many people want to take part, so have them tell you if they're interested in doing something. That's as much as I usually know in advance – I find out what they're doing at the same time as everyone else. It keeps it exciting. Then on the day, you simply get the group to form an audience, read out somebody's name on your list, and with a whoop and a cheer from the audience, you let them get up and show you what they've got.

I've got so many brilliant memories of doing this. From knock-out singers, to phenomenal dancers, to one of the greatest magic shows that I've ever seen in my life. Not only can you celebrate their skills, it also allows you to draw on them later if you're doing devising work. Plus, it can often be a huge morale boost for your group because it allows them to support and celebrate each other and can bring a sense of joy to your room.

One other thing to say is that some people in your group may be on the fence about doing this, so it's a good idea to ask a few times if anyone else would like to show something and to encourage them to do so, as it'll be their only opportunity. Some people might not jump up until your third or fourth bit of encouragement – though it's ultimately a decision for them to make. If they don't want to do it then that's up to them. But for those that do, make sure you all celebrate them for diving in.

Group meal

Being a workshop leader means you'll often have an air of mystery to you, because you'll probably only engage with your group as a professional rather than as a person. Organising a group lunch or dinner can be a great way to bond with your group and to develop your relationship with them. They'll likely appreciate the time.

A group lunch or dinner doesn't have to be fancy. It can be as simple as everybody bringing in some food to share for a picnic in the park, or having a meal after one of your rehearsal days towards the end of your course. But especially if you're working on an intensive course, spending some time with your group out of hours is a nice thing to do if you can.

Take them to a show

It can sometimes be a good idea to take your group to see a theatre show midway through your course. A lot of what you teach will probably make sense in theory, but some of it won't click until they actually see some theatre in practice. It'll help to solidify their learning. It can also be useful to have a discussion with them about their thoughts on the show and how any of it relates to what they've learnt, which is why you'll probably want to go around the halfway point of your course.

If you are going, make sure it's something that's affordable and accessible for everyone, because you don't want anybody to be excluded because of its price or distance. But if this is a concern, come up with a solution to support the people that need it – because to cancel the idea entirely would be to exclude everyone. Also remember that some theatres will give a discount on ticket prices if you're doing group bookings, so you may be able to arrange some cheaper seats.

Schools

Working in schools, you'll probably see the full range of joy, surprises, challenges and drama that running workshops has to offer – from children bouncing off the walls with energy, to teenagers who think they're too cool to take part. Your experience in a school can massively vary depending on the type of school that you go to, its culture, its location, the size of your group, their age and even the teacher. But, as ever, you should go into these settings with an open mind if you want to get the best out of them.

As with any setting, it's important that you go into school workshops with as much information about the group as possible, so make sure that you look at the 'Get as much information as you can' section on page 9 before going into a school.

" I think the key to success in schools is to bring a different energy to the classroom, but to do it in a way that also harnesses the teacher's confidence and creativity. This'll allow everyone – both children and teachers – to encounter something new, together. A school environment today is largely built on instructional learning from one adult to a group, so the power dynamic is established in that way. A good workshop leader can enable both a class and their teacher to bond in a new way and to see each other in a different light, giving benefits within the classroom beyond the workshop itself.

The way the teacher interacts can define a successful workshop in a school. I usually make sure there's a planning meeting ahead of the session, or an email exchange at least, so they understand the dynamics they'll be operating within and feel completely comfortable. That way, you can work as supportive professionals together within the setting. The relationship with you and the teacher is key!

Sarah Golding
Former Associate Artistic Director, *Battersea Arts Centre*
Freelance Arts and Heritage Consultant

For All Ages

Teachers/staff

If you're in a school, always make contact with your teacher beforehand to discuss the workshop, so that you're both clear on expectations. It's your responsibility, not the teacher's. Some key questions to ask them are:

- Do you want them to step in to discipline if necessary?
- Whether or not you want them to take part in the workshop as a participant.
- Are the group okay to work with people that aren't their friends?
- Does the group have any particular call-and-response signals to get the students' attention?
- Will there be any students with special educational needs?

You need to take the lead on this because if you don't, the teacher will, and their idea of being helpful might not be the same as yours. It's your responsibility to be clear.

Personally, I ask teachers to sit back and relax unless I signal for their support. In my early days, teachers would regularly step in to police bad behaviour, but it's disempowering. It places the power with the teacher when the power should be with you to run the room. It's well-intentioned, but often unhelpful. Also, there should always be a member of staff with you in the room. It's standard practice, and not optional. See the section on 'Safeguarding: Don't be alone with participants' on page 267 for more.

Another possible issue is that teachers can sometimes police students who may need policing in their lessons, but don't actually need it in your session. I've seen it many a time where a teacher overreacts to something that is way out of proportion to what the student's actually done.

'Norman, how dare you make such a comment! Go to the headmaster this instant!'

Norman's contribution may actually have been pretty reasonable, but because Miss Dooley has him labelled as the naughty child in her head – based off a long history of truancy, untucked shirts, forgotten homework and backchat – she becomes trigger-happy and gets far too involved. The advantage for any workshop leader is that by simply being new, you give the group the opportunity to start with a clean slate. But this won't work if the teacher's still holding them to account for who they were previously.

Now this is not to say that teachers are bad or always have a negative impact in a room. Absolutely not. Teachers are a valuable support and can be an absolute godsend of a resource. But in order to have them support your work in the room, you need to actively engage with them about what you need.

Teacher-led assumptions

As with assumptions for any group, your preconceived ideas about a group or particular students can impact how you respond to them. And not always for the best. It's useful to have the teacher give you a heads up on students that you might need to keep an eye on, but be mindful of not automatically labelling a student as 'the bad kid' or 'the troublemaker' simply because the teacher says they are. They might be with *them*, but they may not be with you. But if you treat them how the teacher does, they might give you the same reaction. All things considered, listen to the insight that the teacher gives you about the group, but still try to go in with an open mind.

Setting up the classroom

The classroom can quickly and easily become your worst nightmare in a school. Most classrooms will have the traditional set-up of tables and chairs throughout, which means you'll need to push everything to the side before you can begin, which is no small task.

Request a more suitable room if it's possible. Some schools will have a drama or dance studio, a hall, or a library that can be booked. If it's possible to use one of these spaces, absolutely take up the opportunity. Even if they happened to be the same size as the classroom, the fact that you're not having to shift around the tables and chairs will save you a massive amount of time. Plus, the change of space will make the session feel different to their regular classroom lessons, simply by being in a different environment. Just make sure that the space won't be impacted by the rest of the school, such as by dinner ladies who need to set up the tables for lunch; or if the space is a passageway for other classes who might walk through if you're running a session over a double period.

In an ideal world, it's better to have the room set up before the students arrive. This isn't always possible, but if you can, definitely do it. It'll save you heaps of time over having to arrange the room with the students there.

Ask your teacher about the best approach. They may have done this before and already have a strategy. I've seen some teachers spin tables around like a basketball being spun by LeBron James, with the room transformed in minutes. But even if they're used to rearranging the room, you both need an agreed plan for how it will be done. Will it be before the students arrive? After? How long before the end of the session will they need to be put back? Make sure you're both clear on the plan.

Get all hands on deck (if you're allowed to). Sharing is caring, so the quickest way to get everything moved is to have the students help you. But check with your teacher first. It's only happened to me once, but there was one occasion where I was told that the students weren't allowed to help because of health and safety (though another teacher in the same school said no such thing for their class...). It threw a huge spanner in the works, as Miss Foley and I had to move everything ourselves while the thirty students just stood and chilled.

Plan it into your schedule. I guarantee you that moving all those tables and chairs will not be a two-minute job, so your hour session will not be an hour. Not only will you have to clear the space, you'll also have to put them back again, so factor this in to your plan from the outset, rather than being surprised that you have less time than you expected.

Chairs

You: Christina, come off the chair and sit on the floor.

Christina slides onto the floor

...

Christina: But I'm not sitting on the chair, sir...!

If there are empty chairs in the space, students will sit on them. If you don't want this to happen, plan ahead.

If you want people to be on their feet, you need to make getting a chair an ordeal. Stack 'em, turn 'em around, put 'em behind tables – whatever you need to do. You don't need to shuttle them to Mars, but the more difficult they are to get, the harder it'll be for them to sit. The odd person may manage to nab one, but stopping one person will be far easier than stopping a whole class.

Also, if you're going to need chairs, make sure you have enough in the room for the number of people you're expecting. Count them beforehand. You don't want to have to send Barry to fetch another five chairs for your hour-long workshop when the nearest spares are on the other side of the campus... and it's lunchtime.

Be aware of the class's reward, punishment and classroom-management systems

Every school will have a system for rewarding good behaviour, punishing bad behaviour, and managing behaviour such as getting the group's attention or bringing them to silence. It can be helpful to know what these are, because it'll mean you can use what's already in place, rather than establishing something from scratch. There's no point reinventing the wheel. Do whatever works for you. You don't have to use their systems, but being aware of them will allow you to make an informed decision.

Your resources need to be efficient

'Sir! Which bit are we looking at?'

'Miss! I don't have page three!'

'Ronald won't let me see the sheet so I don't know what we're doing!'

If you're giving a group a handout for an exercise, make sure that the only information it contains is the information for that task. Nothing more. So if you've got three tasks for them to do, you should have three separate handouts – one for each task. You might think that you're saving the planet by getting all of your information onto one page, but you'll be sacrificing your workshop to do it. Information that isn't relevant to the exercise will often get groups confused because they won't know where to look, regardless of how many times you tell them or how clear you are. You'll end up spending your time clarifying what they should look at, which is time that could be spent on other things.

You should also be as clear as possible with your teachers about how you want your resources if they're printing them for you. I always tell them what I need by email in advance, but I also write it in the document's filename, for example 'Romeo and Juliet, Double Sided, 8 Copies'. It can also be helpful to send your files as PDFs when you want a file's layout to stay the same – it can sometimes shift around in a Word document when a different computer opens it, but PDFs won't change. Make sure you have access to your files digitally as well, either through a USB stick or by email. That way if you need to access the files, you'll still be able to load them from the teacher's computer when you arrive. Though be mindful that some schools have a 'stick free' policy and won't allow USB sticks to be used, to avoid cyber intrusions.

In some cases, it may also be better for students to have one each of a document rather than to share one between their small groups. A small group sharing a document quickly falls apart if they don't want to work with each other, if their reading or listening skills aren't great, or if they're generally not used to working in a team or sharing in that way. So make sure your approach is one that allows them to get the best out of the workshop, rather than the best approach to save paper.

Lastly, it's essential that you have spare copies of your resources. I've seen groups lose handouts within sixty seconds of me handing them out, in drama rooms so empty I could only conclude that somebody ate them. It'd then take me ten minutes to print another because I didn't have spares. So don't do that. Be better.

Your phone needs to stay in your pocket

There may be times when you need your phone, such as when you're using it to play music, but unless you're in the staffroom or have a very clear reason to use it, your phone shouldn't see the light of day in a school. This includes in the school corridors. Child protection is a big deal in schools, and phones are seen as a risk because they allow people to take pictures or videos of young people, which is categorically not allowed (see the section on safeguarding on page 262). So when you're working in schools, your default position should be to keep it on silent and to leave it be.

Fewer, longer exercises can sometimes be better than several short ones

School groups can sometimes take a while to follow instructions and to settle. It's often the case that what you think will be a thirty-second task can end up taking five minutes. This can be a particular problem if you've planned a lot of short tasks to try to make your workshop more dynamic. Because of this, students will often get frustrated about the stop/start nature of your workshop. So bear in mind that sometimes it can be better to have fewer exercises that you do well, rather than lots of shorter ones. This'll mean you'll have fewer transitions between exercises, and therefore fewer moments of having to call your group to attention.

I once ran a session in a school for the Barbican where I wanted the group to make five freeze-frames based on the five time-periods of prehistoric Britain – the Palaeolithic, Mesolithic, Neolithic, Bronze and Iron Ages. I put them into groups and planned for them to do a quick freeze-frame on each era, giving them a few minutes to create one, watching them back, having a quick discussion, then setting them off on the next one. Each freeze-frame was supposed to take a few minutes, but I realised by the second that it was going to be quite the slog to get through. The stop/start nature of the tasks meant I constantly had to regain their attention, which was as draining for me as it was tiring for them.

I had no choice but to push through with the plan because that was the workshop's main focus, though I varied the length of the discussions and the ways that they presented the work back, to provide a bit of variety. This plan would've worked fine for a more disciplined group who would've been more focused and able to work quicker, but it taught me not to plan in this way for a similar group in the future. An alternative could've been to have each of the five groups focus on one age each, before discussing each one, rather than all five groups doing all five ages. But ultimately, like any workshop, the key is to be able to assess the needs of the group and to adapt to them.

Getting people into groups

Sarah doesn't want to work with Larry who also doesn't want to work with Greg... John is tired of walking now so doesn't want to cross the space to Peter... and Larimey only works with boys and there's no way he's working with Susan because girls are ewww.

Getting people into groups in a school can sometimes be a huge ordeal. The way some students react to being told they can't work with their friends... you'd think you banned them from the internet for life.

It can cause a huge amount of unnecessary drama and take up a lot of time if people don't want to work with each other, and it can easily send students into a sulk. There's no easy solution. Even now, I still don't always feel that I get it right.

It's a good idea to ask your teacher what the best approach is for the groups, as they might be able to suggest the best way forward. It'll be hard for you to group people by ability or personality because you probably won't know them well enough to do that, so ultimately there are three options that you have:

Have the teacher choose the groups. This takes the responsibility away from you completely. The upside to this option is that the teacher will know the class far better than you, so they may have a better idea of the social dynamics of the group, and who's more suitable to work with who. It also means that the students have less reason to complain to you because you won't be the one making the decision (although some still will). Just remember that if you do want your teacher to do this, give them notice in advance. Ideally before the lesson. And tell them what the task will be so they can bear it in mind.

Letting them choose their groups. If, say, people are working towards a performance for a school assembly, you're going to want people to spend their time actually working with their group, rather than protesting. In this situation it can sometimes be better to let them choose who they work with if it means they'll be more productive. However, if you're letting them choose, you need to make it conditional. Be very clear that you're allowing them to work in groups on the condition that they work productively, and if they don't, that you'll separate them. This shouldn't be a fake consequence. That's the deal, and if they break it, split that group up. The rest will likely fix up because of it.

The other halfway to this is to get them to get into pairs of their choice, then to put those pairs with other pairs who they usually wouldn't work with. This gives them at least one person in the group that they'd be happy to work with, while still mixing people up a bit.

Mixing them up
Mixes up the groups

'Sir! Nooooo!'

'Oh my days!'

''Low it, fam!'

This becomes less of an issue if they're working on a general task or an exercise where there's not much at stake. You might get a few wails and curses to the heavens from Karim and Antonio that they're not working with Jay and Ricardo, but it's not the end of the world. It's not that deep. This is normal and happens a lot in this environment, so you'll just need to take it on the chin. Stand firm in your decision and hold your ground, and explain why it's important that they work in mixed groups and not just with their friends all the time. They might not necessarily buy your justification, but the fact that there is one will make it harder to seem like a punishment. Make sure that you read the section on 'How to get people into groups effectively' on page 81 for strategies to get them into mixed groups.

There are different perspectives on whether or not you should ever allow people to choose their groups in a school at all. Although my default position is to mix the groups up throughout a workshop, I do think there are occasions when you should let them choose; it simply depends on the circumstance and what the aim is of your task. Regardless, it's important to bear in mind the pros and cons of each approach:

Letting them choose their groups	Mixing the groups up randomly
+	+
• They may naturally form groups that they're happy with. The social dynamics in a school are usually complex and wouldn't be easy for you to take into account.	• They get to work with different people. This can expose them to different ways of working and get them away from the familiarity of their friendship groups.

• You may get less resistance, given that they'll be choosing the groups.	• People may take on a different role in the group to what they'd usually do, such as stepping up to be a leader when they otherwise might not. • It's fairer. Nobody gets to choose so they're all in the same boat.
-	-
• They can be unproductive if they're too comfortable with each other. Just because they're happy working together, doesn't mean they'll be productive. • There may be conflict if the groups are bigger than what you asked for, e.g. you want groups of four but a friendship group of six don't want to separate. • Some people can feel left out if they don't naturally fit into a group. Spreading these people amongst the other groups can then make them the odd one out, but forming a new group between them all can make them feel like the 'reject' group. This can be awkward to organise.	• There might not be a good social dynamic between the groups, with conflicting characters. • There may be some resistance to not being given a choice about their groups. • Given that it's random, it won't necessarily stop unproductive groups forming.

Ultimately, the thing to remember is that whatever your decision, you need to absolutely commit to it. For example, if you mix the groups up, but are then persuaded by one person's plea to work with their friends, it'll unleash a hornet's nest of other students wanting the same, which will make your life hell on earth. So commit to your decision.

Be as fair as possible

'Ayesha, you need to sit on the floor, not a chair.'

'But, sir! Luke, Caitlin and Caroline all are. Why can't I?'

'Oh, um...'

Students often have a heightened sense of fairness, so make sure you're as consistent as possible with them throughout your workshop. There can sometimes be one student who'll try to be the exception to your rules, but don't fall into the trap of allowing it unless there's a good reason for them to be exempt. For example, if your instruction is for everyone to sit on the floor and one person sits on a chair, letting it happen could invite the other twenty-nine to do the same. You've got better things to do than to be processing seating requests. But this goes for anything. Be as consistent and as fair as you can from start to finish.

Don't be afraid to apologise if you mess up

You'll gain a lot of goodwill and respect if you apologise when the moment calls for it. It's not always something that students will see from teachers, so owning up to your mistakes will make you more human and relatable. I'm not suggesting that you apologise for the sake of it or that you actively look for moments to say sorry; it's about being genuine when the moment requires it. So if you tell someone off but then realise it was unjustified, or you gave a fact that you later found out to be untrue, acknowledge it and apologise.

Enlist the support of the influential students

Some students will hold more power over the group than others. These may sometimes be the leaders, but they may also be those who are the loudest or simply the most enthusiastic. Sometimes these students use their powers for good, but at other times, they can be an absolute menace.

The social dynamics in a school will always be too strong for you to influence directly, but these students can help to do it for you. If they or your group are misbehaving, you can:

- Take them to the side and say you want to speak to them for a moment.
- Acknowledge something positive about them as a person, the work they've done or any positive behaviour they've shown.
- Tell them what could be achieved if they did the action or behaved in the way that you want them or others to do.
- Encourage them to be a leader.

For example:

'Dennis, I need to talk to you for a moment. So look, you've done some really great work today, and I was really impressed with some of the comments you made in the discussion. You seem really switched on, which is great. But your group aren't focusing and some of the jokes you're making are getting them even more distracted. If you really put your mind to it, you could make one of the best scenes in the group right now. So I need you to step up and to be a leader, and to keep your group together. Can you do that?'

Younger pupils will often jump at this kind of opportunity and step up their game in no time, though it may be less effective for older students, particularly in the upper years of secondary school. Regardless, the key here is to be absolutely genuine, because if you don't, it won't work. Even if they don't manage to get their group on board, at the very least, it should transform them from being a negative influence to a force for good.

Don't be called 'sir' or 'miss'

'Sir!' 'Miss!' 'Sir!?' 'Sir!!'

'Miss!!!' 'Sir!' 'Sir!?' 'Miss?' 'Miss!' 'Missss!'

'Sir?' 'Sir!' 'Miss!?' 'Siiiiiir!'

...

'What's your name again, sir!?'

You're not a teacher. Sure, you may be teaching them something, but have a group call you by your name. It'll clearly mark you as being a workshop leader and differentiate you from being seen as a teacher.

Primary-School Age

(For the younger years) They will have energy...! Primary-school children are usually full of energy, and will likely love you from the moment you walk in, just for walking in. It's important to give primary-school groups tasks where you can set them off to work in groups, because they'll probably only be able to sit and listen for so long, given the energy that they often have.

Expect a degree of carnage. Setting them off on a task will likely see the group unleashed. The noise will go through the roof, the children will become animated... this is all to be expected. It's a good idea to speak to the teacher beforehand to let them know that you'll be in control (it'll be a controlled chaos). Classes in schools can often be quite regimented, but drama workshops tend to be much freer, so it'll likely be more chaotic than what the teacher is used to. But what might seem like carnage will likely just be down to their age and their energy. So expect things to be a bit mad, but don't hesitate to reel them in if their behaviour does become a bit too much.

Put yourself at their eye level as you need to. When you're working with young children, kneeling down and speaking to them at their level can sometimes be more powerful than if you're standing up. It can make an interaction feel more personal by talking to them at their level; but it can also be more powerful if you're setting a boundary or putting your foot down. You can either kneel down, or grab a small chair to reduce your height. This can be especially effective if you're over seven feet, or a Big Friendly Giant.

Don't be afraid to call for backup from miss/sir, but only in exceptional circumstances. If things get really bad, don't be afraid to call for reinforcements. You won't want to rely on it, but it is an option if you need it. Having the teacher support you can often be a good ultimatum, because it might not mean much for a student to get in trouble with you if you're only there for a session or two, but it can have huge repercussions if they get in trouble with their teacher.

Secondary-School Age

Starter exercise. This can be a useful technique if you know the group won't all be coming into the room at the same time, such as if they're coming from different classes. This works by setting your group a task for the start of the session when they enter, as you're waiting for everyone to arrive - though it needs to be relatively easy to set up because it's the prelude to your workshop rather than the workshop itself. An example could be to have pictures around the space related to the theme of your workshop, where they guess the time period of the production they're going to see. Starter exercises give the group something active to do in the space, rather than simply waiting around.

Be aware that the group dynamic in the class will likely be quite strong. The social dynamics in secondary schools may be more challenging than with other groups. They may be less willing to work with people they don't like, be less willing to do tasks that embarrass them, or the social aspects of their school lives may impact how they are in the room. The fact that the group will still see each other once the workshop is done will impact on how they respond to the work.

They may be less willing to make themselves look silly. This age group will probably be much more self-conscious and cautious about how they come across. Be careful not to make them do anything that could mean that the rest of the group will take the piss out of them. If students do take the plunge and are brave enough to give things a go or to make themselves look silly, make sure that you really recognise and appreciate them for it.

They'll probably be less enthusiastic than primary-school young people. This is a generalisation, but this age group is more likely to be laid-back compared to primary-aged students. There's a greater chance that you'll need to put more effort in to get them engaged, whereas with primary-school children it'll likely be more about calming them down. Don't let this sway how you enter the room or work with the group. It's fairly normal.

Alternative provision settings may require a slightly different approach. These are settings such as pupil referral units, where the young people have been removed from mainstream education. Many of the pointers above will still apply because of their age and similar learning style, but you may need to make some slight tweaks. It'll be important to find out how they learn best – whether through discussions, visual aids or physical work. Also, be mindful that you may not be able to work with these groups for long periods of time in quite the same way as you could in a mainstream setting, so it might be an idea to think about what resources you can leave behind to allow for some extended learning.

> “When an artist runs an effective session in school, it can be transformational for the participants. The 'rehearsal-room approach', with its emphasis on practical learning, offers a truly creative space for children to explore and be more curious. The nature of being up on their feet and often collaborating with others in physical games or exercises, empowers children to take risks and unleash their imagination. A successful teaching artist will guide this learning skilfully so that the participants understand all of the key teaching points while feeling a sense of joy and engagement. There is a special kind of energy in a well-run session led by an experienced artist, which is new and exciting for children in school, and they often remember how they learnt and what they learnt for a long time after.
>
> **Rachel Dickinson**
> Education Consultant, *Barbican Centre*

Disabled People

Adapting for disability

Working with disabled people and people with learning disabilities can sometimes make practitioners apprehensive, for a number of reasons. Practitioners will often have a fear of getting things wrong, a fear of the unknown, or a fear of not knowing what to say or do. Mostly due to having less experience in this area.

The good news is that for the most part, the things that'll make a workshop successful in a regular setting are the same as what will bring you success here. There are some extra points to bear in mind, but once you can get over your own apprehensions, you'll likely have a great time.

On one end of the scale, you may have people with mild learning difficulties who won't require you to adjust much at all. On the other end you could have people that have, say, one-to-one or two-to-one support, meaning that they have one or two members of staff with them at all times. Somebody having dedicated staff members assigned to them will usually mean that they need more support, but this can be for a variety of reasons – from behavioural issues to medical needs. Regardless, any person that needs that level of support will almost certainly have staff members on hand to support them. Plus, in special educational needs schools, it's normal to have up to five teaching assistants for a class of nine or ten.

All of this is to say that you don't need to be an expert at working with disabled people to be able to work in this area. Any specific knowledge or expertise should be in the room with you through the support staff, allowing you to focus on your job.

> "It's important to understand that young people with additional needs will not only be in special educational settings, but they'll also be in most mainstream settings. So anywhere that you work educationally, it's important to consider how you will work with people with physical impairments, sensory impairments, learning disabilities and neurodiversity.
>
> **Claire Hodgson**
> Founder of *Diverse City* and co-founder of *Extraordinary Bodies*
> Artist and activist

Like any workshop, your experience of working with disabled people will massively vary depending on who you have in the room. The following tips are from what I learnt over seven years of working with people from those with the mildest special needs to the most profound:

Don't lose sight of the fact that disabled participants are people, with disabilities. Treat them like any other group (while making the relevant accommodations). It's easy to get so caught up in the disability aspect that you lose sight of this. Ultimately, so long as you're good with people, can be flexible, and can adapt your exercises to people's individual needs, you'll be great. So take the same approach of entering the room with an open mind as you would with any other group.

Find out in advance if there are any particular needs that you need to be aware of. This includes mobility adaptations, for example. It's far easier to adjust your workshop plan in advance than it is to do it in the moment. You don't need people's medical records, but a general overview of who's going to be in the room can be helpful. Many schools and organisations will give this to you in advance, so feel free to ask if they haven't suggested it already.

It's often counterproductive to research a person's specific medical condition. It's usually less helpful than you'd think. For instance, if someone in your group is autistic – what does that actually mean in practice? Some people with autism can't speak, some can say a few words, some will repeat the same words over and over again, while others won't stop speaking from the minute they wake up to the minute they go to bed. Knowing the ins and outs of autism doesn't tell you anything about the person because the person isn't defined by their disability, and disabilities affect people in different ways. Similarly with wheelchair users – do they have a traditional wheelchair that can be pushed? A highly mobile sports wheelchair? Or a motorised one which is heavy and can't be pushed at all? They all require different adaptations. People's medical conditions are good to know in advance, but beyond that, the rest should come from meeting the individual(s). It's not that you should be ignorant to people's conditions, far from it. It's just that researching a condition won't necessarily tell you who the individual is.

The key to this area is having exercises that you can break into stages and adapt. If you're working in a special needs school, the range of abilities (physical and psychological) will often be much greater than in a mainstream setting – but you won't be able to gauge that until you meet them. For example, you could reasonably assume that a mainstream Year 9 group can all read, whereas a special needs class may have some who can read a bit, some who are fluent readers and some who are unable to read at all. Having exercises that you can scale and adapt based on their skill level will give you the ability to adjust. See the sections on 'Breaking your exercise into stages' on page 60 and 'Adapting exercises for disabled people' on page 207 for more on this.

Don't water down the work. Ultimately, this is about bringing people in, rather than taking things out. For example, don't remove script work from your planning just because one person can't read, otherwise you're essentially planning as if nobody can. Instead, find a way to support that person so that they can engage in their own way. This can include asking a member of staff to feed them the lines, or getting them to improvise the script based on the story.

Don't be afraid to simply ask the person or someone who knows them, if you're ever in doubt. You could never be expected to know somebody's needs from the get-go when you don't know the person. So don't try to. Ask, if you're in doubt. Support staff in particular will be invaluable for this because they should know the group far better than you. They'll know the best ways to handle people and will have the best understanding of them, and they'll know if somebody's behaving out of character.

You may need to give people a bit more processing time. It might take a few seconds for your instructions to sink in for a mainstream group, but it may need a little bit more time for some with special educational needs. This also applies if you've asked somebody a question – be mindful that you may need to wait a bit longer than you usually would for a response. Learn to wait patiently in this silence, rather than feeling like you have to fill it.

Distinguishing between the condition and the behaviour is challenging, but important. It's easy to think that people's behaviour is a result of their condition, but it's important to be able to separate the two. You should absolutely make allowances for those with medical conditions, but bad behaviour should be dealt with just as you would for anybody else. As an example, there's no medical condition that means an autistic person has to snatch somebody else's food at lunchtime. So how would you respond if that happened? In the same way you would if they didn't have autism. The behaviour is completely unrelated. This is important because you don't want to reinforce behaviours that could lead to problems for those participants outside the workshop with people who don't know them. There are no easy guidelines to know the difference between the two, other than through insight from someone who knows them or by getting to know the person, but don't automatically assume that you can't challenge somebody's behaviour simply because they have a medical condition.

Makaton can be helpful, but isn't essential. Makaton is a form of communication that uses both speech and signs. A simple comparison would be that it's similar to sign language, although that's not entirely accurate. Sign language is a replacement for verbal communication, whereas Makaton is a communication aid and supports what's being said. For example, you wouldn't give the Makaton sign for 'hello' on its own. You'd say 'hello' at the same time as giving the sign.

All in all, Makaton can be helpful in this setting, but it's not essential. Don't feel that a non-verbal group won't understand you if you don't know Makaton. They most likely will. Though it's good to know some signs so you can use them to support your key points, or so that you can understand if somebody's doing the sign to you. Good signs to know are 'my name is', the first letter of your name, 'waiting', 'toilet', 'finished', 'drink', 'food' and any snack that you have on offer (e.g. 'biscuit' or 'cake').

Just because somebody's non-verbal, doesn't mean they don't understand what you're saying. The chances are they do. Don't make the mistake of talking about people when they're in the room as if they're not there. You wouldn't do it around anybody else. This also goes for things such as talking to somebody's carer or assistant without acknowledging the disabled person at all. They're right there! Some disabled people might not actively engage with you, but I can almost guarantee you that the level of understanding people have will be higher than you think, regardless of the disability. So make sure that you acknowledge people just as you would anyone else.

> The real eye-opener for me on this was reading a book by Martin Pistorius called *Ghost Boy*, an autobiographical book about how the author acquired an unknown degenerative disease that left him severely disabled, unresponsive and unable to communicate, having lived a fairly regular life before that. 'Most people speak at, around, over or about me so anyone who treats me like a cut above the average root vegetable is unforgettable.' He went on to write a book about his life and later delivered a TED Talk, called 'My Way Back to Words'.

Being aware of people's default energy and behaviour can be really helpful. This is true for everyone but is particularly helpful here. Everyone has a default way of being, a sort of factory setting. For example, if your friend who has infinite patience snaps for no reason, you know that something's wrong because that response is out of character for them. This kind of awareness can help in this sphere because people won't always have the ability to express how they're feeling through words, so you'll have to gauge how they are through their behaviour. It can also help you to distinguish between which behaviours are typical for that person, which are out of character, and what your response should be. The more you work with a person, the easier it is to figure this out. Failing that, you'll need insight from people who know them better.

For example, one student I worked with, Yung, would constantly smile and say 'You okay?', with a thumbs-up, which he'd do all day. But it wasn't being asked as a genuine question, it was something he did on loop more out of habit. Or Ali, who had to go to each class to say hello to every teacher first thing in the morning before he could go to his own class. Or Karl Harris – the life and soul of the school who was always talking and cracking jokes (and would only allow people to refer to him by his full name, Karl Harris). We could tell when something was wrong because he'd go silent and became completely unresponsive. Being aware of the behaviours that were normal for these students allowed us to adjust to their behaviour. In these cases: by discouraging Yung from asking the question and not feeling like we needed to give him a genuine answer every time; allowing Ali to do his morning routine rather than panicking that he's dashing around school when he should be in registration; or encouraging Karl Harris to talk about what's troubling him on a bad day so that we could address what was going on.

Find out how you should deal with challenging or unwanted behaviour. It's important to make sure that the way you respond to unwanted behaviour is consistent with the setting you're working in. This is especially important if you're in a school, because sometimes they'll try to be consistent in how they manage behaviour across a student's school and home life, so it's useful to speak with the staff to find out how you should manage any particular behaviours, or if you need to manage them at all. Some settings will prefer to have the staff handle any unwelcome behaviours, rather than you.

I sometimes frame my approach to challenging behaviours here in terms of 'yes/no/ignore'. For example, for some participants, preventing a negative behaviour can be a case of positively reinforcing what you want to see (yes). For others, you'll want to directly address the behaviour and say no (no). But for others still, you'll want to outright ignore it (ignore). This can sometimes be a challenge because using the wrong one might result in the behaviour becoming worse, but as I mentioned, the key here is to really understand the people that you're working with, and to ask a member of staff what their thoughts are on how best to react to unwanted behaviour.

Keep your language straightforward and simple. This should go for all your workshops anyway, but it's particularly important for this demographic. Leave your big fancy words in the dictionary. Keeping your language as simple as possible will make it far easier for your group to understand you. Simplicity and being understood is far more important than sounding intelligent.

You might be surprised by how language-efficient SEND staff are for those with profound learning disabilities, or very young children. Rather than saying 'Hannah, it's time to sit in your chair for circle-time', they might say 'Hannah, sitting, circle-time.' Fewer words means there's less for the brain to process!

Open questions can often be unhelpful and intimidating. Closed questions are often much more suitable in this environment because open questions can be too broad. This also goes for giving people an option to do something. Rather than asking 'What do you want to do?', make it into an either/or question, where people have a choice of two. This can also be done with 'yes or no?', such as 'Do you want a chocolate biscuit, yes or no?' Having too much choice can be paralysing for most of us, but it's even more so for people with special needs. Don't be afraid of using closed questions more than you otherwise would, and to build in open questions and more technical language as you get more familiar with the group.

" Expect the unexpected and underestimate at your peril.

I once led a workshop where one of the young people was blind and used a stick. As we were doing a balance-the-space exercise, she started to head towards the edge of the stage. I tapped her on the shoulder and said: 'It's Nadia, you're going the wrong way so if you just turn back around...' She interrupted me and said: 'I know, this exercise is boring, I'm trying to escape.'

But ultimately I feel that your creativity and facilitation skills only improve when you work with people who are disabled and neurodiverse. You can make new discoveries in old texts and really explore your creative practice, both in terms of staging and rehearsal techniques.

Nadia Nadif
Actor (*National Theatre*, *Shakespeare's Globe*, *BBC*)
Freelance facilitator, *National Youth Theatre*, *The Old Vic*

Adapting exercises for disabled people

There may be instances in which you need to adjust your exercises for people with disabilities. Sometimes this will be relatively straightforward, other times it'll require more creative thinking.

Some say that all exercises can be adapted for disabled people. I disagree. There are some elements that are so essential to an exercise that they're impossible to change, or else it creates an entirely different exercise.

Here are three examples:

Game	Disability	Adjustment
Stop/Go Clap/Jump	Wheelchair user	'Clap/Jump' becomes 'Clap/Touch' (your knees)
This takes virtually no effort or planning, and is a simple tweak.		

<table>
<tr><td>Name Game: Throwing tennis balls across the circle, saying the person's name as you throw it to them, to ultimately create a sequence/order.</td><td>Cerebral palsy, limited hand–eye coordination.</td><td>Remove the balls and have people set up the name sequence by walking to people in the circle.</td></tr>
<tr><td colspan="3">This is a bigger change as it completely removes the ball aspect. The game still works, though you could argue that it's a variation on the game rather than a tweak. Also with cerebral palsy, you probably wouldn't be able to do any games that require throwing or catching, or if you did (and still wanted to be inclusive), you'd have to radically change the game itself.</td></tr>
<tr><td>Quad</td><td>Wheelchair user</td><td>Don't do the game</td></tr>
<tr><td colspan="3">Quad has people jumping on the spot and turning around on a single count. You could tweak it by, say, having people pump their arms in the air instead of the jump, but the 180-degree turn still wouldn't be possible for a wheelchair user. Even if there were a way to adjust the game, it'd probably be such a change from the original that it'd be an entirely different game. You'd be better off doing something else that achieves the same outcome.</td></tr>
</table>

The first two exercises could stay the same with some minor tweaks, but you'd need to choose an alternative game for Quad. The question you'd then need to ask yourself is: 'What is the aim of the game/exercise?', and then to choose a game that achieves that same outcome. For example:

Quad	Shoal of Fish
Key aspects of the game: Movement Team game/Ensemble Focus Rhythm Remains in the same spot	**Key aspects of the game:** Movement Team game/Ensemble Focus Rhythm Moves around the space

Because Quad and Shoal of Fish both have the same qualities, you could substitute Quad and do Shoal of Fish instead. It's definitely not a like-for-like replacement because they're completely different to each other and you could easily do both within the same workshop, but because they achieve similar things, Shoal of Fish would be a reasonable alternative.

Not every exercise will have an easy alternative, but so long as it achieves the same or a similar outcome as your original exercise, you're good to go.

Quad
(For this example: a group of twelve.) • People stand in a grid formation in four rows with three people in each, each row standing a couple of feet behind the person in front of them. • The front row jumps seven times in unison on the spot and then turns to their right to land on the count of eight. • The second row then do the same, then the third, then the fourth. • The fourth row, who should now be facing in the opposite direction, will then jump five times, before turning to land on the sixth. This sequence repeats, with two fewer jumps on every round. • Once at the end, create some form of miniature celebration.
Upscaling the exercise • You can add gestures or other moves to replace the jumps in certain numbers. For example, jump number four can be a star-jump or a duck. • These can also be related to the theme of a play, e.g. a war zone, with the added gestures being related to the theme.
Variation • You can rehearse it a few times, with the final attempt as if they're at the Olympics going for the gold medal. You can also put music on, but be selective about the rhythm of the song, given that the exercise depends on the rhythm.

Number of people: 4+	Standing in the space
Movement Focus, team-building	Cooperative

Shoal of fish

(For this example: One group of four.)

- People stand in the following formation, all facing the same direction:

- The aim is for the group to copy the movements of the leader – the person at the front of the formation.
- When that person turns around, whoever is now at the front become the new leader, whose movements the group then copy.

Upscaling the exercise

- Put on music to change the dynamics of their movements. Change the music to see if different songs have a different impact.
- If there's more than one group in the space, encourage them to start joining with other groups: for example, to have a group of four become a group of eight fluidly, without talking.

Number of people: 3+	Moving around the space
Movement Focus, team-building	Cooperative

I once ran a workshop in a special educational needs school with a handful of other practitioners. The company was expanding its remit to work with more young people who had special needs, but it was an area that most practitioners in the company had no experience in (though I'd already had a lot of experience with special needs young people by this point).

Each person was responsible for leading a different section of the workshop, so we were all clear on when we needed to lead and when we needed to support or take part. Most people in the room were experienced facilitators or assistants, and the group we were working with were generally an engaged group.

Things started to fall apart though during a game of Zip Zap Boing. The facilitator had set the game up as you would any other workshop, but the group then began to mess about, adding new moves, not listening to the rules and generally not taking it seriously. There was a stunned silence from all the practitioners in the room, who didn't know how to react and were clearly apprehensive about putting their foot down with a group of special needs young people. What do you do or say in that situation?

It's simple. The same thing you'd do in any other situation. After seeing the paralysis from the other practitioners, I stepped in – stopping the game and telling the group that they needed to focus and play the game properly, and restated what the rules of the game were. We then played the game again and a good time was had by all.

What I did wasn't any different to how I would've intervened with any other group. The problem the practitioners had was that they felt unsure about how to respond to a group with disabilities. Make the necessary adjustments for the people that you have in the room, but remember that they're people just like anyone else, so don't overcomplicate things with your assumptions.

Online

Theatre workshops have always taken place in person, because that's the essence of theatre. But that all changed when the Covid-19 pandemic happened, with all corners of the industry scrambling to get their work online; and practically overnight, the words 'Zoom' and 'Teams' gained a whole new meaning.

You'll need an understanding of the technicalities and limitations of these platforms to deliver workshops in this area successfully, but they're fairly straightforward once you know how. So here are some pointers:

Have a solid internet connection. Laggy internet can mean choppy audio, stop-motion video, and sometimes total darkness for anybody trying to communicate with you. Even a three-second delay between you speaking and the listener receiving can make communication challenging, so make sure your connection is as strong as an ox. This may also mean avoiding internet cafés, closing down other internet applications on your computer, and switching off your VPN if you have one. Turning your camera off can help if your internet does happen to be slow, but ideally you'll want your camera on at all times.

Have shorter sessions, and schedule more breaks. Sitting in front of a screen on a video call for any length of time is enough to make anyone crazy, and 'Zoom fatigue' is very real. There's simply no way you can hold a two-hour session online without melting people's brains, so make sure that your sessions are an absolute maximum of an hour at a time, and that you allow people to have breaks to get away from the screen and move around bit. This applies to you as well, because you'll need the brain break too.

Keep the group actively engaged. Get them participating. Ask them questions, have them write in the chat box, give them activities, you name it. People will disengage if you're just talking at them and they're not actively interacting: the longer you have people sitting and listening to you, the more they may as well be watching YouTube. It's much easier for people to switch off in an online workshop so make sure that you're keeping them actively engaged.

Make sure you're well framed and have a presentable background. It's best to have your camera positioned at eye level with your head and shoulders well in frame. Stack your camera or laptop on top of some books if you need to give it height. Tilting your laptop upwards isn't the same because it'll give people a nostril shot, which... isn't what we want to see. You should also avoid sitting in front of a window or bright light, because the camera will find it hard to adjust between you and the light source and it'll struggle to focus on you.

Also, in terms of background, you don't need to have a plain white background as such, but you do still need to come across as presentable, so make sure that it isn't too distracting or cluttered. And take off any underwear that's hanging on the radiators. It's also a good idea not to have any doors in shot too, in case any children, pets, nannies or partners happen to walk through.

Look directly into the camera. It'll make people feel more engaged, and will feel more like you're giving them eye contact as if you were looking at them in real life. Just make sure you balance it out as you would do in the real world. You wouldn't make eye contact and not look away in real life, so apply the same thought process here.

Feel free to have notes. You can have as many Post-it notes, notepads or journals around your workspace as you need. What the camera can't see, your group won't see. So feel free to stick any reminders or useful aids anywhere you like, so long as they're out of shot. Even on your screen.

Welcome people as they enter. A simple 'hi' to each person will do. It instantly acknowledges them and will actively bring them into the session.

You can choose who speaks next, or have them choose. Let's say it's the start of the session and you're having everyone introduce themselves. If you're running a session in person, you can simply go round the circle, because it naturally gives people an order in which to speak. That doesn't work online because the layout of the group on-screen will be different for everyone. So you as the workshop leader can either directly call for each person to speak, or you can have each person nominate who'll speak next after they've finished. Just be mindful that having them nominate each other is more suited to small-/medium-sized groups, because with larger groups it can be harder to keep track of who's spoken and who hasn't.

Be aware of people's environment. If their grandma's sleeping on the sofa opposite them, it might not be the best time to ask them for a fully committed Greek Tragedy monologue. Likewise, if they're in a London studio flat and can touch either ends of the room with both hands, don't ask them to do any grand running or movement activities. You can ask them to be in a certain type of space in advance, but unless your group are minted and can buy themselves a new studio, they'll probably be limited with their options. If you're running a course, it can be helpful to ask about the type of space they'll be working in so you can cater your content with it in mind.

They might not be in an ideal environment. In the car, on the train, on the way to the gym – you'd be surprised at some of the locations from which people dial in. Don't assume that people's environment will be anything close to what you'd consider normal or reasonable for the work you're doing, and be prepared for them to be less engaged with the work because of it. It's hard for someone to fully participate in a vocal warm-up when they have one hand on a steering wheel. This also means that some people may not even be on camera or have a microphone set up. Don't let it faze you, but be aware that it can mean that some people may end up as observers more than active participants.

People can dial in from anywhere in the world. This is great. Just be mindful that any references you make and any advice you give needs to be relevant to the people in your group. Don't suggest that they can find good monologues in the National Theatre's bookshop in London if they live in Japan. Make sure you have an idea of where everyone's based.

Don't be afraid to ask for people to turn their cameras on or to mute themselves. These are reasonable requests for everyone to get the most out of the session, so own your role as a workshop leader and don't be afraid to ask for these. It's far better for people to have their cameras on than off, and it'll make it easier for you to deliver as you'll be engaging with humans rather than a black square. But it'll also keep them more engaged as it'll be harder for them to put on Netflix or do their washing. Likewise, requesting that people mute themselves will eliminate any background noise and keep away distractions – though there are some platforms that'll allow you to mute people yourself, which you should use if you need to.

Make sure that any visual material you use is as engaging as possible. If you're delivering a presentation, make sure that it's s***-hot, because people just won't take the information in if it isn't. Make sure you have at least some understanding of what makes a good presentation and what doesn't, and know that if you have a presentation that's full of text, they're either going to read it and not listen to you, or listen to you but not read it. The brain can only do so much. Also, make sure that your font size is big (no smaller than 16 pt), and that you only show the information that you want people to see. If you have ten bits of information on screen, the audience either won't know where to look, or they'll all be looking in different places, so make sure that you're clear with your content and only show what you need at any given moment. Lastly, if you want to use animations, keep them simple. Animations will never be as smooth for your audience as they will be for you.

Break-out rooms. These can be a great way for you to send people off to do group work. It's the equivalent of putting them in small groups in an in-person workshop. Make sure you put this feature to good use because just as with an in-person workshop, you need to allow people the space to explore the work on their own. As ever, you'll want to be one step ahead of the game with this one. If you're organising groups, have them organised in advance – set them up while the group are doing a task if you have to. Pausing the workshop to arrange them will drop the pace of your workshop. Also, make sure that the settings send people into break-out rooms automatically, so the group don't need to do anything themselves. You should also avoid creating separate meeting links that people have to click in and out of, because there's a high chance of things going wrong and people getting lost in cyberspace. Several platforms also allow you to send messages to the groups when they're in break-out rooms, which is useful for letting them know how much time they have left.

Shared documents and the whiteboard. Google Docs is an example of software you can use to have everyone working on the same document, which allows people to work more collaboratively. A lot of online platforms also offer a whiteboard feature, which allows the group to interact together. Make sure that you experiment with these tools beforehand so you're ready to use them when you need.

If you have an assistant, have them take charge of the technical aspects. This can include admitting new people as they enter the session, monitoring the chat, creating the break-out rooms, sharing documents, or muting the microphone with the barking dog in the background. This'll allow you to focus on running the session, rather than worrying about the technology.

“ Many theatre companies and practitioners are experimenting with new ways of facilitating drama online, such as with C&T's 'Prospero' digital platform. This is a rapidly changing landscape, so explore what other resources are available to support your workshop activities.

As workshop leaders, we all know the power of a provocative stimulus in drama. Challenge yourself to find new ways of integrating what the web has to offer to your drama processes. For example, video games might offer themselves as opportunities for drama, or 'breaking news' on news websites could be starting points for documentary drama.

Streamed performances can be valuable to watch, but workshops are about active participation: interactivity and connectivity are what young people in particular love about being online, so make the most of those possibilities. We created Prospero to do just that, to maximise those possibilities, where we're building a growing library of theatre workshops made for the digital space and engaging with young people on their terms.

Dr Paul Sutton
Artistic Director, *C&T* and *prospero.digital*

4 Yourself as a Workshop Leader

Empowering Yourself

An overview

While every facilitator will have a different style and approach, the best practitioners will have the same things in common. They're confident, genuine, self-assured; they're friendly and treat everyone with respect; they listen to and trust their group; and they're always in control of their room. Who you are as a person and the way you carry yourself will have a huge impact on how the group respond to you, and the better they respond to you, the better things will be.

How you embody these behaviours will be down to you as an individual, because the best person you can be is the most effective version of yourself, rather than trying to be somebody you're not. But it's important to remember that you're a workshop *leader*. This means that while it's important to be friendly with your group, it should never be at the expense of your responsibility to run the room effectively. Being too nice will turn you into a doormat, which isn't good for anyone.

Being in a position of leadership will mean there'll be times when you have to make decisions that people won't like, or when people won't get what they want. This is normal. Giving in to every whim and request that comes your way will make you a pushover, and no group will respect you if they can walk over you or if they feel you've got no backbone. So don't confuse being liked with being effective. Regardless, you should always treat your group with dignity and respect. This is the arts, not the military, and you're not a drill sergeant.

In this section we'll cover how you can manage yourself to be the best workshop leader and person that you can be. Because there's no use knowing how to empower your group if you're a nervous wreck quivering in the corner in fear.

"When I was asked to facilitate at a drama school for the first time, I asked the principal why he asked me. I'd never done it before. He said: 'Look, you're approachable, you're affable, you're very funny when you're on form, but ultimately, you enjoy it.'

The biggest thing for me is that when I walk into a room, I know that what I've prepared will be a lot of fun if they take it on board. And I make them comfortable. You have to make yourself amenable, you have to make yourself approachable, you have to share something of yourself just to make sure that you're all on a level. I hope to be somebody they can trust. Plus, I think the fact that I enjoy it rubs off on people too.

All that being said, you need to own your position as the facilitator. There's a hierarchy, but it isn't to bash people over the head. There's always an order to every room, and it helps because everyone knows where everybody's meant to be. Otherwise, if somebody's more forceful than others, half the room will say: 'I'm not gonna say anything because I'm not going to be listened to.' Or half the room will think: 'Right, I'm running this.' And then you've got anarchy.

Is there an anarchist in me? I suppose there is in what I do for a living. But as much as we sometimes want to be structureless, we all need structure, and we all need a leader who's able to hold their base and say no when it's needed. Because we don't have time to lose. And I want people to have the best experience possible.

Andrew Dennis

Actor (*Royal Shakespeare Company*, *National Theatre*, *Royal Court*)

Freelance Facilitator, *Mountview*, *ALRA*, *East 15 Acting School*

Owning your space and your role

Different careers have different requirements. Being a gardener will mean getting your hands dirty. Being a pilot will mean flying at high altitudes. Being an actor will mean standing in front of a crowd or a camera. Therefore, being a clean freak, being scared of flying or scared of public speaking will rule you out of success in those careers. Likewise, to be a workshop leader, you need to be comfortable being in charge of a room.

Make no mistake: there's a hierarchy when you're running a workshop, and you're at the top of it. I've seen people agonise over trying to eliminate this hierarchy from the room. But I've yet to see a workshop work without it.

This is a good thing, and it's something you should embrace, rather than reject. Think about the responsibilities you have when you're running a workshop, some of which include:

- Planning the session.
- The group achieving the workshop's aims.
- The physical safety of the group.
- Making sure that everyone participates and is as engaged as possible.
- Making sure that everyone has a good time.
- Allowing everyone to be heard as much as possible.
- Maintaining the pace of the workshop.

Without those responsibilities you'd be a participant. Yes, you'll want to empower your group. And yes, you'll want to get the best from them. But you can only achieve those if you take charge of your role and the session. Being in control of the room doesn't disempower your group, it empowers them.

So don't ever apologise for doing your job and leading the room. It doesn't make you a tyrant – there's a difference between being in control of the room and being controlling; they're not the same thing. You're in the space to lead the workshop, so own your position and don't be afraid to take the lead.

I once worked in a school for a term with a team of other workshop leaders. The Year 5 group we were working with struggled with authority, so the teachers asked us to explore the topic, with me leading on the session. Some of the team supported the students' view that all authority was bad and felt that we should support the students, but when you're given a brief... stick to it! Or don't take the job.

To start the session, I set up a simple Heads Up, Heads Down game, whereby if two people made eye contact they'd be out. I then had myself and the other facilitators sit down and let the group play it for five minutes without any intervention or guidance from us at all.

It was a shambles. Arguing, confusion, irritation – it didn't work. We then played the game again, this time with me facilitating. I asked them afterwards which version they preferred. They unanimously said the one that was facilitated.

My point was that it's easy to have an idealistic view that authority is universally bad and we should rise up and challenge it, and that even we as facilitators should be equal in the room to our participants. That might be your outlook on life, but in a workshop it just doesn't work. Someone needs to be in the driver's seat to guide the session and to take responsibility. So don't apologise for leading the room. You can't empower people if you've disempowered yourself. Own your space.

Carry yourself with purpose

Our bodies tell people far more about us than our voices do, so it's important that you carry yourself with confidence. Being shy or timid isn't part of the job description. If you're not a confident person, pretend, it'll come in time. Your workshop depends on it.

Nobody wants to be led by a leader who's unsure of themselves, so make sure your body language and non-verbal communication give the impression that you are. It sounds simple, but standing up straight, with the weight equally distributed between both your feet, while being relaxed and open, will go a long way to making your group trust you as a person. Otherwise, you'll leave a talented group uninspired, and be obliterated by groups that are challenging.

The power of 'no'

'No' is one of the most powerful tools in your toolbox. But it's a word that many of us are often afraid to use, both in workshops and in life. Unfortunately, we sometimes remove the word 'no' from our vocabulary without even realising it. This can come from a place of wanting to be nice, not wanting to hurt people's feelings, or being afraid of conflict or disappointing others. But you need to remember that your role first and foremost is as the facilitator. Your job is to lead the workshop and to be a conduit for their creativity; your job isn't to be liked by everyone at all costs and to be their best friend.

This isn't me suggesting that you should be mean or unlikeable – absolutely not. Without a doubt, you should be friendly, you should be likeable, you should be pleasant. But embodying those qualities as a person is different to you wanting to be liked by everyone, which can lead facilitators to say 'yes' to everything. Don't be a 'yes person'. And don't fall into the trap of thinking that 'no' is a bad word or that it comes from a negative place, because that isn't true. This is about maintaining boundaries for what's acceptable within the space, while allowing you to make the best decisions for everybody in the room. Plus, if you're not willing to say 'no', then your 'yes' has no meaning.

At the end of the day, somebody needs to be in a position to say 'no' in a workshop. And that person is you. This applies to everything. From saying 'no' to unacceptable behaviour or 'no' to a well-meaning but bad idea. People will wipe the floor with you if they know you're afraid to say 'no', and they'll get away with as much as you allow them to.

So get comfortable saying it, and develop a level of assertiveness that can command the room and won't allow you to be knocked around. This isn't about doing power poses or trying to be an alpha, it's about you having the self-belief to hold your space and to say 'no' when you need to. So don't feel like you always need to say yes. You don't.

Firm but fair

There's often a debate about whether being strict or soft is the best approach to running a room, particularly when it comes to young people. Most people will have a view on this and you'll probably lean one way or the other based on your temperament, upbringing and perspective on the world. But this isn't an either/or debate. Be both. In fact, the job requires it. It's perfectly possible to be strict, while having a joy and comfort about you that warms the room. One doesn't have to cancel out the other.

Being too tender will have you excusing behaviour that's unwelcome or unproductive, while being too stern will make people feel constrained and restricted. The key is to be flexible. To be tough but tender, and firm but fair. This'll allow you to be adaptable and effective. It's all about balance.

Be flexible with your status

You need to own your place in the room, but you also need to be flexible with your status. You'll want to start from a place of being relatively high in terms of how you carry yourself, but too high and you'll alienate people with arrogance; too low and they won't take you seriously. A seven is a good balance, because you don't want to be running a dictatorship.

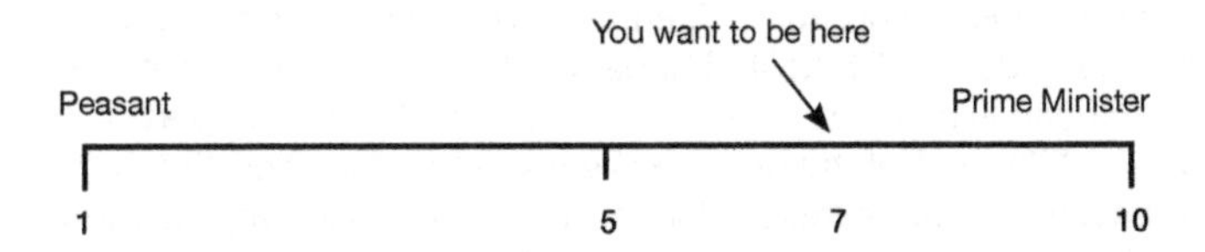

There may be times when you need to put your foot down with your group, but there may equally be times when you mess something up and you all laugh it off. That's all fine, and it's only human. Allow yourself to adjust depending on the situation. So plant yourself, own your status, and adjust as you need to.

There's a status exercise you can do with your group to try this out:

- Have the group form an audience, facing the doorway to enter the room, or something you can stand behind.
- Explain to the group that you'll be entering the room with different levels of status, from one to ten.
- Tell your group the number you'll be entering as, then enter the room.
- Once you've entered, say the line: 'Hi, my name is ___.'
- Exit the room, then repeat step three and four.

The key here is to adjust your body language, tone and stature in relation to each number. For example, a 'one' may have you mumble the line from the doorway, barely even entering. A seven might have you walk in confidently, make eye contact with the room, plant yourself in the centre of the space and confidently say the line. A ten may have you enter arrogantly, take your time, invade people's space and look down on people. You can then have a discussion with your group about their observations.

" I find the idea of status really interesting because when I work in drama schools, I always allocate a student to do the warm-up. I want them to own it, because it fills them with confidence for the rest of the class. And I'll always participate, to show them: 'Look, I'm respectful of the work I've asked you to do.'

For me it's important that I take part, because if I've given you a week and I say that I want you to do a warm-up, and you've gone home and you've thought about it, and on the Monday morning, I've said: 'Okay, your turn…', and you've taken that first intake of breath, going: 'Oh gosh, I hope this goes well,' and I sit in the corner and just watch... nah, come on... no chance. I'm part of the room…! I'm part of the group while we're together. Yes, I'm there to help the group, sure, but I've asked you to do it. Why on earth am I going to sit back and watch you? The least I can do out of courtesy is to be involved.

But…! I would never get involved in the work itself, because I didn't want that to be thought of as me showing off. So if I'm teaching improvisation, I'd never want the students to go: 'Oh my God, I'm doing it with Andrew.' So once the exercise starts, it's not about what I can do in the exercise, it's about them. So yes, as the facilitator you're in charge of the room, but there are times when it helps to adjust your position within it.

Andrew Dennis

Be flexible with your leadership style

There's an infinite number of ways to be a good leader and thousands of books that exist on leadership, so I'm not going to attempt to write one here. However, there are five leadership styles put forward by Daniel Goleman in his book *The New Leaders* that I think are useful when it comes to leading a workshop (although he has six in total).

The first thing to say is that there's no single 'best' style of leadership. It simply doesn't exist. Different situations require different types of leadership and different leaders, so an approach that's effective in one scenario might be terrible in another. You can use this to your advantage because the more flexible you can be with your leadership styles, the more effective you can be as a practitioner.

The leadership styles are:

Commanding

What it is – This is a top-down style of leadership, with you in charge. Although the word 'commanding' can easily paint a negative picture of this style, that's not necessarily true. It's more that this style is direct and decisive, and it has you in control. You might use it if you were putting on a performance and had to restage a scene at the very last minute, or if you were choosing the groups that people were going to work in for an exercise.

Advantages

- Decisions can be made quickly.
- It can be good for inexperienced groups, who may want or need a leader who's decisive.
- It's good when you're under pressure, there's a crisis, or time is short.

Disadvantages

- It can make the group feel that they don't have a voice.
- It might create a negative atmosphere if you use it over a long period of time.
- People may not respond well to this style if they're more experienced than you.

Affiliative

What it is – This style focuses on the people and relationships within your group. It looks to create harmony; to make people feel comfortable and part of a supportive, trusting environment. With this style you'll likely be kind, respectful, friendly and nice. You probably won't challenge people or do or say anything that might make them feel uncomfortable, even if it's at the expense of what the group need or their growth.

Advantages

- It's good at building trust and relationships, and it brings people closer together.
- It creates a strong bond between you and your group.
- It can help to make people feel comfortable.

Disadvantages

- It can be hard to make difficult decisions because your focus is more on making people happy.
- It can stop you from addressing problems or holding people to account for their behaviour.
- It can turn you into a 'yes person', preventing you from saying 'no' when you need to, through trying to avoid conflict.
- It can allow people to take advantage of you because you're trying to be too nice, friendly or popular.

Democratic

What it is – This is when you empower people to contribute their ideas, and decisions are made with everyone's input. An extreme version of this would be for your group to have the final say on decisions, rather than you.

Advantages

- It can boost morale, because it allows people to have a voice and to feel valued.
- It can bring in a range of new ideas and perspectives.

Disadvantages

- It can create conflict if there are opposing views or if people aren't willing to compromise.
- Decisions could be made by the loudest voices or the strongest personalities, rather than by everybody.

- Making decisions and the creative process can take longer.
- It isn't effective for people who don't work well in groups, or for groups who don't work well together.

Coaching

What it is – This style supports people to grow and develop through guidance and support. An example would be to have one-to-one feedback sessions with people, or to give thorough, individual feedback to support their development.

Advantages

- It can build a strong relationship between you and the participants.
- It can be a good way to motivate people.
- It's a good way to develop your group and their skills.

Disadvantages

- It's time-consuming. If you want meaningful results, you can't speed up the process.
- It requires you to really understand each individual.
- It can be challenging if you're working with a large team, or if you have a lot of other demands or are under pressure.
- It only works if people are willing to be coached.

Pacesetting

What it is – This style focuses on your group's performance, setting goals or targets for the group. For example, this could be through setting a task with a time limit and sending your group off to do it.

Advantages

- It can encourage a high level of performance.
- It can push people to achieve more than they expected.
- It keeps people focused.
- It works well over short periods of time and in high-pressure situations.

Disadvantages

- It can be stressful for the group, and can become tiring and cause burnout.
- It can be difficult to maintain over a long period of time, for your group and for yourself.
- It can be stressful for anybody who's not used to working at a fast pace.

It doesn't matter which style you prefer, if you're only comfortable using one, you're going to be incredibly ineffective as a facilitator and you're not going to get the best out of your group. You need to be able to adapt. Some of these styles you may look at and warm to, while others you might not. But they all have their place.

You don't need to overanalyse your approach, but it can be helpful to reflect on your practice to see if you use a range of styles or if you're stuck in the same one.

Don't pretend to know something you don't

Frankie: Sir, what's the capital of England?

You: Las Vegas.

Co-facilitator: Um...

The difference between an experienced person and a newbie is that the experienced person will say when they don't know something, while the inexperienced one will blag. If you don't know something, say it. You're not expected to know everything. If you're asked something you don't know the answer to, say that you'll look into it and get back to them, otherwise you're only going to give out incorrect information.

This is especially important if you're working with a co-facilitator. If you say something that's definitively wrong, your co-facilitator then has the choice to either not say anything and to leave that person with an incorrect answer, or they can correct you and make you look silly. It's a lose-lose situation. Obviously it's fine to make a genuine mistake and to say something wrong from time to time, but if you know that you don't know, you should say. You know?

The flip-side to this is that it removes your option to blag, which means that you need to have a thorough understanding of whatever it is you're teaching. Make sure that you're clued up on your subject area, and if you're not, you probably shouldn't be teaching it.

Don't take yourself too seriously

You need to be able to laugh at yourself. And so do your group. If you're serious to the point that you're a drill sergeant and no one is allowed to put a foot wrong, it's going to make your group really tense. Being able to laugh at yourself and being easy-going will allow your group to relax and to be more willing to say what they feel.

> “ As a workshop leader, you need to create a space that's rigorous, but crucially, also fun and enjoyable. Showing your group that you're human and can laugh at yourself creates an atmosphere that will encourage them to feel free to enjoy, take risks and challenge themselves. This doesn't diminish your authority or ability to lead, but with the right balance, should enhance it.
>
> **Ashley Zhangazha**
> Actor (*National Theatre*, *Royal Court*, *Donmar Warehouse*, *West End*); Freelance Facilitator, *National Youth Theatre*

Your reaction shapes their response

> “ There is nothing either good or bad, but thinking makes it so.
>
> **William Shakespeare**

Your group will see the world through whichever lens you give them. If you frame a task to be difficult and challenging, it will be; if you're relaxed, your group will relax; if you panic, they'll panic. Be mindful of your response and how you frame things because it'll have a direct impact on how everything is received. So frame things in a way that empowers them to engage, rather than restricting them.

I found this out first-hand in a show with Battersea Arts Centre. As part of the show, the audience went on a quest around the building to piece together a story, with a mini-performance in each room by a commissioned artist or performer. One of the performances, by Bryony Kimmings, was set in the theatre's attic, with Bryony stuck to the ceiling after a (pretend) bomb had gone off. The lighting, sound and set design was exceptional to the point that anyone under the age of ten would genuinely believe it was real. But this created a slight dilemma with the school performances. Which I found out all too soon.

It was my first school group, and we knocked the door and heard the (pretend) bomb go off. Peering through, I told the group it was really scary and dangerous and that we had to be careful.

The group freaked the f**k out.

It was as if they were entering a horror movie. They refused to enter. Based on how the play worked, we had no choice but to go in, otherwise every other group's sequence would be knocked off-course. But there were children screaming and wailing all around me.

Having been an observer during my (horror) show, my director debriefed with me by saying that by framing the room as being scary, it would be. It was my job to do the opposite.

From then on, my response changed. 'It's okay. Yeah, it's a bit dark, but it's okay. It's alright, I'm here; and I've got my torch, we can do this.'

The difference between the two approaches was staggering. With the second strategy, every group without fail went in almost without a beat. I'd get two children at most who wouldn't be so keen on going in, but even they would enter with some mild reassurance, and they always came out having loved the experience. It was a lesson that completely transformed my practice. And my life.

Favourites

Let's be real, everybody has favourites. Bosses, teachers, everyone. Even your parents.

But as a workshop leader, you need to treat everyone equally to the extent that no one should be able to tell who your favourites are. Having favourites can make a group bitter, resentful and divisive in a way that's difficult to come back from, and it can quickly ruin your group dynamic. It can be especially toxic in drama schools.

Of course, this isn't to say that you should treat everyone exactly the same. You'll have a different relationship with each person in your group, and you'll naturally get on with some people more than others. And that's fine. It's only human. But you can't let it impact how you treat the rest of the people in your group, or the decisions that you make. They'll be able to tell when you're giving special treatment.

Ultimately, keep your favourites to yourself, and treat people as fairly as you can.

Buy a watch

Keeping track of time is essential for every workshop, and you'll be in a world of pain if you don't. Not every room has a clock, and checking the time on your phone looks less professional than having a watch. So buy yourself one. Though this isn't an excuse to buy that expensive Gucci timepiece. A simple one will do.

If you have an e-watch, setting it to 'always on' during a workshop can be a huge help too. Their touchscreens can sometimes demand one thousand taps before they wake up, so switching this setting on could save you the embarrassment of pausing your workshop while you hammer away at the screen to get the time.

Be cool under pressure

> "...be cool!
>
> **Samuel L. Jackson**

There'll be times when things go wrong. It'll happen. But there's nothing worse than having a leader who freaks out when the pressure's on, or a leader who catastrophises and makes situations far worse than they need to be. Don't be one of those people. It's probably not that deep.

Even if you are truly on a sinking ship and it seems like the end is nigh, as the workshop leader, you are the last person who can lose your head. It's your job to get things back on track. As soon as you lose it, everybody else will. So you need to stay calm under pressure at all costs.

Everyone has different ways of managing themselves under pressure so I'd encourage you to find what works best for you, as it can be quite individual to each person. But here are some general pointers that should help:

Breathe. We often stop breathing when we get stressed, so remind yourself to breathe. Not breathing will only make things more stressful. And if you don't breathe for long enough, you'll die.

Focus on the solutions, not the problem. The problem is what it is. There's no use dwelling on it, mulling over it, worrying about it, looking for who's to blame, wondering how you got there... Stop all that. Focus on the solution. What are you going to do about it? Time and energy spent focusing on the problem is time and energy that could be spent focusing on solving it.

Disconnect yourself from the situation emotionally. Think logically. There are times when it's good to be in touch with our emotions. This isn't one of them. The more connected you are to the emotions of the situation, the more you're going to freak out. Panic, fear, worry, stress – how will they help you to solve the problem you're faced with? They won't. You'll end up spending more energy on those negative emotions and holding yourself together than you will on the problem. So switch your emotional connection to the issue off. I know this is a logical way of looking at an emotional situation, but that's the point. This doesn't mean that you'll become unempathetic or that you won't care about people or the situation – not at all. It's about separating yourself from the emotion of the issue so that you can see a situation with a clear head and good judgement.

Reassure your group (and yourself) that you'll get through this. You've probably dealt with worse. Trust yourself. You're capable, and you'll get through it.

You don't need to react right away. Your initial response to a situation might not be a helpful one. Sometimes it's better to pause, breathe, and take a second before you react or respond. Remember that you're the one in control of the workshop. If you need to pause and have a few seconds to think, do it. Respond when you're ready.

Call for a break if you need to. Sometimes even five minutes can go a long way in helping to reset yourself. It's often the breaks when you'll get those moments of divine intervention – where the answer will just come.

Relax. This will likely come with time the more you get used to handling challenging situations. But the more you can stay relaxed and chill in times of stress, the better. Especially when things really go to pot. Being relaxed will also reassure your group that everything's okay, because if you panic, they'll panic. If it's a stressful time then they may still worry a bit, but far less than if you've clearly lost your mind.

> Notice that the stiffest tree is most easily cracked, while the bamboo or willow survives by bending with the wind.
>
> **Bruce Lee**

Know that things are often far worse in our minds than they are in reality. Our minds love imagining the worst possible outcome. The star of your show is late and isn't picking up their phone? Well obviously that means they were out last night and drank too much and boarded a plane to Thailand with some Scots they met in a club and now you're going to have to recast and maybe even read the lines yourself and oh my God it's press night! The reality? They overslept a bit and will be there in five minutes. Difficult events are rarely as bad as the mind predicts. Acknowledge the problem you're faced with, but focus on what you're actually going to do about it.

Recognise that a negative outcome isn't inevitable. Chances are, the negative outcome is only likely to happen if nobody does anything to prevent it. Sometimes in life we look at problems and completely undervalue or disregard people's power to act to solve the problem. People look at a boulder hurtling towards them and conclude that the end is nigh. That'll only be the case if you don't step out of the way. The negative outcome isn't inevitable. The world adjusts. And so will you.

Take things one step at a time. Some problems can feel huge, but so long as you're solving something or taking steps in the right direction, you're making progress. If you're struggling with devising a scene, don't try to tackle the whole thing at once. Solve one small aspect, then another, then another. Before you know it you'll have cracked it.

Don't be afraid to figure things out with your group. You're not expected to have all the answers, and sometimes it's better if you work things out together. If you're struggling with a scene, be honest that you don't have all the answers. Ask for their input. A group of people working to try to solve the problem will be better than one person on their own.

Stay positive. Even if you don't feel it. You don't have to pretend that everything's okay when it isn't, but having a doom-and-gloom attitude will make your group feel the same, and it'll demoralise everybody at a time when they need uplifting the most. So be the best version of yourself and stay positive.

Be (the best version of) yourself

'Be yourself' can be a terrible piece of advice for all sorts of reasons.

The problem with it here is that the everyday you probably isn't the best person to carry the attention of thirty people for a few hours. Being yourself is great if you're in workshop-leading mode every day of your life, but if you tend to be shy, nervous or unconfident, 'just be yourself' is a recipe for disaster – and it gives you an excuse not to deal with the parts of you that might hold you back.

It's normal to walk into a room with some slight nerves. Why wouldn't you? You're walking into a room of complete strangers who are hoping for a great workshop. But it's only by being the confident, capable version of yourself that your group need you to be that you can achieve that. You can't let yourself as a person get in the way of achieving your objective. Plus, telling yourself that you're shy or quiet isn't helpful because it's a fixed perspective on who you are, and having a concrete sense of yourself like that is extremely limiting. We're far more complex than that, and you have the power to choose who you want to be in the room.

And this means leading by example. If you're a 'late person' but you've told your group to be on time – be on time. If you're going through a really stressful period and need to rein in your emotions and maintain a sense of calm for the room's sake, then do it. Be true to who you are and be authentic, but if there's an aspect of you that gets in the way of the group getting the absolute best from the session – leave it at the door.

Leave your baggage at the door

Didn't sleep well? Had your phone stolen? Car splashed you with a puddle? Life can suck sometimes. But in the room, you need to put it to one side.

The reality is that you're in charge of leading a group who'll all be relying on you. Don't be tempted to let the troubles of the outside world seep into the space because it'll have a direct impact on your group and the session, especially if it gets to the point that you snap at people or become a negative presence in the room. Under no circumstances should the group bear the brunt of your bad day. Or your divorce. Or anything, for that matter.

If you do have things going on, one of the best ways to manage them is to be as present as possible in the workshop. You won't be able to do anything about your problems while you're in the room anyway, so focusing your energy on the group will actually give you a break from it all. Use the session as an escape. Both yourself and your group will thank you for it.

Leave your life story at the door

At some point, most of us will work with a director or teacher who is 10% content, 90% life story. If only that ratio were the other way round.

While there are certainly times when it's appropriate to use a personal story or experience to highlight a point, keep it to a minimum. That's what autobiographies are for. Time spent on your life story is time that could be spent on the actual content of the workshop – which is, you know, what people are likely to be there for in the first place.

Leave your politics at the door

Unless your workshop is specifically related to a political theme, politics should not be brought into your workshop. Politics is one of the most divisive things you can bring into your room, so the more you bring it up, the more conflict you'll bring in. It's the quickest way to dismantle any trust and team-bonding that you've built.

Practitioners who do introduce politics are usually perfectly well-intentioned. They often feel passionate about a cause or they want to change the world. But unless the purpose of your workshop is specifically related to politics, that isn't your job. It goes back to the fundamental question: 'What's the objective of your workshop?' If politics isn't directly in line with that, you need to chuck it out.

One of your most important jobs as a workshop leader is to bring the group together, which is especially true on longer courses. Anything that can cause divisions in your group needs to be cast out, and this is no exception. From what I've seen, the more that people actively include politics in their room, the more fractured and divided those rooms become – which is the opposite of what you want.

One problem that isn't talked about enough with politics is its impact on people's mental health. The reality is that most things related to politics are completely out of our control. We don't have any direct control over who gets elected, we have a miniscule amount of influence on a country's carbon-emission targets, and we have very little say on the policy decisions that guide our society. So by introducing politics, you're actively encouraging people to dwell on the things they have no control over. This is a recipe for disaster. It's literally the opposite of what therapy does. So even if by some miracle your two-hour or two-week workshops were able to change society, you'd be doing so at the expense of your group's mental health.

But there are some other, more direct impacts it can have. Unless you have the least diverse group possible, in which everybody thinks the same and agrees on everything, there are always going to be people in your room that have different views or opinions; and the more contentious the topic, the greater the chance of there being conflict or disagreements. It can also:

- Lead to arguments between yourself and members of the group.
- Result in participants censoring themselves to avoid disagreeing, arguing, or being 'othered'.
- Alienate people that disagree with the consensus of the room.
- Create tensions in the group outside of your working hours.
- Create tension between their parents and yourself or your organisation (if you're working with young people).

It's good that people want to make a difference to society, but trying to channel that through your workshop isn't about your group, it's about you. It's about you wanting to make a difference. But that isn't your job. Your workshops should be about your group; so if you do want to go and make a difference to society, there are thousands of groups, causes and campaigns you can support who have the specific purpose of achieving those things.

Once you embrace the fact that changing the world or the political landscape is out of your control as a facilitator, it gives you much more power to embrace the things that you can. Theatre itself can be life-changing. Bringing people together and bringing joy to the room can too. Giving people the gift of in-person interaction and a break from social media and the continuous news cycle can be therapeutic in itself. So by embracing the limitations of what you can actually achieve with your workshops, you empower yourself even more, not the opposite.

If you ever did need to step into the territory of politics, Jonathan Haidt's book *The Righteous Mind: Why Good People are Divided by Politics and Religion* would be an essential read, as it looks at the moral roots of the political left and right. It does a fantastic job of giving a level-headed, in-depth understanding of both sides of the political divide, and puts into perspective some of the most controversial debates of our time. It'll allow you to engage in a genuinely well-meaning discussion that respects all sides of a debate, which is essential for navigating difficult topics, especially around politics. He did a TED Talk in 2012 called 'The moral roots of liberals and conservatives', though the book expands on it and adds a sixth moral foundation that I think is invaluable.

But, ultimately, politics is creeping ever more into every aspect of our lives, and most people would prefer to experience the joy and wonder of theatre, so give them that.

I first realised this when I ran my first two-week National Youth Theatre junior course. The first week had been fantastic, with a brilliant group of thirty-one young people aged fourteen to seventeen. As far as I could tell, there wasn't any conflict within the group, and everyone had grown incredibly close and supportive of each other, without any real problems, other than an abundance of energy which was hard to control at times.

In the second week, as was custom at the time, we did a director-swap, and I took another course for half a day while another director took mine. We had a chat beforehand to give an overview of our groups and to see what each group needed. I planned some Shakespeare work with the other group, while the other director planned some vocal and music work with mine, meaning that we both covered what the other was weak at. I also explained that my group were talkative, but otherwise shouldn't be too much of a problem. Plus, our assistants would stay with our groups to support.

Following the session, my assistant explained to me at lunchtime that their session had been absolute chaos. The director had started the session with an agree/disagree exercise, where the director reads out a statement and each person stands at different sides of the room depending on whether they agree or disagree with the statement. The questions came around to politics, with one of the boys (who was very well respected by the group) expressing an opinion that did not go down well.

A huge rift was created in the group, with two girls in particular being absolutely furious. One of them told me afterwards that they got even more enraged because they weren't invited to speak during the discussion – most likely because the director had realised that their anger would cause even more conflict. The director ended up moving on, which meant that the debate wasn't resolved, which impacted the rest of the session because the group were restless, wouldn't listen, and just wanted to carry on the debate.

While I get that the group had a responsibility to listen and compose themselves following the exercise, the reality is that it shouldn't have been done in the first place. What did the exercise have to do with vocal work or music? The political aspect had no connection to the work whatsoever and was only ever going to bring conflict. Plus, this was never agreed or mentioned to me in our planning discussion beforehand.

The group were still able to work constructively together, but there's no denying that it caused issues. Even if the group hadn't vocally aired their views in the way that they did, those feelings still would've impacted the group in the background and affected their cohesion, in a way that I wouldn't have been able to be address because I wouldn't even know it was there. I've never had conflicts of that scale when working with people who have never met each other before. And I think that keeping politics out of the space is one of the key reasons why.

You're not a therapist

Similar to politics, if your job is to run a theatre session, run a theatre session. Many workshop leaders have good intentions to help people with any mental health challenges they might have, but if you're not a qualified therapist, just don't. Being passionate or having researched mental health is not the same as being a qualified professional, and it's highly likely that you'll make things worse, not better. You wouldn't operate on someone if you weren't a qualified surgeon, and this is no different.

Just as it's important for you to admit when you don't know something, it's vital that we don't try to solve things that are out of our depth. This goes for anything trauma-related too. And even if you *were* to be qualified, there are two questions you should ask before you put on your therapist hat:

1. What can you actually do to address the person's problem(s) within the few hours or days of working with them?

2. How will bringing up traumatic experiences support your workshop's objectives?

To the first, my hunch would be that if someone really is having severe issues in their lives, there's almost nothing you can do in a session that'll make an impact of any significance. You can't cure somebody's depression or solve their problems. Your workshop can serve as an escape, but actual change in this area takes time and professional help. Time which you do not have, and an expertise that you likely don't have either. It's arrogant to assume that you can solve people's problems in that way.

To the second, if your session's objective was to be therapeutic or to deal with traumatic experiences, it wouldn't be a theatre workshop – it'd be therapy. And as I mentioned in the first point, there's very little you could actually do within a session or two. Plus, therapy requires personalised one-on-one attention. You can't provide a therapy session for ten to thirty people, and you run the risk of opening a Pandora's box which you're underqualified to deal with.

Once you embrace your own limitations in this area, it makes things better for everyone. It's reductive and patronising to assume that anyone going through a challenging time in their life needs a theatre practitioner to swoop in and save them. And don't be fooled into thinking that your good intentions are enough.

There are many things in life that can be therapeutic – green spaces, exercise, laughter... Theatre can give people a sense of joy that life doesn't often bring. That's (one of) the life-changing aspects of theatre. And that's what's in your power as a practitioner. So embrace it.

> Facilitators should be mindful of their relationship with their internal rescuer, because you may need to learn to keep it in check while you're running a workshop. People haven't come to be rescued from their problems... they've probably come to get away from them for a bit. Our need to be liked can activate a messiah complex, which isn't helpful in a drama workshop.
>
> What you can do to help is to do some research about organisations that offer mental health in the area you are working in or nationally. Being able to signpost relevant support is an essential resource. This would allow you to refer people to specialists who are able to provide help, and may give you relief that you'd been able to do something within your own limitations.
>
> **Delma Walsh**
> Psychotherapist

Co-facilitation

Co-facilitation is when you have more than one lead facilitator in the same session – usually two people, but sometimes more. It's a different power dynamic to if you're working with an assistant because you're more likely to be working as equals. Here are some tips to making the most out of co-facilitating:

Have a planning conversation beforehand. Being 'too busy' is not a good enough excuse to avoid this. You are not Beyoncé. If you've committed to leading a workshop, either meet up early on the day, or speak on the phone or do a video call. A phone or video call is probably more practical, because meeting before the workshop can fall apart if either of you are late (which hopefully you shouldn't be after reading the 'Arrive early' section on page 46). If you don't have the time for this, don't do the job. Give it to somebody that does.

Be clear on your roles and the sections you're leading on. Having a free-for-all as you both find your way through and take things as they come doesn't work. It's often unbalanced, with one person dominating and the other in the background, with both of you being unclear on where the responsibility lies. Only one person can drive a car at a time – facilitating is no different.

Have one person lead per section. The other person can still contribute and jump in to support when necessary, but it should be one person leading per section. It makes your roles infinitely clearer.

Be active in the space, even when you're not leading. Model how you want your participants to be. So no chillin' on the sidelines on your phone. You don't necessarily have to turn into a participant (you can still be at the side of the space), but there's a difference between being on the sides and still engaged, and being on the sides but switching off.

Your co-facilitator can be a good source of ideas. They'll also likely have a different approach to you and a different perspective, which is great to complement yours. Make sure that you embrace this and allow them to fully contribute to the process, as you can learn a lot.

Compromise. As with any task in which you're collaborating with someone else, there'll be times when you get your way, there'll be times when you won't. Accept it and embrace it. Sometimes your way will work, sometimes theirs will – but remember that you're working together. You won't be able to have everything your way, and that's a good thing.

Stay communicating, even if you don't like each other. Some practitioners you won't get on with, it's only human. It's easy to disengage with your co-facilitator when this happens, but don't. You need to keep communicating otherwise resentment will build. You don't have to fall in love with the other person, but you still need to work together for the benefit of your group, so it's important that you don't let your working relationship impact the workshop. You can't control the other person, but you can control yourself. Make sure that you're trying to maintain as productive a working relationship as possible.

Check in with your co-facilitator during the breaks or group work. These are the moments when you can check in with each other and see if you need to make any adjustments to the work. It allows you to keep the channels of communication open.

Don't take over the other person's section unless it's absolutely necessary. Taking over when someone else is leading is patronising, and it's not your responsibility. The only time you should take over is when something's going absolutely haywire. Raphael may actually be perfectly capable of running the room, and he won't necessarily need you to swoop in and play superhero, even if you think he does. Stepping in and taking over will usually make the other person think they're incapable. This goes for your assistants as well. Let them do their job. And they should let you do yours.

Leave the behaviour management to the person leading. Intervening on bad behaviour when you're not leading can be more of a hindrance than a help. This includes going round and having quiet words with people while the other person's facilitating. It undermines the lead facilitator and suggests that they can't manage the room. Giving the person next to you a look or a nudge if they're doing some mild chatter is relatively okay, and there may be some clear occasions where you do need to actively intervene – but for the most part, let the other person lead.

Give your co-facilitator a heads up if you're going to hand over to them. This can be through simple eye contact or a signal as you're nearing the end of an exercise, or telling them that you're coming to the end of your section as the group are working. This also applies if you're asking them a question. It's bad practice to put your co-facilitator on the spot without some kind of warning first. For example, rather than saying: 'What do you think, Kieran?', you could say: 'Kieran, it'd be good to get your thoughts on this – we've got a choice between having the actors come in from stage-left or stage-right, what's your opinion?' What you say isn't really that important – it's simply to give the other person a bit of notice that you want them to come in, without catching them by surprise.

Don't contradict your co-facilitator unless you have a good reason to. Generally, you both want to be working from the same page, or at least to disagree constructively or to offer a different perspective. But otherwise, unless there really is a genuine error that needs to be corrected, try not to contradict each other. It's bad practice, and can make it seem like you're working at odds with each other, rather than working together.

Assistants

Being an assistant is a rite of passage for most facilitators. It allows people to learn from lead facilitators in a safe and supported way. One of the best things about assisting is that you get to see different styles of working in practice, because once you become a lead facilitator you'll be working on your own for most jobs, which means that your opportunities to learn from others will be limited.

An assistant can be a brilliant source of support. Unfortunately, some practitioners view assistants as an inconvenience, or worse, they barely see them at all. Do not be one of those people. I definitely remember being on the sidelines when I was an assistant on a course, in the past, where I was essentially just an observer. I balanced it out by taking the lead on the pastoral work and building a bond with the group – but even that was entirely of my own doing.

So I can say first-hand that it's important to actively involve and use your assistant. It's not a bonus. Just as you have a responsibility to your group, you have a responsibility to your assistant. You may be perfectly capable of running the session yourself, but it's vital that you include them. They're the practitioners of tomorrow.

> It's important that you communicate with your assistant before you start working together. It's good for you both to get to know each other, and for you both to be clear on what the expectations are. Plus, if it's a course, your assistant will want to give both you and the participants their full attention once the workshops are underway, so being clear on what's required will give them time to plan ahead. They may want to adapt their warm-ups after knowing what you want to do, or build playlists for exercises to be explored in the sessions.
>
> **Molly Walker**
> Actor (*National Theatre*, *Secret Cinema*, *The PappyShow*)
> Freelance Facilitator, *National Youth Theatre*, *The Silver Lining*

Here are some pointers on making the most of the opportunity:

Actively involve them. Assistants shouldn't be sitting on the side the whole time, it doesn't matter how experienced you are. Assistants will come with a range of experience and expertise, so it's important that you get to know them so you know who they are and what they want from the experience. Some will want to actively lead while others might not, but it's your responsibility to take the lead and to start the conversation about what your working relationship will look like.

Give them opportunities to lead if you can, because there's only so much they can learn from observing. Games are easy for assistants to lead on because they're more straightforward to run than exercises, but don't necessarily limit them to this. Some assistants will be more experienced and would benefit more from leading sections or exercises that are more in-depth, and by letting them lead a section, you'll allow them to use their unique skillset and share it in a safe environment. It can be helpful to support where necessary, but only as much as needed – you don't want to lead the session for them. I'll usually only step in if I absolutely have to, because if a group isn't responding well to their delivery, they need to learn to adapt for themselves – they won't have anyone to step in for them when they're facilitating on their own. Also be mindful that assistants may ask for feedback after their session, so it's a good opportunity to observe and to guide them as they find their feet.

Don't outsource your workshops to your assistant. If you're the lead facilitator, be the lead facilitator – it's likely to be that way for a reason. The majority of your sessions should still be led by you.

They can bring different or complementary skills to the table. Just because somebody's not an established facilitator doesn't mean they can't be skilled in other areas (some of which you may be weak at) – such as music or dance. Drawing on these skills can be of huge benefit for everyone, and you ignore them at your peril.

They can give you an insight to your group that you might otherwise miss. Because they'll probably be working much more closely with the group than you, they'll likely have a better understanding of the social dynamics and be able to influence them in a different way. They'll be closer to being an equal with your group, because your role will be more firmly set as the workshop leader. This is really useful because it means that they might be able to give you a more accurate picture of how the group are, and it'll be easier for them to support the group from the inside, in a way that you can't.

Regularly check in with your assistant(s) if you're running a course. You need to make sure you have a strong working relationship, and the only way to do that is to maintain an open channel of communication. *You* need to take the lead on this because they're not going to do it for you. In your conversations, you can cover how they're doing, how the group are doing, or any adjustments that need to be made to improve things for both of you. It doesn't necessarily need to happen for every session, but it's important. And 'not having time' isn't an excuse. You-are-not-Beyoncé.

Have a chat about whether they should actively take part in the session or not. Assistants can engage in the workshop as a participant, they can observe, or do a mixture of both. It's often good to give them a choice, because their views on this might be different depending on their level of experience and the exercises being done. Regardless, the usual approach would be for them to step in or out as the exercise requires for pair work or group work, based on the number of people that are needed.

It's sometimes helpful to give them an insight into your planning. On longer courses, some directors will plan their sessions alongside their assistants, which is more collaborative. I don't personally, but I do debrief with my assistant at the end of each day, explaining why I planned what I did, any changes I made and any reflections that I had. This allows them to see my thought process as a practitioner. Doing this isn't essential to working with assistants and I'd only do it for longer courses, but it goes a long way towards their development.

If you have two assistants, make sure you check in with them both individually. Even though they'll be a partnership, you'll still be working with two individuals, who'll both have unique skills and backgrounds and will likely have two different experiences from the workshop(s). There may be nuances or challenges between them that need your support, which they'd only be willing to share on an individual basis, rather than together.

> “The best use of an assistant is when they're welcomed to become an extension of you. Allow them the space to springboard creative ideas and feel that their voice is appreciated inside and outside the rehearsal room.
>
> A lot of assistants come into the role with an apprehension of hierarchy. They might not be so forward in telling you that they've actually facilitated for ten-plus years, or that they specialise in drag skills or trained at Lecoq. Don't patronise them, or worse, plonk them in the corner of the room to disappear into stacked chairs and disused flipchart paper. Nine times out of ten they want to be in your position at some point in their career and are keen to learn.
>
> **Kenny Cumino**
> Actor/Writer
> Artistic Director, *Pint Sized Poetry*

Finding work

Like most things, getting jobs gets easier the more you work, so often the inital stages of your career can be the trickiest. But once you've got some decent experience under your belt, it should hopefully get much easier.

The first thing to say is that it's important to commit to every job you do and to deliver as best you can, regardless of the job. It's a small industry, and it's perfectly normal for a contact in one theatre to pop up in another. So, depending on the quality of your work and your relationships with people, this can open doors that were otherwise closed, or close doors that otherwise would've opened.

There's also a huge range of settings and demographics that you can work with. These include schools, drama schools, pupil referral units (PRUs), prisons, special educational needs (SEND) settings, with refugees, and the corporate sector for businesses (which usually pays the best), such as through the National Theatre's Theatreworks programme.

Here are some pointers to find work if you're looking for more:

'Low-hanging fruit'
The concept behind this is to start with companies you have a connection to, then to build from there. The chances of you working for the National Theatre if you've got nothing on your CV are relatively slim, but you'll probably find it easier to get work with your local theatre company or your old drama school. Alternatively, you can ask any contacts you have about any opportunities they know of, or if you can assist on any workshops. The key here is that they don't have to be big opportunities. Just a start.

Once you've got that experience under your belt, you can approach companies that are a little bit higher up the food chain, gaining experience there. That'll get you more experience and more on your CV, which you can then use to access other venues. You then simply repeat the process. The more you have on your CV, the more likely an employer is to pay attention when you contact them.

Theatres and theatre companies

It's important to be aware of the way theatres work and how they're funded, because it usually (but not always) has a link to whether or not they do any education work.

For the purposes of this, there are broadly two types of theatres: subsidised theatres and receiving houses. Subsidised theatres often have an education department because their public funding gives them a wider remit than simply turning a profit. This means they can be a good source of work because they'll often do theatre workshops in schools, the community, or in-house at their venue. Receiving houses are usually those such as the big West End theatres that host musicals. These theatres usually only put on productions and don't have an education department. There are exceptions, though, and some theatres don't quite fit those rules.

Subsidised Theatres	Receiving Houses
• Receives public funding, i.e. Arts Council funding. • Often has a creative learning department; examples include: ▪ The National Theatre. ▪ Birmingham Rep. ▪ Manchester Royal Exchange.	• Don't receive public funding. • Don't have a creative learning department; examples include: ▪ The Lyceum Theatre (*The Lion King*). ▪ Cheltenham Everyman. ▪ Bristol Hippodrome.

Contacting the education departments at subsidised theatres can be a good way to make contact with a theatre and to get involved. As an initial introduction, send a short, well-crafted email explaining your interest in their work alongside your CV. But don't be disheartened if you don't get a response on your first attempt. Even for myself, having worked for most of the major theatres in the UK, there are still some who haven't responded to any emails I've sent, and one theatre company in particular responded to my email two years later...! These things can take time. That's why you should work in the places that you're able to, and if you're good at what you do, the doors should open eventually.

There are also a ton of theatre companies and organisations that use theatre practitioners. From companies such as Frantic Assembly and Complicité, to Punchdrunk Enrichment, to drama schools, LAMDA classes, Stagecoach, Drama Kids, or adult acting schools such as City Academy. The type of places you should contact will depend on the type of work you want to do, but there are companies of all shapes and sizes that you can approach, simply with an email and a CV.

Job websites
Some theatres will post facilitator job openings directly on their website, but there are also other websites where employers post jobs. Two of them are:

Arts Jobs – www.artsjobs.org.uk
Managed by Arts Council England, here you can find job listings from across the arts sector, with a filter that allows you to search by criteria such as pay, location, art form and contract type. The website is free to use, with new job listings going up on a regular basis. You can also subscribe for job alerts by registering your email address.

Spotlight – www.spotlight.com
Spotlight is the largest performers' database in the UK, which most professional performers will be registered to, as it's more-or-less an essential if you're seeking professional work in the industry. Although it mainly caters to performance work, facilitation jobs are still posted there occasionally. It requires a yearly membership, so if you're solely looking for facilitation work rather than performance opportunities then you may not think that it's worth it. But if you're already a member, it might be an idea to set up your job alerts to capture any work that might be suitable.

Develop your skillset
Developing a specialism is a big way to differentiate yourself from other practitioners. Do you have skills in music and song? Physical theatre? Stage combat? Young people with special needs? Shakespeare? Banjo? All these things can be invaluable

in finding work. If you have those skills, develop them. If you don't, learn some. Failing that, become s***-hot at what you do. The more you can do, the more employable you'll be, and the more reason they'll have to employ you over somebody else who's equally qualified as you.

Assisting

You'll almost certainly assist on workshops when you're starting out – which is only a good thing. Don't turn your nose up at it. Every facilitator's style is different, and the more people you can learn from, the better you'll be. One of the realities of this type of work is that it's unusual to see other practitioners at work once you establish yourself as a lead facilitator, so the best chance you'll get to learn from other people is when you're assisting – make the most of it. It's only in the rare instance that you get to co-facilitate or you have an assistant yourself that you'll get to see other people working. In the early days, assist as much as you can. It'll give you far more contacts and expertise than if you don't.

How to Use Your Voice

The voice is often the most overlooked and underappreciated element of running a workshop because you often won't even think about it... until you lose it. And losing your voice midway through a project will be a nightmare of an experience, unless you're a skilled mime artist.

Your voice is one of your most essential tools, so it's important that you know how to use it. But knowing how to use your voice effectively won't only help your voice go the distance, it can be the difference between your group switching off whenever your mouth opens, and having them on the edge of their seats, listening to your every word. So be sure to use it to your advantage.

"I learnt the importance of using voice correctly the hard way: working as a children's party entertainer delivering up to six two-hour parties every weekend. After packing up, saying a charismatic goodbye and leaving the venue, I'd collapse into my car seat and think: 'This is a lot!', with a lump in my throat and pain in my head. It wasn't because I'd been working with overly enthusiastic children, it was because I was using my voice and body overenthusiastically.

I was overexerting myself. I needed to maintain my energy but protect my voice. Being high in energy both physically and vocally was putting a real strain on me.

I realised that I'd hold tension in my body and was using a higher vocal register when interacting with parents and children. Being aware of these meant I could learn to engage the diaphragm when speaking, which increased the power in my voice.

When we're nervous or unsure, I find we can tense up and often restrict our vocal passage. A wonderful way to open up the vocal cords and increase the clarity and warmth is to perform vowel sounds, rubbing of the cheeks or lip trills. Having your own vocal warm-up or routine before a session is never a bad idea.

Shireenah Ingram
Creative Director, *Red Lens,* www.red-lens.co.uk
Actress (*BBC*, *British Film Institute*)
Board Member, *Birmingham Royal Ballet*

Upward and downward inflections

Upward inflections can quickly rob you of all authority, making it seem as if you're asking permission to be in the room or to speak. Upward inflection is when you go up in pitch at the end of the sentence as if you're asking a question, and it's important to be aware of because the last thing you want is to sound unsure in what you're asking people to do.

On the other hand, downward inflections are when you drop the energy at the end of your sentences, which can sap the energy from your speech and give it a dead weight. These are things that actors need to be aware of when performing, but also facilitators. To give yourself more authority, you'll want to keep the energy up towards the end of your sentences, while finding a midway point between the two.

Make your questions questions and your statements statements

Own what you say. Don't make your statements into questions. Common examples of this that people use are:

'Can you get yourself into pairs?'

'Would you mind...?'

'Could you...?'

This probably comes from a place of being polite. But if you're giving an instruction – give the instruction. Otherwise, you're essentially asking for your group's permission. Alternatives would be:

'Get yourself into groups of three. Go.'

'Take a seat on the floor.'

'Find yourselves a partner.'

You also need to be mindful of this because with more challenging groups, you can end up negotiating to get your instruction done, rather than it being carried out. For example, giving the instruction: 'Can you stand in the circle please like everybody else?' to young, fit and healthy Jeremiah, could easily lead to the response: 'But I can't, I've got a bad leg', which then automatically puts you on the back foot. So your instructions always need to be clear and direct.

Being direct isn't rude unless you use a rude tone. By not turning your questions into statements, you'll give yourself more authority in the space and will take more ownership of your position. Otherwise it'll seem like you're apologising for being there, or it'll open you up for a response that you don't want. There'll be occasions where you do want to be more indirect with your requests, but unless it's an active choice, commit to your statements.

Filler words

'So, um, er, let's, hmm, just sit, erm, on the floor, um, then, like, basically, we can, er, make a start... You know?' :(

'Let's all sit on the floor.' :)

As with upward inflections, fillers can massively reduce your status in a room. Although they're a part of everyday language, try to use them as little as possible – you'll come across as far more confident and self-assured, and it'll make your group respond to you far better. I'm not suggesting that you outright eradicate every last 'um' and 'er' or that you worry about them endlessly, but you need to be mindful of them. Solving this partly comes through confidence and committing to what you have to say, and not apologising for your place in the room. Pausing is far more effective than fillers, and knowing how to use pauses effectively will make you far more engaging than if you don't.

“ In my personal experience, fillers tend to occur when we're unsure of where we want to go. This is sometimes okay – some exercises are a journey of discovery. However, when leading an exercise it's important to reduce the number of filler words you use as these create a distance from the instruction. The use of a pause is far more powerful, or even a moment of breath. Good breathing and the voice go hand in hand.

You should also bear in mind the importance of pace. Filler words sometimes happen when we haven't found the natural pace required to deliver an instruction. Think about the pace of your delivery and how a well-planned pause or intake of breath can allow you time to think your way through an instruction.

Marcia Carr
Artistic Director, *Arts Outburst*
Artistic Director, *Creative Blast Company*
Freelance Practitioner, Senior Lecturer and Deputy Chief Examiner, *Royal Opera House*, *National Youth Theatre*, *Royal Central School of Speech and Drama*, *LAMDA*

Talk like a human

'I would take this opportunity to displace the situated recognition of care as an existential mode of coexisting in the established hierarchies of value and the coercion of capital.'

An extract from a real-life arts application

Well-educated people and creatives often have a talent for making the simple overly complicated – either by using language that's more complicated than it needs to be, or by creating new words where suitable ones already exist. William Zinsser puts it nicely in his book:

> Our national tendency is to inflate and thereby sound important. The airline pilot who announces that he is presently anticipating experiencing considerable precipitation wouldn't think of saying it may rain. The sentence is too simple – there must be something wrong with it.

William Zinsser
On Writing Well: An Informal Guide to Writing Non-fiction

Straying away from everyday language makes the arts far less inclusive than it should be, because it means that artists are speaking a different language from the rest of the population. With the exception of genuine theatre terminology, if a random member of the public wouldn't be able to understand a particular word without an explanation, you shouldn't be using it. Time spent having to explain a new word or term is time that could be spent actually delivering the workshop. Plus, don't assume that people will be willing to put their hand up and ask you what you mean. They probably won't. So your message could go entirely in one ear and out the other.

Some may argue that new terminology is created to be more inclusive. Okay. But it goes back to my previous point. If you're speaking words that people don't understand then you may as well be speaking a different language. And having to teach somebody a new language to engage with you when you already have a language in common is far from being inclusive.

High volume – low volume

It's standard practice to speak loud enough for people to hear you – but there's also something to be said for bringing your volume down. Actors with a strong grounding in vocal technique will definitely be at an advantage and be able to fill the space, but I've also seen people do the opposite. One director I worked with was so softly spoken and quiet that her participants were too – partly because everybody had to be quiet to hear her. But this wasn't by accident, it was a conscious choice, one that you can use to your advantage. Intentionally bringing your volume down can really draw your listeners in. Use your volume to your advantage.

Don't speak when anyone else is

This is important to establish early on. If in the first five minutes you set the precedent that the group can talk while you're talking, they will, and it'll be an issue throughout your workshop. By stopping what you're saying when somebody else starts talking, it'll bring the workshop to a halt. Most people won't want to be the person holding the workshop up for everyone else, which will stop most people from talking over you. It might seem over-the-top to commit to this, but not doing it can make your life much harder.

BUT. You do have to be careful, because its effectiveness depends on the level of respect that the group has for you and your perceived authority in the room. If you're not respected and don't have any authority, this can massively backfire. We can probably all remember a time in school when kids would deliberately use this to their advantage: Miss Davis standing around for ages at the front, waiting for silence while Jane and Lisa natter away without a care in the world, deliberately trying to hold the lesson up. If this happens then you need to have some form of consequence for people who don't listen, because you can't allow yourself or the workshop to be controlled in that way.

One of the benefits of this is that it should make your group listen to you more, and because you won't have to compete vocally to get your words over other people's, it should make workshops much easier on your voice.

Try not to speak over groups while they're working

Linked to the previous point, speaking over groups as they're working is a sure-fire way to lose your voice. If you need to give a message to your whole group, either use a call-and-response or a signal to get your group's attention (like putting your hand in the air), or give them a countdown from three to get their attention, before telling them whatever it is that you need to say. If you've got good vocal technique then you may find it easy to speak over people as they're working, but even then, it's better to use it to get people's attention, or for very short messages, such as reminding them of how much time they have left. Try to keep it to a minimum, otherwise you'll find your voice getting tired really quickly.

Glottal stops

Glottal stops can ravage your voice in no time if you're not careful. In everyday life, glottal stops aren't so much of a problem, but they can decimate your voice when you're running a workshop.

A good example of glottal stops in this sense would be with the word 'okay'. 'Okay' is made by the back of your tongue making contact with the glottis (at the back of your throat). Because it's made at the back of the mouth, saying this without good vocal technique and with volume and force can be like slamming a hammer to the back of your throat, creating an explosive sound. And because it's a common word to get a group's attention, it can have big consequences quite quickly.

The solution would be to add a small 'h' at the start of the vowel, which will take away its punch and have less impact on your voice. You'd essentially be saying 'h-okay', but it should be subtle enough that people can't hear it. Another word that can have a similar impact is the word 'go', which has the same level of explosiveness because, again, the sound mainly comes from the back of your throat. But the same thing applies. You'll want to actively reduce the explosiveness of the 'oh' sound, to have it be a softer, smoother sound instead.

Try it for yourself. Say the word 'go' loudly and forcefully ten times in a row and see how your voice feels. Now imagine doing that with even more power for a whole day's workshop. And then a week. Your throat would become mincemeat. Then try that same word again but with a much softer vowel sound or with the 'h' in front of the vowel and see the difference. Again, it should be subtle. In no way should a group be able to hear you say 'hhhhhhhhhhhhhhhhhh-okay!' It's just a minor tweak.

If you can reduce the explosiveness of your glottal stops, or failing that, replace any words that you know have a negative impact, you'll massively increase the endurance of your voice.

Repeat the instructions

'...so that's what you need to do. You've got five minutes to make your scene. Go!'

They get into groups

...

'Sir! What are we supposed to do again?'

It's helpful to repeat your instructions when you're giving your group a task. For whatever reason, people don't always take them in the first time. Even me. Sometimes when I'm in a workshop as a participant, all it takes is one rogue thought and my mind ventures off on a tour of the universe. So by giving the instruction twice, you should hopefully prevent people asking: 'So what do we have to do?' as soon as they get into groups.

It's better to be too clear by repeating yourself than it is to try to save time by saying it once, only to then have to go round to each group and explain yourself again. You can also repeat the instructions but rephrase them the second time. This is a great way to make sure that people understand what you said if they didn't understand the way it was phrased the first time. A good example of this is when you're using technical jargon.

Technical jargon

'Ensemble, traverse, casting director, proscenium arch, fourth wall...'

'HUH!?'

Every industry has technical language that is complete jargon to the everyday civilian, and theatre's no different. You need to be careful with technical language because not everyone will have an understanding of the technical terms used in the industry, and it can create a barrier between you and your groups. One of the best young actors I ever worked with was completely new to acting, and once put his hand up to ask the question 'What's the RSC?' (Royal Shakespeare Company). Good on him for asking.

Technical language is so often taken for granted. I once told a group to make a freeze-frame (a still image) and they looked at me in stunned confusion with no idea what I was talking about. Most people won't have the guts to ask what you mean if you use technical jargon – but you shouldn't outright remove it. Instead, frame it in such a way that everybody can understand. One way to do this is to use the technical word, then to repeat it in everyday language. For example:

'This exercise will help us to work together as an ensemble, to get you working together as a team.'

Or:

'You'll want to make sure that you're on the radar of casting directors, because it's the casting director's job to find the actors to audition.'

That way they're exposed to both the language and its meaning at the same time, and can learn it without being alienated by it.

> "The voice can help to break down terminology by using a differing vocal tone to add sense and meaning to the instruction. For instance:
>
> 'I'd like you to create five tableaux – frozen pictures – that use the ideas you've just discussed.'
>
> By giving the words 'frozen pictures' a different vocal pitch (lower, for instance), you'll make connections between the technical language and the meaning of your instruction.
>
> **Marcia Carr**

Economy of language

Keep your instructions simple. Say as much as you need to, and no more.

Take a step back

Designing your workshop so that you're not talking the whole time can massively save your voice. If you're talking for the whole of your two-hour session, there's a good chance it'll get tired – almost certainly if you're talking for the whole day (unless you've had vocal training). The way to achieve this is to have a good sprinkle of exercises for people to get on with themselves, without you leading. For example, a forty-five-minute devising exercise will mean you're not actively projecting your voice for forty-five minutes, which will give your voice a break – though this is something you should be doing anyway because you always need a good mix of exercises that are led by you, alongside others that have the group engaging with each other. See the section on 'The basics: Who the group interact with' on page 5 for more.

Demonstrating exercises

Demonstrating exercises is a great way to support your explanation, and can sometimes remove the need for an explanation entirely. Some exercises are easy to understand once people do them, but are actually difficult to explain. So in some instances, it's easier to give a quick explanation of how the exercise or game works, and then just to jump in and demonstrate it. Use your assistant if you have one, or pick a volunteer in the room. But don't feel that you always need to explain. Sometimes it's better to show.

Safeguarding for Children and Young People

In the UK, safeguarding is a legal requirement for anyone working with children and young people, to ensure their safety and wellbeing as well as yours. Every organisation should provide you with safeguarding training, or they need to make sure that you've done the training recently. This chapter isn't a replacement for it, but it covers some of the key points that you need to be aware of.

Safeguarding policies will vary between organisations and may change slightly from year to year, but it should broadly be the same across companies.

For more guidance on safeguarding for children and young people, visit: learning.nspcc.org.uk/safeguarding-child-protection

“It's important to recognise that safeguarding is far more than a policy. For me, it underpins the culture of who we are at the National Youth Theatre and how we work with the participants, artists and staff. It allows us to create a brave space where everyone can do their best work.

As an organisation, we have a cross-departmental team of trainers who deliver safeguarding courses, but they also meet monthly to discuss any safeguarding concerns and any updates in governmental policy. However, it's also a peer support group; a space to decompress and share challenging days. This allows the team to share best practice, acknowledge challenges, and reset for another day amongst a team of peers and experts.

So you're not on your own. Sometimes holding safeguarding responsibilities can feel overwhelming and isolating, but it's important to remember that there'll always be a team to support you. They're on your side, and they're there to support you to create an environment where everyone can thrive. So if you ever have any safeguarding questions or concerns, I'd always encourage you to speak to a member of the safeguarding team for the organisation you're working for.

Anna Niland
Associate Artistic Director and Head of Safeguarding,
The National Youth Theatre

Professional boundaries

There are some professional boundaries that you'll need to keep in mind when you're running workshops. These apply to working with adults as well, but they're even more important when working with young people.

- Maintaining a professional boundary includes:
  - Not sharing unnecessary information about your life. Some of your experiences might be relevant to talk about and you don't need to be a completely closed book, but you shouldn't be sharing unnecessary information about your personal life or oversharing.
  - Contacting or meeting participants outside of the professional environment is a no-go. This includes driving people home or doing one-on-one sessions with young people without the school's or parents' consent.
  - Forming a personal or inappropriate relationship with young people is not allowed under any circumstances. Your relationship with the group should always be a professional one.
  - Not posting about young people on your social media accounts, regardless of whether you explicitly name them or not.
  - Not introducing anything of a sexual nature. This includes:
    - Inappropriate sexual jokes, comments, themes or conversations.
    - Nudity or sexualised content.
- Maintaining a healthy level of personal space. This includes:

  - Not engaging in unnecessary physical contact. It might be that you need to make contact with somebody to demonstrate an exercise, but this should only be just as much as is necessary, and only for just as long as needed.
  - It's best practice not to initiate hugs, though it's usually okay if the other person initiates them. You don't want to be cold and detached, but you also need to remember your boundaries.

- Using appropriate language. What's appropriate will depend on the type of group that you're working with and their age, but in general, you should:
  - Keep swearing to a minimum. With younger age groups you shouldn't be swearing at all. You might have more leeway when it comes to older young people in a non-school setting, but even then, swearing can often be distasteful and is largely unnecessary.
  - Stay away from terms of endearment: 'Darling', 'babe', 'gorgeous', etc. They can all give off the wrong impression, and like swearing, just aren't necessary.
- Images and video:
  - Don't take pictures or videos of children and young people unless you have written consent.
  - If you are taking pictures or videos of young people, you should ideally use a device that belongs to the organisation, rather than your own. But if this isn't possible, you must delete the content as soon as possible.
  - Don't upload any images or videos of young people to social media. If media content needs to be uploaded for a project, this should always be for and through the organisation or school and with parental consent. It should never be through your personal social media accounts.

Disclosures

A disclosure is when a child or young person lets someone know that abuse is taking place. While it's important that you honour people's confidentiality when you're working with a group (so that what happens in the room, stays in the room), disclosures are a definite exception. Because they relate to people's safety and wellbeing, it's important that you report disclosures if they ever come up.

Every school or organisation for young people should have a designated safeguarding lead, and in large organisations, such as in a school, there'll often be a team. The designated safeguarding leads are responsible for handling safeguarding issues and will have an in-depth knowledge of safeguarding guidance. You should be told who the relevant person is that you'd need to speak to if you needed to, but if you're not told, you should find out. They're the people you should raise concerns with if you have any, and they're there to support both the young people and yourself.

There are a few ways that disclosures can become apparent. They can be:

- *Direct* – The person specifically says what's happened to them.
- *Indirect* – They say something ambiguous that suggests that abuse is taking place.
- *Through behaviour* – They display signs or signals that something's wrong. This might be deliberate, it might not be.
- *Non-verbal* – Through writing, pictures, or other means.

If somebody does make a disclosure, you may naturally want to ask a lot of questions. But this isn't your job. Your job is to find out just enough to be able to make a decision about whether or not it needs to be referred, so it's important that you're aware of how to handle them.

Here are some dos and don'ts about how to respond to disclosures:

Do:

- Listen carefully and take the young person seriously. Be patient. Try not to express your opinion, or appear shocked or confused.

- Reassure them. Acknowledge how hard it is to share something of that nature.
- Tell them that you'll need to pass it on to the designated safeguarding lead. You have a responsibility to make sure that the young person is safe from harm, and your duty of care to them means that you have to pass it on. This is for their safety and wellbeing, and isn't something you have a choice about.
- Refer it to the designated safeguarding officer or relevant member of staff as soon as possible.
- Make some notes. Write down the date, time, location, and the facts about what was said. It's important to be accurate and factual; not to write down your own interpretations or assumptions.

Don't:

- Ask leading questions.
- Assume anything or jump to conclusions.
- Promise that you'll keep it confidential.
- Try to find out if the young person is telling the truth.
- Discuss it with anyone other than the designated safeguarding lead.
- Confront the alleged abuser if you know the person being referred to.

A key thing to note is that for something to be considered a disclosure, it has to suggest that they're in danger now. So if someone refers to an event from ten years ago, that wouldn't necessarily be classed as a disclosure because it doesn't refer to their safety at the moment. But even then, it'd be worth mentioning it to the relevant safeguarding lead in case it's necessary to check that they're okay.

Be mindful though that things aren't always clear-cut and can sometimes take a bit of judgement, and it's important to remember that your job is to run your workshop, not to go hunting for disclosures. The reason I say this is because I've seen facilitators become so hyper-aware of them that they actively seek them out to a point of fault. A child saying that they're sad at home isn't necessarily a sign of abuse and that social services need to be involved, so while it might still be important for the school or organisation to know, a child being sad doesn't mean that you need to hit the disclosure alarm button. If you're ever in doubt, report it to the safeguarding lead, and be sure that you report it in a way that's accurate to what was said, rather than putting your own spin on it.

Lastly, as daunting as it might seem to have to encounter disclosures, remember that when you're working with young people, there should always be a member of staff to support you. The organisation that you're working for and/or the venue (such as the school) will usually already have systems in place, so ask for help when you need it and never try to handle things by yourself.

Don't be alone with participants

It's best practice not to be alone with a participant somewhere you can't be seen. Many organisations should have systems in place to prevent this, such as a teacher being in the room with you or you having an assistant, but it can still happen.

It's fine if participants want to have a one-on-one conversation with you, but try to do it where you can still be seen by other people, such as in a corridor, an outside public space, or a room that has windows where people can see you. You don't need to run for the hills the second it seems like you're going to be alone with someone, and it doesn't mean that you need to be cold and detached, but you do need to be mindful of it. This is to protect both of you.

Don't share your contact details

As a rule of thumb, you're advised not to share your contact details with your participants. This can sometimes be a bit of a difficult area on courses because you'll often build up a strong connection with your group, and if you're a creative in the industry, it'd make sense that they'd want to be in touch from a professional standpoint and to get advice from you. The problem is that sharing your personal contact details becomes similar to being alone with participants, in that you're opening up a private channel of communication. So it's often better not to share contact details or social media information, to protect both yourself and the young people.

This does vary, however, depending on the organisation you're working for, so it might be a case of checking their policy on this so that you know their stance. For instance, some companies are okay with contact details being shared after a course but not during it, while some will ban it entirely. For schools, it'd almost certainly be an outright no.

If you did have questions about this, then, as mentioned above, you should speak to your organisation about it. As a happy medium, most organisations are happy to act as a go-between and to pass on any messages that you have for students, and vice versa. It can also be helpful to explain your stance on this to your group at the end of your course or your session so that you're all on the same page. This should save people from feeling like you're rejecting them if they add you on Insta and you don't follow back.

DBS/Update Service

To work with children and young people in the UK, you'll need to have a Disclosure and Barring check, which is essentially a criminal record check to make sure that you can work with young people. It's essential, not optional, so you'll need one if you want to work. Borrow the money if you don't have it. They usually last for a few years.

Some companies may still request that you get a new DBS through them even if you already have one. Some will cover the cost of DBS checks for you, but all companies are different, so speak to them to find out their policy. If you already have one and they're happy to use it, it'll save you all time and money.

There's also a system called the Update Service, which I highly recommend you sign up to. For a small fee, registering on the Update Service will renew your DBS every year, and it'll mean that companies can get the most recent information about your

DBS without you having to get a new one. It's not expensive, and it'll save you heaps of time having to completely redo the DBS application system every few years, and it'll be cheaper.

A lot of schools will also request to see your DBS when you arrive, so it's worth keeping it in your bag whenever you work with young people just in case they ask for it. Most places will only accept the original paper copy, but it's always useful to have a digital scan that you can access just in case, and to have the DBS and Update Service numbers saved too. Email them to yourself or save them in cloud storage, so you can access them at any time.

Final Thoughts

Running a workshop is a craft like any other. In writing this book, I spent a long time trying to break down the art of good facilitation. But more than that, I spent even longer learning it in the field. The time it takes to create the art is just a fraction of the time it takes to create the artist.

You won't be able to apply all the guidance of this book to your work overnight, but nobody's expecting you to. You don't need to be perfect to be effective. We're all still learning, and I'm no exception. Some things I learnt over fifteen years ago when I started, while some things I didn't learn until I was writing this book. But I'm hopeful, and confident, that once it all becomes second nature to you, you'll be able to deliver an effective workshop in any room you walk into, no matter what gets thrown your way.

The next part of your journey is to combine all this knowledge with your experience and to find your own style. Figure out what works for you, what doesn't, and most importantly, what brings out the best in your participants. And if something isn't working, change it, and adapt.

Go forth, and be great...!

Thank-yous from the Past

As I came to the end of writing this book, I realised that you'll have heard from me and from other practitioners in the industry, but not much from the other side – the people that we work with. So I figured, maybe you should.

In the introduction, I mentioned how I was all about the work. My work was never about me – it was about delivering the best for my groups as best I could. I didn't set out to do anything magical or to change lives, but by solely focusing on delivering some damn good workshops, it happened anyway.

So what you have here are some of the messages from the thank-you cards, thank-you notes, and extracts from the Compliment Games that came from doing what I do. And I hope, going forward, that the same will happen for you too. So if you're ever in doubt that the joy of theatre itself is enough to change lives, this chapter's for you.

Linden, so I have a lot to say but it will have to be abbreviated. Thank you. Honestly thank you so much, I have reconnected my love for drama and made some of the best friends and memories from this course. There have been days where I felt happy again and not depressed and that's come from you teaching the course and making us feel like a family and welcome. So I will miss you so much, and thank you from the bottom of my heart.

These past two weeks have just flown by, and now that it's time to go home I cannot be more thankful for all the unbelievable training you have offered us – whether it's Shakespeare or an intense game of Splat, you never fail to bring so much energy and excitement to the room. Thank you for showing me so much more to acting and the importance of the ensemble that I never knew before. To me, you are the biggest inspiration (as cheeky as it sounds) because after a day learning and performing with you, there is an incredible sense of fulfilment that I feel, which is exactly what I want to pass on to people when I perform in the future. I cannot wait to continue to perform and learn and I hope to see you (and the fantastic people on this course) in the near future!

Well, I have never felt the amount of care, compassion and enthusiasm you have shown me in these two weeks in my whole life. I'm sure to describe your immense talent to you would be useless as one would hope you know how utterly incredibly you are. In all my years f****** around on a stage, I have never learnt so much and felt so appreciated – you are truly one of the best people I have ever had the bloody honour of being in the presence of. I feel as though this is becoming a fan letter but it's not, don't get gassed. Sometimes in life you meet people who just change your life, it is rare and has only happened to me once before now, however you are one of those people and I do hope I do you justice and make one of the most amazing actors and not only that but the most amazing man I have ever met proud. I hope I can do you proud, thank you for everything.

I just want to say thank you so much for absolutely everything! Our time together is drawing to a close and I wanted to take a moment just to appreciate what a f****** amazing guy you are. Not only are you an amazing actor but you are also such an amazing person with such an electric personality. It has been an absolute pleasure working with you and being a part of such a solid group of actors. You really don't understand how much I will miss you because you're such a genuine, down to earth guy with such a brilliant presence and sense of humour. This might sound creepy but I promise you it's not. Hahaha. When I got the email through about you being my course director I thought… right, let's google him. So I did. I thought wow, he looks like a fantastic actor and well, you met that expectation. I love how when you walk into the room the whole environment becomes so much happier and a lot more uplifted. Just the smallest things you do make me so happy. For example when you make a joke and smile after it instantly. I definitely think… actually, I know that you have made my experience f****** amazing! I get you. I get your acting, I get your directing, I just get everything you do. You my friend are an inspiration to us all and I know for sure that your name, Linden Walcott-

Burton, will remain with me for the rest of my life and if I ever do make it, your name will be the first I will say to people. You're such a credit and such a funny bloke. I also want you to know that you (without knowing) have made my life better. I won't go too deep but things aren't great at the moment with my social life but you have made me so much more resilient and you have refuelled my passion for acting/drama. This definitely isn't goodbye. Thank you so much.

I realise that there is probably no way that I can write you this letter without you thinking that I'm in love with you. No offence, you're a swell guy but this isn't me confessing my undying love or anything. Sorry mate.

I really hope that you don't quit acting because you're so full of talent but more than that I hope you don't quit teaching because I couldn't have dreamt of the shit that you've taught me. I can't express how grateful I am and how much I appreciate you putting my name forward. I come off as a really confident person and I'm very kind to people so I often get taken advantage of and made fun of because people think that I'm confident enough to be unaffected but I'm not.

For example, I didn't get to be a prefect because I 'didn't need the confidence boost'. I don't get main parts in plays because I 'don't mind not being centre-stage'. So to be able to audition and get in based on my ability and not be sent away because I 'didn't need it' was wonderful.

Thank you again, thank you, thank you, thank you, thank you, thank you.

It is difficult to put into words how amazing the past few weeks have been but I can honestly say that I have come away a better actor and person. You have taught me more in two weeks than I have learnt in my life and it has been so much fun coming to the studios every day (even if some of the stuff did terrify me!). Thank you so much for the love and support you have given us over the course. You are a brilliant director, actor and 'lad' (can't believe I said that) and it has been a pleasure and privilege to work with you.

You are such a genuine and inspiring person. Chill but with a very clear vision and it was such a pleasure to work with you. It's been jokes, and built up my confidence so much because of you!

> Thank you for giving us the courage and confidence to be ourselves. You have such a gift of making people feel at ease as well as your kindness. I couldn't have asked for a better course director.

Could spend a long time trying to thank you enough for everything you've done and still not have covered half of it. Thank you for giving me the confidence to be myself again.

> Thank you for everything. I aspire to be as open and creative as you are. You've taught me so much. I'm grateful to have had you as my course director.

Bruvah, I cannot explain how perfect you've made this experience for me. You've shown me that with the voice of the youth this doesn't have to be a competitive industry. It's been a long time since I've found enough comfort in an institution to explore my creative abilities freely. You, my g, have provided that for me. There's too much I want to say man. I am in debt to your greatness for these three weeks. My bruvah!

> I am genuinely so happy we had you as our course director. You get straight to the point, you're down to earth, funny, and an absolute pleasure. Again, so glad we had you as a director! Really respect the lesson you did on moral foundations as well. Seen so many teachers create more division with politics, but you did a fantastic job. Genuinely heartfelt thank you. It's been an honour working with you.

It has been a pleasure working with you over the last three weeks. You've worked so hard for us, and I hope we've been a decent group for you to work with. Thanks for everything you have taught me, I hope I get to learn from you again. I'll miss your infectious laugh.

LINDEN – I cannot begin to tell you how grateful I am for having you as a course leader – you understand my quietness, that it's not me not caring, it's listening, and you helped me with how to work on getting involved more and gave me the confidence to do that. I cannot thank you enough – I really hope I work with you in the future – and thank you for giving me roles that push me outside my comfort zone!

> You've taught me so much. I came here very unmotivated and you have pushed and supported me every step of the way. This has been life-changing and I'm eternally grateful.

Linden I honestly couldn't have asked for a better three weeks. I've learnt countless lessons, not only as an actor but on how to be a positive force in the world. You're the perfect leader, but also such an incredibly humble and down-to-earth friend. This has been an unforgettable experience. I can't thank you enough.

> Basically you are so great and I don't think you realise how great you have been to us. I really genuinely appreciate having such a living legend as a teacher. You're the best, thank you.

Linden, thanks so much for this week! I loved the way you structured the course and I was really grateful to get to work on such a range of things but still feel like we covered it in-depth. Your direction and attitude to the rehearsal room has had such a positive impact this week.

> Thanks for taking the time beforehand to reach out to me in the run-up to the classes and for taking the time with me after the sessions to share your approach (not many people would be so generous). I really appreciate learning from you and trusting me to lead/facilitate.

I love how you created a space which brought the best out of people. You're very comfortable in yourself and your work which has been very inspiring to see and be in a room with.

Your calmness and composure has kept us all focused this week. You have inspired me so much and I'm so lucky to have had you as a director.

You inspire me to be as confident and strong as you. I have learnt so much over this past week and that is down to your incredible leadership and direction.

Thank you so much for creating this family.

I have loved having you as a director this week. You inspire me to be the best actor I can be. You have taught me so much in such a short space of time, and I really appreciate that you treated us like adults the whole time.

Thank you so much for one of the best weeks of my life. You are really inspiring.

Thank you so much for this week! I feel I have got everything I possibly could out of your sessions and more. I am so grateful for everything you have taught and especially for the scene you gave me. It really challenged me but I loved every second. Thanks again!

Hi Linden! I just wanted to let you know that a couple of weeks ago I got cast in a main supporting role on a new HBO show directed by Joss Whedon! I just wanted to tell you so I could thank you for everything you did to help me at NYT because I really think it helped me to improve.

I'm not good with words so please forgive me. I don't think I would have enjoyed this course half as much if I had another director. And I think I can say the same for the rest of us. You have been amazing. Your ideas, your jokes, your acting (which is on point by the way). I'm sorry it's written down but I don't know how to say it to your face. I think I would start crying. You have made this the best two weeks of my life. I never want to go home. Being here has changed me (in a good way) and it wouldn't have happened without you. I never thought I could learn so much in just two weeks. I don't think any of us are joking when we say you are like a dad to us and we love you for it!!! Being here I have made so many friends and I don't think I would have spoken to anyone if it wasn't for what you said about age doesn't matter. And I know it sounds silly but it really did help me. So THANK YOU!

List of Contributors

With huge thanks to the following people for their written contributions throughout this book:

Kate Beales
Senior Artist and Practitioner for *National Theatre Learning*
Associate Artist, *Project Phakama*
Freelance facilitator, *The Drive Project* and *Bravo 22 Company*

Tara Boland
Freelance Practitioner, *Punchdrunk Enrichment, The Free Association, Mountview*

Euan Borland
Head of Education and Community, *The Old Vic*

Marcia Carr
Artistic Director, *Arts Outburst*
Artistic Director, *Creative Blast Company*
Freelance practitioner, Senior Lecturer and Deputy Chief Examiner, *Royal Opera House, National Youth Theatre, Royal Central School of Speech and Drama, LAMDA*

Kenny Cumino
Actor/Writer
Artistic Director, *Pint Sized Poetry*

Josie Daxter
Freelance Director and Facilitator, *National Youth Theatre, The PappyShow, Complicité*

Andrew Dennis
Actor (*Royal Shakespeare Company, National Theatre, Royal Court*)
Freelance Facilitator, *Mountview, ALRA, East 15 Acting School*

Paul Edwards
Freelance Practitioner, *National Youth Theatre, Almeida Theatre, Southwark Playhouse*
Visiting Lecturer, *Royal Central School of Speech and Drama, Brunel University, Italia Conti*

Rachel Ellis
Freelance Practitioner and Head of Drama at *Cambridge School of Visual & Performing Arts*

Louise Fitzgerald PGCE
Freelance Acting Facilitator and Life Skills Coach

Sarah Golding
Former Associate Artistic Director, *Battersea Arts Centre*
Freelance Arts and Heritage Consultant

Claire Hodgson
Founder of Diverse City and co-founder of *Extraordinary Bodies*
Artist and Activist

Shireenah Ingram
Creative Director, Red Lens – www.red-lens.co.uk
Actress (*BBC, British Film Institute*)
Board Member, *Birmingham Royal Ballet*

Nadia Nadif
Actor (*National Theatre, Shakespeare's Globe, BBC*)
Freelance Facilitator, *National Youth Theatre, The Old Vic*

Anna Niland
Associate Artistic Director and Head of Safeguarding, *National Youth Theatre*

Ann Ogbomo
Freelance Practitioner and Trainer, *National Theatre*
Actor (*Wonder Woman, Justice League, The Sandman, Krypton*)

Chetna Pandya
Actor (*Netflix, Channel 4, ITV, Royal Court, Complicité, Royal Shakespeare Company*)
Freelance Facilitator, *Barbican, Complicité, Royal Central School of Speech & Drama, Generation Arts, Guildhall School of Music & Drama*
Artistic & Quality Assessor, *Arts Council England*
Board Member, *Complicité*

Lucy Shaljian
Freelance Practitioner and Consultant, *Leap Confronting Conflict, Playing On Theatre Company, Tender Education and Arts*

Dr Paul Sutton
Artistic Director, *C&T* and *prospero.digital*

Jackie Tate
Primary Programme Manager, *National Theatre Learning*

Molly Walker
Actor (*National Theatre, Secret Cinema, The PappyShow*)
Freelance Facilitator, *National Youth Theatre, The Silver Lining*

Delma Walsh
Psychotherapist

Ashley Zhangazha
Actor (*National Theatre, Royal Court, Donmar Warehouse, West End*)
Freelance Facilitator, *National Youth Theatre*

Acknowledgements

There are so many people in my life who I could thank for helping me become the person I am today. There'd be far too many to name. But I do want to give a special thanks to all of the people who helped me to bring this book to life, whether directly or indirectly. So I'd like to thank Mrs Kibble (Miss Shufflebottom), Miss Basterfield and Miss Mackay – my drama teachers at Hillcrest School and Community College, who believed in me long before anybody else did and were the first to see my flair for drama, even as a geeky teenager who had never had a drama lesson in his life. Pam Stock, Julie Marshall, Mark Woodcock-Stewart and Clive from my sixth-form college King Edward VI – who carried the baton and did the same. Desmond Kelly, Marion Tate, and all the wonderful people at Birmingham Royal Ballet, whose brilliant guidance led me to play Tybalt in Birmingham Royal Ballet's *Romeo and Juliet*, along with Keith Horsfall and all the people at Leaps and Bounds. An achievement far beyond what any of us could've imagined. Paul Edwards, who I assisted for a year on the Saturday community outreach workshops in Brierly Hill for the National Youth Theatre, who taught me all the fundamentals of how to lead a workshop – so much of which served as the foundation of my practice. Daisy Douglas who, without realising, lit the spark that made me write down every exercise that I ever encountered, which saved me a thousand times when I hit a brick wall in workshops, and became the inspiration for this book. Sarah Golding, who gave me my first theatre job out of drama school at Battersea Arts Centre, who taught me so much about working with children and young people that impacted even my relationships with my nieces, nephews and little cousins. Lukas Angelini, whose conversation one day led me to question what good facilitation even is, which set me on a quest to find out. All the assistants that I've had the joy of working with in the past, but Sarah Kenny, Molly Walker and Steph Golding in particular, who taught me more about facilitating than they probably realise. Craig Talbot for looking over my initial pitch and for the support to get me started, along with Sarah Baiden, whose pep talks were always useful when I'd finally finished the book for the tenth time, only to get frustrated that I'd then think up a whole new chapter to include. Francis Ashworth Emmott for explaining to me that a book doesn't need to be finished (and therefore perfect) in order to send it to publishers, which kicked me into gear to do it. Anna Niland from the National Youth Theatre, for everything she's done for me since knowing her as a teenager, but for this book in particular, for putting me in touch with Nick Hern Books, who subsequently went on to become the publisher. Everyone at Nick Hern Books for having the belief in this book, for entrusting me to write it, and for all the incredible work they've done to bring this to life, particularly Sarah Lambie, the book's brilliant editor. Philip Hedley. For everything. And for mentoring, guiding and supporting me. All of the brilliant practitioners whom I admire, who took the time to read through, comment, and provide contributions or suggestions to this book – Paul Edwards, Marcia Carr, Nadia Nadif, Shireenah Ingram, Ashley Zhangazha, Josie Daxter, Kizan Ayton Green, Rachel Ellis, Kate Beales, Ann Ogbomo, Claire Hodgson, Paul Sutton, Euan Borland, Tara Boland, Sarah Kenny, Lucy Shaljian, Louise Fitzgerald, Molly Walker, Chetna Pandya, Delma Walsh, Sarah Golding, Anna Niland, Rachel Dickinson, Andrew Dennis – all of whom have taught me so much, and who I'm infinitely grateful for. Jackie Tate at the National Theatre for writing the fantastic foreword. My family, parents, brothers, sisters, nieces, nephews, cousins... far too many to name; for everything. And last but not least, everyone who I've had the pleasure of working with in a workshop – from schools to courses to adults – who have all taught me as much about life and theatre as I have them.